CARNIVAL OF FURY

Robert Charles. A sketch by Jean Stone based on drawings in the New Orleans newspapers and descriptions from Charles's contemporaries as related to Mrs. Stone by the author.

CARNIVAL OF FURY

Robert Charles and the New Orleans Race Riot of 1900

William Ivy Hair

LOUISIANA STATE UNIVERSITY PRESS

Baton Rouge and London

This book was designed by Dwight Agner, and
composed in VIP Caledonia by The Composing Room
of Michigan, Inc., Grand Rapids, Michigan.

LIBRARY OF CONGRESS CATALOGING IN PUBLICATION DATA

Hair, William Ivy.
    Carnival of fury.

    Bibliography: p.
    Includes index.
    1. Charles, Robert 1865 or 6–1900. 2. New
Orleans—Riot, 1900. I. Title.
F379.N553C424   976.3′35′060924 [B]   75–34856
ISBN 0-8071-0178-8 (cloth)
ISBN 0-8071-1348-4 (paper)   65443
Louisiana Paperback Edition, 1986

To
my mother, ANNA BELLE JAMES HAIR
and my sister, ANNIE JUNE HAIR
and in memory of my father,
WALTER IVY HAIR (1899–1974)

It is only natural that the deepest interest should attach to the personality of Robert Charles. What manner of man was this fiend incarnate? What conditions developed him? Who were his preceptors? From what ancestral strain, if any, did he derive his ferocious hatred of the whites, his cunning, his brute courage, the apostolic zeal which he displayed in spreading the propaganda of African equality? These are questions involving one of the most remarkable psychological problems of modern times.

"Making of a Monster,"
New Orleans *Times-Democrat,* July 29, 1900

CONTENTS

ILLUSTRATIONS

PREFACE One steamy August morning in 1900, the aged editor of New Orleans' official journal sat at his desk, busily composing yet another sulfuric denunciation of a recently killed black man named Robert Charles. But this time a new idea—a new fear—struck Henry J. Hearsey of the *Daily States*. "If the wild and heroic stories of his bloody triumphs are continued," the editor warned, "some Yankee scoundrel will write his life and depict him as the negro Coeur de Lion." For his part, Hearsey promised "to suspend the recital" about "the negro murderer Charles," since he had no desire to encourage such a book. It was a pledge he soon broke—Robert Charles would not let go of his thoughts.

Three quarters of a century later what the old editor of the *States* dreaded has finally happened, at least partly; this book is about the life of Robert Charles, and the world he knew. But no Yankee wrote it (like Hearsey, I am white, was born and raised in Louisiana, and have never lived in the North); nor do I recall being referred to as a scoundrel. Neither is this biography of Robert Charles intended to portray him as an Afro-American Richard the Lion-Hearted; he was a very ordinary man in many respects, and would most probably have spent his life in anonymity, had not a particular situation developed on a New Orleans street one July night in 1900, in his

thirty-fourth year. (Ironically, the same month that Charles's
hitherto obscure existence ended in a storm of notoriety, the
"Births" columns of the local press—which seldom listed nonwhite
families—failed to record the arrival of a black baby who would
someday become Louisiana's most acclaimed celebrity of the twentieth century: Louis "Satchmo" Armstrong.)

I first came upon the name of Robert Charles while starting
research for a projected book that was to survey the political and
social history of Louisiana from 1900 to 1928—a sequel to my
Bourbonism and Agrarian Protest, which dealt with the period from
the end of Reconstruction to 1900. Struck by the extensive newspaper accounts of his clash with the police in New Orleans, my first
thought was that perhaps I had found a meaningful beginning for my
proposed study of Louisiana in the early twentieth century: white
reaction to Charles vividly illustrated the hardening of racial attitudes which occurred around that time; moreover, Charles's defiance of authority might be viewed as a harbinger of the rising black
assertiveness in future years.

For a time my research on the planned survey of 1900–1928
Louisiana continued. But finally I realized that it must wait; the
puzzle of Robert Charles had too firm a grip on my imagination.
Even the hostile New Orleans press of 1900 admitted that few
human beings ever fought death as hard as he did. That he possessed courage was obvious without further investigation. But what
sort of man was he otherwise? What could be learned of his earlier
life? There were various rumors that he had been a lawbreaker
before, probably in Mississippi—but had he been a vicious mul-
tiple murderer, as some reports alleged? What had he experienced
or witnessed in his youth that might have conditioned him for the
hopeless, prolonged siege on Saratoga Street that ended his life?
When I decided upon as thorough an investigation as was possible of
this man's lifetime, I knew that I must avoid the pitfall of caring what
the truth about him was; whether he was at heart a brutal or a decent

man must be of no concern to me; I wanted only substantive information, whatever it might reveal. Actually, the initial paucity of material about him tended to promote objectivity on my part—having committed myself to the project, I was eager for *any* solid evidence, regardless of what it might indicate about Charles as a person. But from the beginning, it seemed reasonable to expect that whatever might be discovered about Robert Charles would interest anyone concerned with black history—and white history—in the American South.

The acknowledgments that follow provide only a partial statement of gratitude to the many persons, too numerous to name all, who helped and encouraged me during my research. My heaviest debt is to a fellow historian and true friend, James H. Stone, who at the time of my research was a staff member of the Mississippi Department of Archives and History. Of all the librarians who gave of their time and talent, Mrs. Nancy Dyer of Georgia College ranks first in a select group; as a reference and interlibrary loan specialist she has, in my opinion, no equal. Other librarians and archivists who deserve particular mention are: Collin B. Hamer, Director of the Louisiana Division of the New Orleans Public Library; M. Stone Miller, Director of Archives at Louisiana State University; Wilbur "Bill" Meneray, manuscripts librarian of the Special Collections Division at Tulane University; Richard Allen, curator of the William Ransom Hogan Jazz Archive at Tulane University; Mrs. Dorothy N. Hulsart of Drew University Library; and two staff members of the Georgia College Library, Mrs. Jody Watkins and Mrs. Peggy Kinns. I am further indebted to two helpful gentlemen whom I met during my weeks of research in New Orleans: Major Henry M. Morris, Chief of Detectives of the New Orleans Police Department; and Philip Mabe, an historian who like me had become interested in Robert Charles while researching another project, and who took the time to drive me to various street addresses in New Orleans where events described in the latter part of this book occurred. I should also like to thank my colleagues at Georgia College as well as my former colleagues at Florida State University, for their encouragement and friendship. Louisiana State University Press Director Leslie E. Phillabaum, along with Marie Jones—a most careful, helpful editor—have earned my gratitude for making less troublesome the problems of publication. To my wife Karolyn and to my sons Steven and Walter, I express my love and appreciation for all that they did toward making this book a reality.

W. I. H.

Milledgeville, Georgia, 1975

1

COPIAH The 1200 block of Saratoga Street, between Clio and Erato, never was a fashionable address in New Orleans. At the turn of the century working-class whites and blacks lived there jammed alongside each other in small duplex cottages. Today, close by the glistening new Superdome, this block marks the edge of one of America's most squalid black ghettos. Overhead, a massive concrete entrance ramp of the Interstate 10 Expressway speeds traffic onto the Mississippi River bridge. Below, along the narrow street, the little Golden Leaf Hotel faces a weedy vacant lot and two rusting, abandoned Oldsmobiles. Elderly blacks in the neighborhood say they do not remember that vacant lot ever being anything else. But once a house stood there— in which occurred the final scenes of a violent racial tragedy that was extraordinary even for New Orleans.

On the afternoon of July 27, 1900, a Mississippi black man named Robert Charles, who had been hiding at 1208 Saratoga with a Winchester rifle and a portable furnace for making bullets, shot twenty-four white people, including four policemen, before he was finally killed and stomped into the mud of the street. Earlier that week Charles had shot three other police officers. Five more would soon be dismissed from the force for cowardice because of him. The *Picayune*, least extravagant in its opinions of all the New Orleans

dailies, averred that "no other man," apparently not even the hated
Union General Benjamin F. Butler whose army occupied the city
during the Civil War, had "ever before so profoundly aroused the
rage and indignation of the citizens" as did this Robert Charles.[1]

During and after the last violent week of Charles's life, white
publications referred to the man as a "monster," "an unreasoning
brute," "bad nigger," "cocaine fiend," "woman beater," "dangerous
agitator," "worthless, crapshooting negro," "ruthless black
butcher," and "bloodthirsty champion of African supremacy."[2]
Many black leaders of New Orleans excoriated him scarcely less:
they called him, among other names, "a demon," "devil in embryo,"
"lawless brute, only in the form of human," and "hideous monster."[3] In truth Robert Charles was none of these.

Yet it would also be a distortion of reality to glorify Charles in the
way that a white liberal historian recently described him, as "one of
the proudest black martyrs in American history."[4] For martyrs seek
death, or gladly give up living for the sake of some fixed belief.
Charles's primary conviction was that his own life should continue as
long as possible, consistent with dignity; and by sheer necessity he
resisted those who, in the words of the New Orleans *Item*, wanted to
"rid the earth of such a great encumbrance as was Robert Charles."[5]

What sort of person was the actual Robert Charles, and why is
his living and dying worth remembering? The few historians who
referred to him at all described him as a back-to-Africa disciple of
Bishop Henry M. Turner of the African Methodist Episcopal

1. New Orleans *Daily Picayune*, July 28, 1900.

2. *Harlequin*, II (August 4, 1900), 6; New Orleans *Daily States*, July 25, 1900;
Baton Rouge *Truth*, quoted in New Orleans *Daily Item*, August 5, 1900; Steen's
Creek (Miss.) *Times*, August 4, 1900; New Orleans *Times-Democrat*, July 25, 26,
August 4, 1900.

3. New Orleans *Daily Picayune*, June 29, August 1, 1900; New Orleans *Times-
Democrat*, August 6, 1900; New Orleans *Southwestern Presbyterian*, August 9, 1900.

4. Sig Synnestvedt, *The White Response to Black Emancipation* (New York:
Macmillan Company, 1972), 57.

5. New Orleans *Daily Item*, October 12, 1900.

Church who, in this cause, distributed pamphlets and sold magazines on the streets of New Orleans, and who, in the aftermath of
a race riot that erupted when he shot several policemen, died
in a spectacular shootout.[6] This has been all that was known of the
man. His life before he became the central figure in a great tragedy
was never probed, except by some wildly inaccurate reports that
circulated in New Orleans newspapers around the time of his
death. But his total existence spanned the thirty-four years from
Emancipation to 1900. Considerable information on his earlier life,
and even more evidence of what it was like to be poor and black in
the places where he lived, has survived on the shelves of air-
conditioned archives, as well as in the disarray of certain sweltering
courthouse attics of Louisiana and Mississippi. Robert Charles was
neither hero nor fiend incarnate, but a human being of rather more
than ordinary courage. Trapped by a problem that neither he nor
the world around him was capable of solving, he and his experience
tell us much about his troubled time and place.

When Robert was conceived, his parents, Jasper and Mariah
Charles, were still slaves. He was born shortly after the Civil War
ended, either late in 1865 or early in 1866. Copiah County, Mississippi, was most likely his place of birth. It was certainly where he
grew up. From Robert's childhood until his father's death there in
the spring of 1900, the Charles family lived as sharecroppers in a
cabin on one of the cotton plantations along Bayou Pierre, in the
northwestern section of Copiah County.[7] For those seeking the

6. See especially Edwin S. Redkey's excellent treatment of Bishop Turner and
the Liberia emigration activity in his *Black Exodus: Black Nationalist and Back-to-
Africa Movements, 1890–1910* (New Haven: Yale University Press, 1969). Charles's
activities in New Orleans are summarized by Redkey on pp. 255–58. See also: John
Smith Kendall, *History of New Orleans* (3 vols.; Chicago: Lewis Publishing Company, 1922), II, 538–40; Dale A. Somers, "Black and White in New Orleans: A Study
in Urban Race Relations, 1865–1900," *Journal of Southern History*, XL (February,
1974), 42.

7. Returns, United States Census, 1880, Mississippi Population, V, Copiah
County, Beat 4, p. 19, in Mississippi Department of Archives and History; Port

combination of natural beauty and good soil, a better land would be
hard to find anywhere. But a less auspicious time and locality for the
arrival of a black baby would be equally difficult to discover, unless it
might be Copiah County prior to 1865.

When the Civil War closed, most of the half million black people
of Mississippi remained on or near the same plantations and farms
they had known as slaves, working either as hired laborers or—as
most preferred—living apart from white supervision on family-
sized portions of the landlord's estate and either renting, or existing
off the proceeds of a share of the crop. Newly freed young blacks
near the few towns of any consequence tended to migrate to those
places—Vicksburg, Jackson, Natchez, Meridian—seeking jobs
that usually were not available and drawing occasional rations from
the Federal occupation authorities. But Jasper Charles was a quiet
and cautious man, disinclined to move about. In 1865 he was
already forty-one years old and had a growing family to support.
There were three young sons, Louis, Henry, and George; and his
wife Mariah, age thirty, was again pregnant with their fourth son, to
whom the name Robert would be given.[8]

Jasper and Mariah Charles had been born slaves in Mississippi.
They would recall to a census enumerator years later that their own
parents were originally from Virginia. The Bayou Pierre bottomland
of Copiah County where Jasper and Mariah lived had been settled
by planters from the Atlantic seaboard states who took their slaves
with them in the 1810s and 1820s—proud white families with
names now filling the old cemetery at Pine Bluff with weathered but

Gibson *Reveille*, August 9, 1900. Like many other black families residing there, the
Charleses are not reported in the 1870 federal census either in Copiah or in any
neighboring county. The 1870 census is notoriously incomplete, and a comparison
with that of 1880 indicates that the enumerators of the previous one did not bother to
list many of the families who lived in the Bayou Pierre region.

    8. Vernon Lane Wharton, *The Negro in Mississippi: 1865–1900* (Chapel Hill:
University of North Carolina Press, 1947), 52–53; Returns, U.S. Census, 1880,
Miss., V, 19.

still impressive marble monuments: Carter, Ellis, Hood, Robertson, Ainsworth, West.[9] Probably one of these families brought from Virginia the slaves who were the parents of the parents of Robert Charles.

Whoever Jasper and Mariah belonged to in the days of slavery they did not—as did so many freedmen—take the last name of their owner after Emancipation. Antebellum Mississippi had several whites named Charles, but none were listed among the slaveowners. The name may have been chosen at random, or possibly Jasper's father was known as Charles (few slaves were awarded last names), or perhaps Jasper and Mariah remembered their parents talking of a past homeland, at Charles City County, in the Tidewater of Virginia. Equally problematic is the Charles family's mingling of ancestry. Descriptions and drawings of Robert Charles indicate some admixture of races in his background. Referred to variously as a "mulatto" and "a Cuban-looking negro," he seems, nevertheless, to have been predominately African, with probably a one-quarter portion of Indian—or more likely both Indian and white—blood.[10] But Robert apparently never talked about, and was not interested in, his mixed ancestry. He considered himself a black man and let it go at that.

Copiah County's 780 square miles of southwestern Mississippi consists mostly of rolling hills, with sudden bluffs dropping off to lowlands and swamps along Bayou Pierre. An interior region more than twenty miles from the Mississippi River, Copiah's natural isolation became less pronounced when, in the 1850s, the tracks of the New Orleans, Jackson and Great Northern Railroad (later incorporated into the main line of the Illinois Central) were laid through

9. Returns, U.S. Census, 1880, Miss., V., 19; S. C. Caldweal, "Copiah County," in *Copiah County Mississippi: Quarter Century Resource Edition* (Crystal Springs: N.p., 1920), 2–4; Personal observation of Pine Bluff Cemetery.

10. Irene S. Gillis (comp.), *Mississippi 1850 Census: Surname Index* (Shreveport: Gillis Publication, 1972); Population Schedules, Seventh U.S. Census, 1850, and Eighth U.S. Census, 1860, Mississippi, both in Mississippi Department of

the county. Copiah's three major towns—Crystal Springs, Hazlehurst, Wesson—grew up along the tracks. With good silt and
loam soils, though not quite as rich as the alluvial bottoms in
adjoining Claiborne County to the west, Copiah attracted small
planters and farmers rather than the masters of hundreds of slaves
and thousands of acres. Few antebellum homes in the county look
impressive. But ownership of from two to twenty slaves was common among the white families, and by 1860 blacks slightly outnumbered (7,965 to 7,432) the white population. Only one free person of
color lived in the county.[11]

The upheaval of the Civil War physically affected Copiah less
than some other parts of Mississippi. Though subjected to Federal
cavalry raids, it never became a battleground. With a few exceptions
the whites supported the Confederacy, and a substantial portion of
the young men who marched off in gray uniforms did not come back
from the war, or returned minus arms or legs. The bitterness of
defeat was compounded by a brief occupation of Copiah County by
black troops during the summer and fall of 1865. Of all former
Confederate states, Mississippi proved most intransigent in recognizing the fact of black emancipation, and the dominant white
opinion in Copiah went along with the militant attitude of the state.
Federal bestowal of freedom and citizenship upon the black majority did not, in the minds of most whites, alter the verity of the
often-repeated slogan that "Copiah is a white man's country."[12]

Archives and History; Albert Phelps, *Louisiana: A Record of Expansion* (Boston:
Houghton, Mifflin and Company, 1905), 397; New Orleans *Daily States*, July 25,
1900.
    11. Lawrence E. Hood (comp.), *Copiah County* (N.p., n.d.), 1–3; Slave
Schedules of the Sixth U.S. Census, 1860, Mississippi, Copiah County, in New
Orleans Public Library; *Eighth Census of the United States, 1860* (Washington, D.C.:
Government Printing Office, 1864), I, 265–67.
    12. Works Progress Administration, Source Material for Mississippi History:
Copiah County, IX, Wars, *ca.* 1938 (MS in Mississippi Department of Archives and
History), 32–34; Hazelhurst *Copiahan*, December 30, 1865; Hazelhurst *Copiah
Signal*, September 27, 1883; letter from "Amicus," in Vicksburg *Evening Post*, July
10, 1890.

Yet in that county lived thousands of blacks—and a surprisingly strong minority of whites—who believed instead in a biracial sharing of the rights of citizenship. For a long time after the Civil War, and even for years after Reconstruction, this coalition would have a vigorous county leader. And thus Copiah would also have one of the most turbulent histories of any county in the South during the late nineteenth century.

There is no evidence that Robert Charles's father participated directly in any political conflicts during the Reconstruction period, although like most adult male freedmen in his vicinity, he was a registered voter who, whenever fraud or force did not prevent it, consistently supported the Republican ticket. Both Jasper and Mariah knew how to read and write, unlike many of their black neighbors. As a voter, Jasper remained on call for jury duty in the county's circuit court, appearing there as late as 1882. Who the Charles family's landlord was, and whether he happened to be their former owner, is unclear; surviving records and reports do, however, indicate that one or more of Jasper's older sons, upon reaching maturity, sharecropped a portion of an estate in northwestern Copiah owned by N. L. Fulgham, a member of one of the area's leading families.[13] The most certain statement that can be made about the Charleses is that they were landless sharecroppers who were desperately poor, but who were no worse off than most black families living in the political subdivision of Copiah County known as the Pine Bluff Precinct of Beat (District) Four.

To live at Pine Bluff would have compensations, even for the poor and black. The locality today has been renamed Dentville, although otherwise it seems to have changed little during the past century. The air is still clean, the water unpolluted. Down from the

13. Returns, U.S. Census, 1880, Miss., V, 19; Hazlehurst *Copiahan*, April 1, 1882; Assessment of Personal Property and Polls in Green's Store Precinct, Supervisor's District 4, Copiah County, 1884, in Record Group 28, No. 423, Mississippi Department of Archives and History; Hazlehurst *Courier*, quoted in Vicksburg *Daily Herald*, August 10, 1900.

hills pour numerous spring-fed creeks, clear except after rainstorms, rushing over sand and pebble beds into the watercourse of Bayou Pierre, which winds sluggishly through alternating farmland and swamp westward toward the Mississippi River. Nearby, steep bluffs with limestone outcroppings are crowned by thick groves of pine trees. Small game is still plentiful, and almost any black or white boy would learn to use a rifle at an early age.

But gone today are certain sounds of nature that young Robert Charles would have heard a hundred years ago: the hammering of big ivory-billed woodpeckers searching out their special insect diet within newly fallen timber, and occasionally at night from deep in the swampland, the sharp cries of prowling large panthers. These great cats had given the county its name. The Choctaw Indians, who inhabited the Bayou Pierre region before any whites or blacks arrived, had a word for the calling panther. It was *Copiah*.[14]

14 Dunbar Roland (ed.), *Mississippi: Comprising Sketches of Counties, Towns, Events, Institutions, and Persons, Arranged in Cyclopedic Form* (3 vols.; Atlanta: Southern Historical Publishing Association, 1907), I, 563.

2
DEMOCRATIC
THUNDER

Reconstruction in Mississippi was scarcely the saturnalia of carpetbagger corruption and Negro ineptitude that conservative Democrats would describe in campaign jeremiads for generations to come. Nor did it last long. Nor was it black dominated, although blacks held many offices. Five years passed after Appomattox before a Republican state government elected by black votes was able to take office; and within five more years, by 1875–1876, the "home-rule" Democrats had reestablished themselves in power throughout most of the state by carefully organized paramilitary demonstrations which, along with other measures, intimidated the black majority. Even during the short-lived period of Republican ascendancy, management of state affairs remained essentially under white control, and a careful student of Mississippi history concludes that the Negro legislators and sheriffs who did hold office generally performed in a satisfactory manner. Corruption evidently took place in Vicksburg, but that town almost never enjoyed honest government anyway.[1]

Nothing short of massive and continued federal military activity

1. J. G. Randall and David Donald, *The Civil War and Reconstruction* (2nd ed.; Lexington, Mass.: D.C. Heath and Company, 1969), 623–24, 684–85; Vernon Lane Wharton, *The Negro in Mississippi 1865–1900* (Chapel Hill: University of North Carolina Press, 1947), 157–80.

could have saved the Republican experiment in biracial, partly Yankeefied government in Mississippi. By 1875 the national mood no longer countenanced such burdensome intervention. Republican Governor Adelbert Ames, an honest but naive idealist who once thought he could transform Mississippi into a southern version of New England, finally recognized the futility of his task and resigned in 1876. Before departing, Ames prophesied to his wife (a daughter of General Benjamin F. Butler) that the freedmen of Mississippi faced an appalling future. "They are," Ames wrote, "to be returned to a condition of serfdom—a new era of slavery."[2]

Actually, an economic "condition of serfdom" already existed for most blacks in Mississippi and every other southern state. Ever since Emancipation the vast majority of freedmen, having insufficient money to purchase land or equipment, either rented or sharecropped the fields they tilled. Moreover, their share of the harvest was usually mortgaged under the crop-lien system, whereby they—and eventually most small landowning white farmers as well—gave the merchant with whom they traded (often the merchant was also the landlord) a first claim, or lien, on the gathered crop. Since few renters or sharecroppers ever cleared enough money to pay cash for store goods during the year, signing a lien agreement with a "furnishing merchant" was the only way to obtain necessary food and supplies from one harvest season to the next. Merchants, whose credit price for goods customarily included steep interest rates, often frowned on croppers raising their own vegetables, but frequently did not or could not prevent it. "Every darkey for miles around has a patch in peas,"[3] observed one Copiah County newspaper.

2. Adelbert Ames to Blanche Butler Ames, October 12, 1875, quoted in LaWanda Cox and John H. Cox (eds.), *Reconstruction, the Negro, and the New South* (New York: Harper & Row, 1973), 295.

3. C. Vann Woodward, *Origins of the New South: 1877–1913* (Baton Rouge: Louisiana State University Press, 1951), 180–82; Crystal Springs *Meteor*, March 17, 1883.

The annual debt at the store—not to mention the landlord's portion of the crop, which was typically one-half but sometimes more—took legal priority over the sharecropper's part of the harvest when the cotton was ginned and sold. The Charles family, under this discouraging system, was slightly better off than many other sharecroppers. By the early 1880s Jasper and Mariah had managed to save enough to buy one mule, one horse, a cheap old wagon, and some equipment; probably they had to transfer no more than half their crop to the landlord, whereas others with no team or tools usually came out with less. But from their half of the crop had to be paid whatever debt there was at the store. Robert's older brother Louis, known as Luke, who lived with his parents until he married and moved away in 1884, had five head of cattle listed under the name. The federal agricultural census for 1880 showed the Charles family as sharecropping eighteen acres, of which thirteen had been planted in cotton and five in corn during the previous season. Like the cotton, the corn was divided with the landlord, and most of the Charleses' portion of the corn would have been used to feed Luke's five cows and the fourteen pigs the family also owned.[4] This was their world; this was all they had, except each other.

In the fifteen years from Emancipation to 1880 Jasper and Mariah's family had grown considerably. The census enumerator who visited them in 1880 began by recording Jasper's age as fifty-six; Mariah was forty-five, and Luke had reached twenty-five. George and Henry, the other living adult offspring, had moved elsewhere. While writing down the name of the next oldest Charles still living at home, the enumerator had to dip his pen again into the ink; then in thick letters the official recorded Robert as black, male, single,

4. Assessment of Personal Property and Polls in Pine Bluff Precinct, Supervisor's District 4, Copiah County, 1882, 1883, 1884, in Record Group 28, No. 423, Mississippi Department of Archives and History; Marriages Prior to 1926, Mississippi, Soundex Code 626 in C to 120 in D, in Mississippi Department of Archives and History; Returns, U.S. Census, 1880, Miss. Agriculture, Enum. Dist. 23 Copiah, in Mississippi Department of Archives and History.

fourteen years old, and literate, but no longer attending school; his occupation was given as laborer. Since Robert's birth the family had expanded to include: John Wesley, age eleven; Aliac, another son, who was ten; a daughter, Alice, age eight; another daughter, Ellen, age five; Ellen's twin and the family's youngest son, Albert (reported by the enumerator as "idiotic"); and the youngest child, a daughter, Floril, age three. Also living with them was an eleven-year-old named Mary Smith, whose relationship was listed as "granDaughter" [sic]; she was apparently the child of an older daughter of Jasper and Mariah who either had died or had left Mary in their care. An agricultural census taken at the same time reveals that the sharecropper and lien contracts for the little farm were taken out in Luke's name instead of Jasper's, although Jasper owned the team and equipment. The total annual value of the farm production of this family of eleven was listed as $375, of which half went to the landlord and probably most of the rest to pay off a merchant.[5] From this there was survival, but no real hope of a better life.

Materially, the lot of Mississippi blacks did not substantially worsen—or improve—after Reconstruction ended. For the remainder of the nineteenth and far into the twentieth century, the overwhelming majority continued as nonlandowning tillers of the cotton fields, or as menial workers and domestics in the towns. A fortunate minority managed to acquire land or enter into the professions. Yet most remained in approximately the same static, disadvantaged circumstances as the members of the Charles family of Pine Bluff Precinct, Copiah County. For employers of labor this situation was clearly beneficial. In an age of unmechanized agriculture black people had, in the opinion of nearly all white plantation owners, a definite and useful place in Mississippi. Indeed, what little prosperity the state knew was mostly based on cheap black

5. Returns, U.S. Census 1880, Miss., V, Copiah, Beat 4, p. 19, in Mississippi Department of Archives and History; *ibid.*, Miss. Agriculture, Enum. Dist. 23, Copiah.

labor for the plantations, especially in the astonishingly fertile Delta counties north of Vicksburg. That much of Mississippi would revert to wilderness without the blacks was commonly understood. "As inhabitants," declared the relatively liberal Vicksburg *Evening Post* in 1889, "negroes are a vast improvement over panthers, bears and wildcats." Yet what must never be forgotten, future governor James K. Vardaman pointed out in 1900, was that the usefulness of black people was confined to only one "function ... that of a menial. That is what God designed him for," Vardaman explained, "and the white people will see to it that God's design is carried out."[6]

While the economic condition of Mississippi blacks remained, from the standpoint of white employers, satisfactorily stationary, there developed after Reconstruction a consensus among most upper and lower-class whites that a change must be effected in the blacks' social and political status. From the viewpoint of white supremacists, release from slavery had given black people dangerous aspirations which must be discouraged. It was decided that Negroes must be more submissive toward whites, more aware of their social inferiority whenever the two races came into contact, and that they must be shut out of the political process altogether. These developments were common to all southern states during the late nineteenth century. That Mississippi exhibited an extraordinary degree of militancy in such matters was due to the fact that, of the three states with more blacks than whites, Mississippi had the largest Negro majority. Particularly in the plantation counties whites developed a siege mentality, feeling themselves surrounded by what one writer described as "a mass of blackness."[7] Greater fear bred greater repression.

The policy of increasing social repression soon achieved a surface

6. Vicksburg *Evening Post*, August 15, 1889; Greenwood *Commonwealth*, August 10, 1900.
7. Wharton, *The Negro in Mississippi*, 274–75; anonymous letter in Vicksburg *Evening Post*, February 28, 1891.

victory of sorts. Mississippi blacks, especially, were made abundantly aware that there was an unwritten code of racial etiquette which had to be obeyed; all whites, regardless of individual merit, must be accorded the deference due to members of the superior, ruling race. The penalty for infractions of the code varied widely with place and circumstance, from the slow death by fire sometimes inflicted upon accused rapists ("ANOTHER NEGRO BARBECUE," read an account of one episode at Gulfport), to the punishment of a Cincinnati black man who "sassed" a telegrapher at a rural trainstop: "IMPUDENT SLEEPING-CAR PORTER RECEIVES A SEVERE THRASHING AT LAKE, MISSISSIPPI." The story below this headline primly concluded: "They did not want to shoot him. Lake bears no such reputation." So instead he was only "badly disfigured."[8] At the more ordinary levels of interracial contacts, minor "impudence" might be overlooked if it happened infrequently, or it could easily lead to a servant's dismissal from his job without the very necessary letter of reference, or result in a landlord's order to vacate the cabin and farm immediately. In order to survive without additional problems, the majority of blacks seemed to acquiesce in the neo-slavery ritual of behavior toward whites. There were those who acted as if they accepted their inferior status cheerfully, even enthusiastically. But there were many others who, when pressed hard, threw aside the mask and demonstrated their true feelings.

Along with social repression, the diminution of black participation in Mississippi's political affairs quickly followed the overthrow of the brief Reconstruction experiment. Yet in this matter there were national complications which caused a delay in the final solution. Black and white Republicans continued to hold some legislative and county offices for years after the Democrats took control of the state government in 1876, and tens of thousands of black voters

8. Dan Lacy, *The White Use of Blacks in America* (New York: Atheneum, 1972), 128–29; Rayville (La.) *Richland Beacon-News,* November 9, 1901, describing a lynching in Gulfport, Mississippi; Vicksburg *Evening Post,* November 5, 1891.

remained on the registration rolls until the last decade of the nineteenth century. Fear of the possibility of federal vengeance discouraged proposals to officially purge blacks from the registration rolls—until the writing of a new state constitution in 1890. That year Mississippi decided to test the national commitment to black citizenship with a clever circumvention of the Fifteenth Amendment; no mention in the 1890 constitution was made of race, but it contained a vital "understanding clause," which provided that every voter "shall . . . be able to read any section of the Constitution of this State; or shall be able to understand the same when read to him, or give a reasonable interpretation thereof." As to what was an acceptable interpretation, the Raymond *Gazette* slyly noted that "there might be honest differences of opinion between a corn-field nigger and inspectors of elections." The United States Supreme Court in *Williams* v. *Mississippi* (1898) upheld this clause, and thereby emboldened other southern states to take similar action.[9] A few Mississippi blacks continued to register and vote after 1890, but most, literate and illiterate alike, soon came to "understand" that attempts to register were futile, and might even prove unhealthy.

Events in Copiah County during the post-Reconstruction era provide more than a mere case study in the processes of social and political repression of blacks. What occurred there was in some ways typical of Mississippi, but in one important respect was not. In Copiah, unlike anywhere else in the state, black voters were able for a time to unite politically with a large segment of the poorer white agriculturists, and together they revived the Reconstruction experiment in a most improbable place.

9. Albert D. Kirwan, *Revolt of the Rednecks: Mississippi Politics, 1876–1925* (Lexington: University of Kentucky Press, 1951), 69–70; Raymond (Miss.) *Gazette*, September 20, 1890; James H. Stone, "A Note on Voter Registration under the Mississippi Understanding Clause, 1892," *Journal of Southern History*, XXXVIII (May 1972), 293–96; Alfred H. Kelly and Winfred A. Harbison, *The American Constitution: Its Origins and Development* (4th ed.; New York: W. W. Norton & Company, 1970), 497.

There were, to be sure, other examples of political "fusion" between whites and blacks in Mississippi during the late 1870s and early 1880s; yet without exception these others took place in heavily black counties, by agreements made among conservative Democratic planters and accommodating black politicians who received a few minor offices.[10] But in Copiah, with a population about equally divided racially, the coalition was between blacks and poor whites who acted together in defiance of the will of virtually all the upper- and middle-class white property holders of the county. Not surprisingly, this novel political experiment failed within a decade. For a time, however, it succeeded remarkably, and showed every sign of continued vitality until the Democratic leadership adopted the desperation policy of assassination.

A coalition of this sort, in this place, required a leader of more than ordinary daring. Such a man was John Prentiss Matthews, known to friends and enemies alike as "Print." No one else quite like him lived in Mississippi. Born in Copiah County in 1840 to one of the wealthier families (his father owned thirty-five slaves), Print seemingly never cared what others of his class thought of him. A strain of nonconformity ran in the Matthews line. Once in the antebellum period a band of vigilantes had "ordered the Matthews family out of the county" for some unstated violation of local customs; but through the protection of neighboring friends they managed to remain. Print weighed only 130 pounds, walked with a pronounced limp, and moved and spoke with intensity. As a young man he had opposed the secession of Mississippi and survived the Civil War in Copiah County as an outspoken Unionist. Predictably, he became a Republican activist during Reconstruction; he was first appointed, then, with black votes, elected sheriff.[11]

10. Kirwan, *Revolt of the Rednecks*, 15–17; Walter Lord, *The Past That Would Not Die* (New York: Harper & Row, 1965), 19–22.
11. Slave Schedules, Sixth U.S. Census, 1860, Miss., Copiah County, in New

What was most extraordinary in his career was his relative success in organizing, after Reconstruction, an "Independent Party" coalition of blacks and white farmers.

Print Matthews was in private life an unlikely leader of a biracial agrarian coalition. He lived in a big, comfortable home at Hazlehurst, the county seat; his wife and daughters dressed fashionably; his two sons attended the University of Mississippi. The brick store of J. P. Matthews and Brothers on Hazlehurst's Railroad Avenue was one of the largest mercantile establishments in the county and, in addition to selling groceries and dry goods to the townspeople, the store furnished supplies on credit to a rural clientele of mostly white farmers. One of his partner-brothers also owned a 1,400-acre plantation in southwestern Copiah, and the family held another plantation in neighboring Simpson County. By usual definitions Print was no economic radical. It is not realistic to assume that he made, as was charged, communistic and incendiary speeches to his followers; and many of his political foes conceded that the man had a reputation for personal charm, generosity, and honesty. But he did enjoy exercising political power, and, what was most unsettling to majority white opinion, he maintained a fixed belief that black people were "entitled to all the rights, privileges and immunities of American citizens." He also dared to criticize the two most powerful businesses in the county, the Merchants and Planters Bank at Hazlehurst and the textile factory (Mississippi Mills, Inc.) at the town of Wesson.[12]

With few exceptions the blacks of Copiah County loved and trusted Print Matthews. Many were said to rank him alongside Abraham Lincoln. Democratic lawyer J. S. Sexton testified to a United States Senate subcommittee investigating affairs in Copiah

Orleans Public Library, 3–4; *Senate Reports*, 48th Cong., 1st Sess., IV, No. 512, xxv, 422.

12. Hazlehurst *Weekly Copiahan*, June 17, 1882, March 1, 1884; letter from J. P. Matthews, *ibid.*, September 15, 1883.

that of the 2,500 black voters in the county, Matthews could count on the unswerving support of at least 2,200; they would, Sexton grumbled, "vote for the devil if [Print] put him on his ticket." Along with his black support, Matthews held the loyalty of 600 to 700 of the county's small white landowners, men who were squeezed, increasingly, between falling crop prices and rising interest rates, and who believed Matthews' argument that they, like the blacks, were victims of what he termed "the Democratic aristocracy" of the county and state.[13] With the county's 5,000 registered voters almost equally divided between white and black, the Matthews biracial coalition would, in a free election, outpoll the Democrats by at least three hundred votes.

But elections were hardly more free in Copiah than elsewhere in Mississippi during the 1870s and 1880s. As Judge J. B. Chrisman, who knew the county and state as well as anyone, observed with honest sadness years later: "Sir, it is no secret that there has not been a full vote and a fair count in Mississippi since 1875." Intimidation, however, was preferred over outright fraud, or murder. What came to be termed the "Mississippi Plan" of carefully orchestrated displays of armed white strength became the particular trademark of Copiah, Hinds, and Rankin counties, although it was by no means isolated to those three. During the week or so prior to election day, private military companies of white Democrats, usually hauling a cannon with them, would parade into heavily black precincts and, as one Copiah newspaper approvingly headlined it, make the valleys echo "WITH DEMOCRATIC THUNDER." The cannonade and rifle fire was as a rule aimed into the air instead of at people; and, in fact, beef barbecues often accompanied the military demonstrations, enticing black voters to listen to Democratic orators who urged them to join the conservative crusade "against venality, corruption and Radi-

13. *Senate Reports,* 48th Cong., 1st Sess., IV, No. 512, p. 1, 723, lxii (Appendix); letter from "Pearl River," in Hazlehurst *Weekly Copiahan,* October 1, 1881.

calism."[14] Then if verbal means failed, other methods could be used.

As a child, Robert Charles heard the cannonading of Democratic thunder on several occasions, and may have, like other impoverished black children in the area, accompanied his parents to Democratic rallies in order to taste the free barbecue. Pine Bluff Precinct drew both artillery and food during the critical elections of 1875 and 1876. Robert's ears would also have caught the sound of even heavier barrages from the fifteen cannons hauled to a big rally-barbecue at Utica, a few miles away, across the Hinds County line in 1875. There, local blacks were summoned to hear that it was "very necessary" for the Democrats to win "the next election, or for one of the two races to emigrate." The speaker "also endeavored to persuade them it would not be the white race."[15]

Black responses to such political pressure, as well as to social repression, varied in Copiah County from quiet submissiveness to armed defiance. At one extreme stood "Uncle" Lewis Adams, an humble former slave who, when interviewed a half-century after Reconstruction, related his tireless efforts in behalf of the Democratic party. "I wo' my lungs out," Adams was reported as saying, "tawkin to dem niggers, tryin' to show dem . . . dat de white folks wuz de bes' frens. But dey wuz po' deluged chilluns." Another apparent believer in white supremacy was "Uncle" Howard Divinity, who, having done menial service for the Confederate army, proudly wore a gray uniform to several Confederate veterans' reunions, and displayed his jingling reunion medals until he died near Bayou Pierre in 1930. Quite the opposite was the response of Lewis

14. Judge Chrisman, quoted in Woodward, *Origins of the New South*, 57–58; Crystal Springs *Monitor*, October 26, 1876; Hazlehurst *Mississippi Democrat*, September 1, 1875.

15. Hazlehurst *Mississippi Democrat*, September 1, 1875; Crystal Springs *Monitor*, October 26, 1876; letter from "U.T.K.," in Crystal Springs *Monitor*, July 22, 1875.

Brown, who lived in southwestern Copiah County. During the politico-racial crisis which developed in 1883, Brown organized an armed group of black men for the purpose of resisting any white aggression at his precinct. "You talk about these lamb-like negroes," remarked one Democrat with grudging admiration, "that negro, Lewis Brown, is as brave as Caesar."[16]

The majority of black people in Copiah adopted the flexible, survival-value technique of appearing to acquiesce whenever directly confronted with white demands, but immediately asserting themselves when there was a reasonable chance for success, or when it seemed there would be no serious retaliation. Time and again during the years following Reconstruction, black men in the heavily Negro precincts of Copiah were reported by Democrats as "beginning to appreciate the situation," with scores solemnly joining "Anti-Radical" clubs, while others held white-promoted meetings in which they pledged to "withdraw from politics." But it took direct fraud, or violence, on election days to prevent most black registrants from voting the Republican ticket—or from supporting any sort of coalition ticket which stood in opposition to the "Conservative Democracy." This kind of stubbornness was one of those "diseases," decided the Wesson *Herald* in 1881, which required "stern treatment."[17]

Most black families in Copiah owned a gun. So did virtually every white family, but the whites had more and better fire-arms. It was of more than passing concern that so many blacks as well as whites habitually carried concealed pistols whenever away from home. This particularly worried the editor of the *Copiah Signal*, who was convinced that the hidden emotion of most blacks toward

16. Works Progress Administration, Source Material for Mississippi History: Copiah County, X, The Negro, *ca.* 1938 (MS in Mississippi Department of Archives and History), 7–8; *Senate Reports*, 48th Cong., 1st Sess., IV, No. 512, lxxx, Appendix.

17. Crystal Springs *Crystal Mirror*, September 9, 1876; Hazlehurst *Copiahan*, July 10, December 4, 1875, August 21, 1880; Wesson *Herald*, November 19, 1881.

whites was one of hatred. He believed that, if they could, they would exterminate the white race.[18] With males of both races going armed, it might seem surprising that there were not more homicides—and particularly more interracial killings—than actually occurred. Murders took place often enough, but usually whites shot whites, and blacks shot blacks.

As far as the prospect of interracial warfare was concerned, Mississippi whites were not inclined to start any large-scale killing unless they felt their supremacy threatened, and blacks were all too aware that the whites were better armed and organized.[19] In any sustained conflict, there was absolutely no hope of a black victory. The white state militia would have been on its way to the scene by train within an hour if news reached the state capital that a black uprising had overwhelmed the whites of any locality; and even in the unlikely situation of a statewide insurrection of blacks, the federal army would have been called in to restore order, which would have meant a restoration of white control.

If blacks in Copiah County tended to conceal their true feelings toward the other race, most whites did not. The attitude of the white leadership class, at least, is well documented. Though sentiment varied, the typical person responded out of a jumble of fear, contempt, and paternalism. What the very poor whites thought about blacks is hardly clearer than black opinions. But certainly among the articulate upper- and middle-class whites of Copiah there were deviations in attitude, both to the right and left. Some viewed the blacks as worse than inferior humans—they were "apes" and "monkeys," said one newspaper editor in Hazlehurst and another in

18. Crystal Springs *Crystal Mirror*, May 27, 1876; Hazlehurst *Copiah Signal*, July 11, 1889.

19. In the decades after Reconstruction, Mississippi witnessed several "race riots," embellished by local legends into the status of warfare, but outside of a conflict in the Delta county of LeFlore in 1889, none amounted to more than white overreaction to imaginary threats. Wharton, *The Negro in Mississippi*, 222–23; Jackson *Clarion-Ledger*, September 5, 1889; Vicksburg *Evening Post*, September 4–6, 1889.

Crystal Springs. Men of this opinion occasionally spoke as if they actually *wanted* a race war, hoping the blacks would provide an excuse for their extermination.[20]

On the other hand, there was Print Matthews, and he did not stand entirely alone. Nor is there reason to doubt that, even among those who believed in the further social and political subjugation of blacks, there often appeared feelings of affection and acts of kindness toward individual Negroes. Even an intensely racist milieu could not totally extinguish the better side of human nature. It is impossible to read the obituary of an aged black woman of Hazlehurst, Peggy Sims, written by a white woman who signed herself "A friend," without being touched by the love expressed therein.[21] To ignore such instances would be to diminish humanity.

Copiah County's nearest approach to outright racial war came in the election of 1883. Print Matthews, though out of the sheriff's office since Reconstruction, was still the most powerful man at the county courthouse. All local officials in Mississippi served two-year terms. In 1881, Print's Fusion Independent ticket, as it was called, had elected a majority of the county's district supervisors, officials who then—and now—constituted a potent local legislature in Mississippi's counties. The Board of Supervisors held the power of assessing taxes, directing county expenditures, and selecting grand jurors. Print himself was narrowly defeated in 1881 in his bid to become sheriff once again (beaten officially by 2,075 to 1,991), but his ticket won the county treasurer's post and three of the five supervisors' seats. He lost the sheriff's office because the hundred or so ballots in the virtually all-Negro precinct of Mt. Hope were "eaten"—so chortled the Democratic inspectors—by a hungry mule who thrust his head through a window and into the box before

20. Hazlehurst *Copiah Monitor*, January 15, 29, 1880; Crystal Springs *Meteor*, February 10, 1883; Hazlehurst *Copiah Signal*, October 27, 1882.

21. Hazlehurst *Signal*, July 23, 1885.

those decisive votes could be counted. The "bad mule of Mt. Hope" became a standing joke in Copiah County and made several future appearances.[22]

Eighteen eighty three was, for most Americans, a year notable only for its special quietude. President Chester Alan Arthur's benign presence occupied the White House, and the major news story of the year was that Congress had finally authorized a national Civil Service Commission. The army and navy were tiny and the State Department almost comatose; no international crisis disturbed the American calm. One of the few instances that year of what the New York *Times* termed "unseemly excitement" came from a Negro bishop of the African Methodist Episcopal (A.M.E.) Church, Henry M. Turner of Atlanta, who harshly criticized the Supreme Court decisions which in effect encouraged further racial segregation, by declaring unconstitutional the congressional Civil Rights Act of 1875. The decisions in the Civil Rights Cases (1883) reinforced Bishop Turner's belief that blacks in America should "prepare to return to Africa or get ready for extermination."[23]

In Copiah County, Mississippi, natural disaster and human culpability gave that small portion of America in 1883 the most tragic year it ever knew. About three o'clock on the windy, rain-swept afternoon of April 22, residents of the southern portion of Copiah watched continual flashes of lightning from an unusually dark cloud to the west, and then down from this cloud appeared, with a "rumbling, howling noise," a long black funnel that swayed to and fro and gathered in density as it approached. The tornado killed

22. *Senate Reports*, 48th Cong., 1st Sess., IV, No. 512, xvi; Hazlehurst *Weekly Copiahan*, November 19, 1881; Hazlehurst *Copiah Signal*, July 14, November 10, 1882, October 11, 1883; Hazlehurst *Signal-Copiahan*, July 1, 1886.

23. New York *Times*, November 9, 1883; Henry M. Turner, "Negro Emigration to Africa," *Independent*, LI (September 7, 1899), 2430–31; Edwin S. Redkey, *Black Exodus: Black Nationalist and Back-to-Africa Movements, 1890–1910* (New Haven: Yale University Press, 1969), 41–42.

seventy-five people and injured over three hundred before it crossed the Pearl River and dissolved at the edge of the next county. Fifteen miles to the north of the tornado's path, where the Charles family lived, high winds caused damage; but there were no deaths. All of Copiah, however, suffered during the remainder of the April–September growing season from a prolonged drought that severely reduced both the cotton and vegetable crops. By the time cotton pickers were gathering from the dusty fields what little yield there was, the campaign had begun for the biennial county election, set for November 6. The kindly editor of the *Weekly Copiahan*, least racist of the local newspapers, feared that a new calamity approached, and he was right.[24]

Print Matthews summoned a mass meeting at Hazlehurst in August of 1883 to once again nominate a ticket for his Fusion Independent party. The gathering was attended by Negro Republicans, along with white farmers who in national politics identified with the Greenback-Labor party, and a few dissident Democrats whom conservatives referred to as the "Sore Heads." All nominees the Independents put up for county offices were white, and so were the candidates for district supervisors—except Anderson McGrew, a black man nominated for supervisor in Beat Four. This time Print sought no office himself, but his brother, Leon H. Matthews, was selected as the Independent candidate for sheriff. Everyone knew, however, that Print remained the coalition's leader. It was equally clear that a majority of the registered voters supported his slate. But by now the Democratic leadership of the county had reached—or were in the process of formulating—a grim decision. Thus the *Copiah Signal*, edited by the chairman of the Copiah Democratic

24. *Report, Executive Committee Associate Society Red Cross, Copiah County Mississippi, on account of the Great Cyclone of April 22, 1883* (Jackson: Clarion Steam Publishing Company, 1883); Hazlehurst *Weekly Copiahan*, April 28, November 3, 1883.

Executive Committee, announced in October: "No more Matthews rule in Copiah. Break the back bone and the thing can't wiggle."[25]

There were a few white men of old families who, like the Matthews brothers, became active Republicans in Copiah after the Civil War. But not all of them were willing to go along with the Matthews post-Reconstruction coalition. Next to the Matthews brothers, the most prominent Republican in the county was Uriah Millsaps. In 1883 Millsaps declared he was voting Democratic in this election and made public statements against the Independent ticket. "The handwriting is on the wall," said Millsaps, that a party based largely on Negro votes would no longer be permitted election victories. The Matthews party, he pointed out, "is not organized statewide" and could expect no help from the outside if trouble came. For his part, Uriah Millsaps was content to maintain a low-profile identification with the national Republican party, stay at peace with his Hazlehurst neighbors, and "hope to live to see the day when a man can be a Republican and be respectable." Millsaps would, it turned out, hope in vain, but his attitude allowed him to outlive Print Matthews by many years.[26]

Print and his supporters, black and white, appear to have been quite unprepared for the violent chain of events that began two weeks before election day. "This thing," Uriah Millsaps noted later, "came on them like a clap of thunder." The Matthews party's previous successes, and the relatively tame methods of repression hitherto used by Copiah Democrats, permitted them to think that there was little physical danger in opposing the party of the majority of whites. A gathering of what was termed "the fighting element" of

25. Crystal Springs *Meteor*, August 4, September 8, 1883; Hazlehurst *Weekly Copiahan*, July 21, 28, September 15, 1883; Hazlehurst *Copiah Signal*, October 11, 1883.
26. Hazlehurst *Copiah Signal*, August 10, October 18, 1883; Crystal Springs *Meteor*, October 6, 1883; Uriah Millsaps tombstone, Hazlehurst Cemetery.

the county's Democrats had been held late in August to "consider what is to be done with Print," but nothing serious happened until late October. Meanwhile, however, the militantly Democratic Crystal Springs *Meteor* announced to all concerned that "incendiary speeches have but one counter-irritant—lead."[27]

On the afternoon of October 25 the Democratic "fighting element" mounted their horses and set out on what was euphuistically called "The Procession" into the heavily black precincts of western Copiah. Special attention would be given to District Three, where the Matthews party had its strongest support. From then until election day, 150 armed and mounted men, commanded by Erastus (Ras) Wheeler of Hazlehurst, conducted nightly forays into the region, galloping along the dirt roads by moonlight, firing at intervals the artillery piece used in previous elections, and stopping occasionally to pay surprise visits to the cabins of Negro families. But this time there was a difference—some of the guns were aimed at people instead of the sky. That the men involved were not ordinary rowdies was testified to by Democratic Congressman Ethelbert Barksdale, who made a speech in Copiah County shortly before the election. Of the procession Congressman Barksdale remarked, "So far as I knew, the men who composed it, were among the best in the county, a good many of them planters and men of various professions."[28]

Tom Wallis was a black man who owned a small farm in District Three. He "took a good deal of interest in politics" and was a friend and supporter of Print Matthews. About 2 A.M. on October 26, several members of the procession broke into his home, and while dragging him from bed, attempted to throw a rope around his neck.

27. *Senate Reports*, 48th Cong., 1st Sess., IV, No. 512, p. 429; Jackson *Tribune*, quoted in Hazlehurst *Weekly Copiahan*, September 15, 1883; Crystal Springs *Meteor*, September 15, 1883.

28. *Senate Reports*, 48th Cong., 1st Sess., IV, No. 512, xvii; Crystal Springs *Meteor*, March 15, 1884.

Apparently their intention was to carry him outside, threaten him with death, and severely whip him as an object lesson in leaving politics alone. This had been the experience of another black man in the neighborhood named Henry Fortner, earlier that same evening. But Wallis put up a fight, and the intruders fired several shots, killing him instantly. One of the bullets passed through him and into his wife's arm. Mrs. Wallis later gave testimony before a United States Senate subcommittee investigation, but soon afterward died from an infection of her wound.[29]

The campaign of terror intensified in the last days before the election, but after the Wallis killing no one died until the day of balloting. Almost nightly, however, the procession entered the homes of blacks who were known to be politically active and threatened the inhabitants with death. Mr. and Mrs. Frank Hayes were shot by the procession but later recovered. A black church where political rallies had been held was burned. The most typical visitation was that accorded Benjamin Sandiford, a black leader in District Five. He was dragged from bed, warned of death, and again visited two hours later, with shouts of "bring in your rope and let us hang the damned son of a bitch." Numerous other black men were forced to swear they would either vote the Democratic ticket or stay away from the polls.[30]

Robert Charles was at the impressionable age of seventeen when the procession descended on his area of Copiah County. The Charleses' cabin was probably not directly visited since the father, Jasper, was not a political leader among blacks in the neighborhood. No member of the Charles family was listed among the casualties of the campaign, or appeared to testify at the subsequent Senate hearings held in New Orleans. But if their experience was typical of

29. Hazlehurst *Weekly Copiahan*, November 3, 1883; *Senate Reports*, 48th Cong., 1st Sess., IV, No. 512, xviii.
30. New York *Times*, February 19, 1884; *Senate Reports*, 48th Cong., 1st Sess., IV, No. 512, xviii–xxiii.

most blacks in western Copiah, the Charleses spent the last few days and nights prior to the election hiding in the nearby forest. Several local white families who supported the Matthews ticket decided to take the same refuge. One black man from the area who did give testimony was quoted as saying: "Dar is a mighty big settlement of cullud people up our way, an de biggest part of dem laid out at night, for dey dasn't stay at home. Some white men was in de woods, too, but dey was all Republicans. We all had to lay out like possums when de dogs are after dem."[31]

It was obvious that most of Matthews' supporters, black and white, would be afraid to go anywhere near the polls on election day. Print was in a hopeless situation; his followers were demoralized and there was no outside authority to expect assistance from. There were, it is true, a number of armed blacks under Lewis Brown's leadership in District Three, and they seemed willing to fight; but to call upon them would have been to ask their sacrifice of life with no hope of victory. Realizing all this, Print issued no appeal for armed resistance. But as a point of personal honor he decided to ignore a written ultimatum handed to him, at his home, the day before the election:

Whereas it is thought that the public interest will be subserved by Print Matthews absenting himself from the polls on election: Therefore,

Be it Resolved, that Print Matthews be ordered to keep within his own enclosure tomorrow.

Adopted by the citizens of Copiah County, this 5th day of November, 1883.[32]

Print's wife and daughters were present when the ultimatum was delivered, and according to them he replied, "I think I have as much right to vote as any of you. I have never done any of you any

---

31. *Senate Reports,* 48th Cong., 1st Sess., IV, No. 512; New York *Times,* February 19, 1884.

32. *Senate Reports,* 48th Cong., 1st Sess., IV, No. 512, xxvii.

harm. I have tried to be useful to society in every way that I could. . . . you have got it in your power to murder me, I admit. But I am going to vote tomorrow, unless you kill me."[33]

Early the next morning, Tuesday, November 6, Print dressed, ate breakfast with the family, and then walked across the street to the precinct called Hazlehurst East. Several Democrats carrying shotguns stood outside the door of the polling place. They watched Print approach but did not attempt to stop him as he entered the little room where the election inspectors were gathered. Also in the room was Ras Wheeler. Although he served as "Captain" of the procession, Wheeler was a relatively poor man and was not considered a decision-maker among Copiah Democrats. But he was loyal to those who were. And he would be quoted as saying that he had "pledged himself" to perform an unpleasant task. "It was," he explained, "my lot." He thought well of Matthews as a person, and had an account at his store.[34] This was not going to be one of Wheeler's enjoyable days.

Ras Wheeler sat quietly on a bench, next to the wood box for the stove. Upon entering the room, Print looked around, saw Wheeler, and went over to sit beside him. The two men talked in low tones for a minute or so. Wheeler finally said: "Print, I would not vote today if I were you." Matthews then got up, walked over to an election official, and presented his ballot. He was asked to fold it. He was doing so when Ras Wheeler reached inside the wood box, lifted out a double-barreled shotgun, and taking quick aim, fired first one and then the other charge of buckshot. Print Matthews died instantly.[35]

The news raced across the county by telegraph and by horsemen that Matthews was dead. Among white Democrats there were said

33. *Ibid.*
34. *Ibid.*, xxviii, 21.
35. This account of the killing of Print Matthews is based upon eyewitness testimony in *Senate Reports* cited above, along with stories about the affair in two Copiah newspapers. See Hazlehurst *Weekly Copiahan* and Crystal Springs *Meteor*, both for November 10, 1883.

to be "extravagant demonstrations of joy." A band at Crystal Springs played martial music for an hour. Whites at the predominately black precinct of Tailholt gathered for a jubilant demonstration, where, as one witness described the scene, "old men and leading men, that you would think would shudder at murder and be horror struck, just yelled and fairly shouted." A rumor spread that seventy-five armed Negroes had been spotted preparing to march on Hazlehurst; the sheriff telegraphed the governor for troops to help put down a black insurrection, but this request was soon rescinded. Armed riders from nearby towns sped toward Hazlehurst; "they came," said an admiring Democratic paper, "like gallant and chivalrous Knights at ancient times to render assistance to their threatened brethren and, if need be, to defend the women and children with their lives." Their services would not be required. No trouble developed from either black or white supporters of the Independent ticket. Near Crystal Springs there was a gathering of blacks, but of peaceful intent: "The niggers," reported the *Meteor* a few days later, "met one mile South of here last Tuesday and passed resolutions of sorrow." [36]

Resolutions not as sorrowful were adopted the day after election by a meeting of white Democrats at the courthouse in Hazlehurst. By then the anticlimactic counting of ballots was finished. The ticket of the late Print Matthews had been defeated overwhelmingly, the Democratic candidates winning by uniform totals of about 2,900 to 870. Pine Bluff Precinct was one of only two that returned majorities for any Independent candidates. [37] At the courthouse on November 7, Joseph L. Meade, chairman of the Copiah Democratic Executive Committee, presided over the adoption of resolutions aimed at discouraging any future efforts by the Matthews coalition. As duly

36. New Orleans *Times-Democrat*, November 7, 1883; *Senate Reports*, 48th Cong., 1st Sess., IV, No. 512, xxix; Crystal Springs *Meteor*, November 10, 1883.
37. "Official Vote of Copiah," Hazlehurst *Weekly Copiahan*, November 17, 1883.

printed in the local press, the significant portions of this document read:

Whereas certain rumors are current that the relatives of the late J. P. Matthews have threatened the peace of society, in order to avenge his death, by killing Democrats and destroying their property: Now therefore,

Be it resolved by the people of Copiah County in mass meeting assembled this day, at the court-house of said county, that if any person shall be injured, or an attempt made to injure him, either in person or in property, in any manner, by the said relatives or friends of J. P. Matthews, that we hereby declare that we hold his said relatives and friends who participate accountable for the same, and that we will regard them as without the pale and protection of the law and common enemies of society, and that we will visit upon them certain, swift retribution. . . .

Resolved further, that in the opinion of this meeting it is necessary to the safety of society and the welfare of all races and classes in this county that the Matthews family shall keep out of politics in Copiah County.

Resolved further, that from henceforth no man or set of men shall organize the negro race against the whites in this county, and if it shall be attempted in the future, we hereby give notice that it shall be at the peril of the person or persons attempting so to do.

Resolved, that we do hereby pledge ourselves, each to the other, our lives and fortunes and our sacred honor, that we will, all and individually, from henceforth, hold ourselves in readiness to enforce the foregoing resolutions, and to meet at any time upon the call of the chairman of this meeting. . . .

Resolved, that the thanks of this meeting be extended to the Hazlehurst brass band for their services on this occasion.

J. L. Meade, Chairman.[38]

There were some white Democrats in Copiah who regretted the recent violence and who thought these resolutions by their leaders too strongly worded, and in poor taste. Yet there were others whose

38. *Congressional Record*, 48th Cong., 1st. Sess., 715. See also Hazlehurst *Weekly Copiahan*, November 17, 1883.

impulse was to state even more bluntly the real purpose of what had transpired. The editor of the *Meteor*, along with publishing the above resolutions, added a more succinct declaration: "Keep the nigger down." [39]

39. Crystal Springs *Meteor*, November 10, 1883.

3
THE PISTOL

Copiah had its hour upon the national stage early in 1884, when the county's recent political violence became the subject of a United States Senate investigation. National Democratic leaders charged—with truth—that the Senate's Republican majority decided to investigate Copiah's affairs "for the purpose of aiding the Republican party in the approaching Presidential [election] by reviving the stories of outrage and crime."[1] The Copiah inquiry was, indeed, an echo of the Reconstruction-era "bloody shirt" exposés of southern violence. But this partisan motive did not make the outrages described by eyewitnesses any less real, or less repulsive.

The hearings of the special Senate subcommittee took place inside the granite walls of the United States Customhouse in New Orleans in February of 1884—not at Copiah County. After all, New Orleans during Mardi Gras season (or any time) was a more interesting community to visit than Hazlehurst; and it was assumed that dozens of witnesses, mostly blacks, could speak more frankly away from home; moreover, among the northern senators there was an uneasy feeling that "the people of Copiah might become unduly

1. "Views of the Minority," *Senate Reports*, 48th Cong., 1st Sess., IV, No. 512, xliii. See also "The Sherman Resolutions," *Harper's Weekly*, XXVIII (February 9, 1884), 87.

excited by the presence in their midst of a Senate committee."[2]
Certainly, the mood of Copiah's white leadership toward the investigation was one of defiance, and of fierce resentment that any
outsiders would presume to question their conduct. The fact that
the committee was headed by a Massachusetts man (Senator
George F. Hoar) made the inquiry all the more odious. Of all
northern states, Massachusetts—the home of abolitionism—had
long been held in lowest esteem by white Mississippians.[3]

The report of Senator Hoar's committee laboriously attempted
to attach blame to the Democratic party generally for the crimes of
whites in Copiah County. But it became increasingly obvious from
the statements of local politicians and newspapers—from the time
of the 1883 campaign violence up through the investigation—that
the dominant class of Copiah was quite unconcerned with national
politics or national opinion. Even the criticism of other white Mississippians was regarded as outside meddling.[4] Copiah was—or
wished to be—a world unto itself. Such intense county-centered
provincialism has always been common in Mississippi, a state with
no large cities with which to identify. But the whites of Copiah
displayed this trait to an extraordinary degree.

Seldom has a Mississippi county shown such utter disregard for
outside opinion as did Copiah in the weeks following the election
disturbances of 1883. Ras Wheeler, who had assassinated Print
Matthews in front of several witnesses, was shortly thereafter appointed city marshal of Hazlehurst. One of the aldermen, asked by
Senate investigators why he had selected a known killer for this
position, replied: "[Wheeler] has a good heart." Wheeler went
through the formality of a murder trial in May of 1884, but was found

2. New York *Times*, February 9, 1884.
3. Hazlehurst *Copiahan*, October 16, 1875; Crystal Springs *Monitor*, May 22,
1879; Crystal Springs *Meteor*, February 16, 1884.
4. Hazlehurst *Copiah Signal*, September 14, November 15, December 6, 1883;
Oxford *Falcon*, quoted in Hazlehurst *Weekly Copiahan*, March 1, 1884; *Senate
Reports*, 48th Cong., 1st Sess., IV, No. 512, p. 21.

innocent on grounds of self-defense, even though Matthews had been unarmed.[5] The murderer's popularity was such that a Hazlehurst drugstore used a testimonial from him endorsing their locally concocted patent medicine, for which another ad read: "Don't waste your money and endanger your life by trying Northern trash. Use a genuine Southern chill remedy... Burnley's OMNICURA." While still under indictment, Wheeler was elected to represent Copiah's church-sponsored prohibitionist movement in presenting the state legislature with a memorial in its behalf. There was some talk of running him for governor of Mississippi.[6]

Most of the black witnesses who appeared to testify at New Orleans were said to be planning to settle a safe distance from Copiah County. Such was the sentiment of some whites as well as blacks in the aftermath of the murder. A number of whites who had supported Matthews moved elsewhere. The black man who dug a grave for Print left shortly afterward because he was threatened with death. Matthews was buried on his family's property in Hazlehurst; the family either was not allowed or did not wish to place him in the town cemetery. A tall marble column inside a wire fence marks his grave today, along Georgetown road. Most of the Matthews family departed the county shortly after the funeral (though some of them returned years later); moreover, one of the Print's brothers paid the transportation of several black families to Kansas. One of Print's sons, J. P., swore that he would someday avenge his father's death, but he did not. J. P. was fatally shot on Christmas day of 1890 in Carrollton, a northern Mississippi town where he was postmaster and Republican party leader. He was politically unpopular there.[7]

5. *Senate Reports*, 48th Cong., 1st Sess., IV, No. 512, p. 405; New Orleans *Daily Picayune*, May 8, 1884; Hazlehurst *Weekly Copiahan*, May 10, 17, 24, 1884.

6. Hazlehurst *Weekly Copiahan*, November 1, 1884; Hazlehurst *Signal*, November 6, 1884; *Senate Reports*, 48th Cong., 1st Sess., IV, No. 512, xxxi; Friar's Point (Miss.) *Gazette*, quoted in Hazlehurst *Weekly Copiahan*, March 22, 1884.

7. New York *Times*, February 16, 19, 22, 1884; Port Gibson *Reveille*, December 31, 1890.

For a long time many black families in Copiah had indicated a desire to move somewhere else. Economic advancement and human dignity were goals that seemed unobtainable where they were. The increasingly repressive social and political climate that followed the violence of 1883 heightened blacks' unhappiness with the role that the ruling class—and their own lack of training for anything but raising cotton and corn—had decreed for them in Copiah County. Unfortunately, there was no clear prospect for a better life anywhere else. But beginning 1876 the white-edited newspapers of Copiah occasionally reported, as did papers in neighboring counties, that a number of blacks were anxious to move to some other state or nation. Jamaica was sometimes spoken of, as were other places in the Caribbean. The state of Kansas became the actual destination of about six thousand Mississippi blacks during 1879 and 1880; nearly one hundred families from Copiah left for there. And some dreamed of a return to Africa.[8]

Mississippi white reaction to migration talk among the blacks varied usually according to economic interests, but Negro-phobia among some whites eclipsed any material considerations. In the Delta counties the large planters were virtually unanimous in wanting more—not fewer—blacks, even though some parts of the Delta were already over 80 percent black. Negroes are, explained one spokesman for plantation interests, "the animate machinery which has largely produced our wealth."[9] But in Copiah as well as in the other transitional counties between the lowlands and the

8. Crystal Springs *Monitor*, June 8, 1876, January 10, 1878, January 16, April 17, July 31, 1879; Hazlehurst *Copiah Monitor*, December 18, 1879, January 22, 29, 1880; Vernon Lane Wharton, *The Negro in Mississippi: 1865–1900* (Chapel Hill: University of North Carolina Press, 1947), 115–16; Jackson *Comet*, August 16, 1879; Vicksburg *Evening Post*, March 19, 1889.

9. F. R. Guernsey, "The Negro Exodus," *International Review*, VII (October, 1879), 373; Vicksburg *Evening Post*, March 19, May 28, 1889, January 6, 1890; Natchez *Democrat*, quoted in Vicksburg *Evening Post*, May 28, 1889.

clay hills, where the racial division was about equal, white opinion on the possibility of a massive black departure was certainly mixed.

Copiah's few large planters, along with the furnishing merchants to whom the black peasantry was in debt, strongly opposed black departures. The sentiments of those whites who were not dependent on Negro labor seemed to vary from indifference to euphoria over the prospect of such an exodus. Among whites, the most vigorous supporter of black movement to anywhere was Walter L. Birdsong, editor of the *Copiah Monitor*. Most blatantly racist of the several county weeklies, Birdsong's paper during the Kansas migration activity of 1879 and 1880 adopted as its motto "The nigger must GO!" For the benefit of obstinate planters, the editor added: "Why not let them go, the colored apes." He conceded that "if all the niggers were to leave without paying their debts," the merchants would be financially hurt, but for the sake of upgrading what was already "the best county in the State" people should be willing to make sacrifices. For his own part, Birdsong proposed to contribute money toward a fund for purchasing additional tickets to Kansas. It also occurred to him that Massachusetts deserved to have a selected sampling of Copiah's black population.[10]

Even so, the same whites who said they wanted black people to leave sometimes enjoyed heaping discouragement and ridicule on their dreams of doing so. A Crystal Springs weekly (also named *Monitor*), hearing in 1878 that New England philanthropists were proposing to send shiploads of southern blacks to Liberia scoffed that those who went on such a journey would not have the fortitude to cope with the African environment; such a move meant "death to the nigger." Later the *Monitor's* editor claimed to have seen a letter an expatriate Mississippi black wrote to his local friends which

10. Hazlehurst *Copiah Monitor*, October 9, November 20, December 4, 1879, January 8, 29, 1880.

contained the depressing information that in Liberia monkey meat had to do in place of pork. He quoted from this alleged letter that "roast monkey is mighty dry eating, and needs lard; but that you can't get [here] for love or money."[11] As to the occasional talk among Copiah blacks of migrating to the Caribbean, the same paper insisted that the following conversation was overheard on the streets of Crystal Springs between a young black woman and her boyfriend: "Gawge," she softly murmured, "down dar in Jamaky whar monkeys frow coca-nuts at niggers, and war dar is no work, dar's whar we mus go. No work no nuffin, Gawge."[12]

The vision of returning to the African homeland has recurred time and again among the poorer blacks of the United States. It was by no means confined to Mississippi and Louisiana or to the post-Reconstruction period. Certainly those who were first brought over in chains dreamed of return. But as an actual movement the idea of a wholesale migration of former slaves and their descendants began with the white-sponsored American Colonization Society (ACS) in 1816. With congressional funds, the ACS saw to the establishment of the Republic of Liberia during the 1820s, as a nation into which free American blacks would voluntarily resettle. Many white southerners at the time supported the society; viewing slavery as uneconomical and immoral, believing also that blacks and whites could not peacefully live together in a free society, the founders of the ACS looked forward to the eventual emancipation and departure of all Americans of African ancestry. A few thousand free blacks did settle in Liberia, but the ACS's ultimate plan collapsed during the 1830s, as the South became more economically committed to slavery and more blind to the moral evils of its "peculiar institution." It

11. Crystal Springs *Monitor*, January 10, 1878, January 16, 1879. See also Hazlehurst *Copiah Monitor*, December 18, 1879; Crystal Springs *Meteor*, January 14, 1887.

12. Crystal Springs *Monitor*, June 8, 1876.

is a startling irony, as a modern writer has pointed out, that the "'Back-to-Africa' movement was in its inception mainly a white man's fantasy for Negroes." [13]

But once the mass of southern blacks could express such ideas, however cautiously, the lure of Africa would become to some of them a compelling attraction. It was never a popular movement among the black elite. Booker T. Washington and W. E. B. DuBois, the two most prominent black Americans of the late nineteenth and early twentieth centuries, quarreled over what strategy black people should follow in their struggle for a better life; but both agreed that the answer was not in Africa, or in migration anywhere outside the United States. [14] Their disagreements—which reflected a division among the black leadership generally—were of little concern to the lower-class rural peasants who made up the majority of the race, and for whom there was no real hope in America of that era, either with Washington's plan of accommodation toward whites or in DuBois' perilous call for militant protest.

Both in Mississippi and Louisiana a reawakening of interest in African migration was noticed in 1883 and became more apparent among lower-class blacks in the years ahead. During the summer of 1887 an organization called the African Emigration Society was incorporated to promote migration specifically from those two states "to Liberia or some other place that is desirable." One of the leaders was a former slave from Mississippi named George Charles. Early in 1888 Charles and two associates were reported by the New

13. Philip J. Staudenraus, *The African Colonization Movement, 1816–1865* (New York: Columbia University Press, 1961), 23–103; Theodore Draper, *The Rediscovery of Black Nationalism* (New York: Viking Press, 1970), 9–13. The Draper book is an excellent survey of nationalism among American blacks from the early nineteenth century to the present.

14. August Meier, *Negro Thought in America, 1880–1915: Racial Ideologies in the Age of Booker T. Washington* (Ann Arbor: University of Michigan Press, 1963), 66–68; Edwin S. Redkey, *Black Exodus: Black Nationalist and Back-to-Africa Movements, 1890–1910* (New Haven: Yale University Press, 1969), 3–5.

York *Times* as preparing to visit Liberia to obtain firsthand knowledge of its potential "for the colored people of this country."[15] Exactly what became of their organization is not known. Since nothing further was heard of it, the African Emigration Society evidently had a short and unfruitful life. It is not even mentioned by historians who have written on back-to-Africa movements.

Who was this George Charles, and was he related to the future "bloodthirsty champion of African supremacy," Robert Charles? Robert had a brother named George, but this man was positively not him, as census records show that Robert's brother was born in 1859; and the George Charles of the society was a much older man, who was born a slave in Mississippi during the 1840s. He may have been a brother of Jasper Charles, and thus Robert's uncle. Robert had one uncle, name unknown, whom he seems to have been close to, and who later wrote a letter apparently defending his nephew's conduct in New Orleans. The letter no longer exists. Much of black history is recoverable by diligent use of surviving records, but to trace family relationships that date back to the antebellum period (before slaves' names were listed by census takers or tax assessors) is not possible unless recollections have been orally handed down within the family. In the case of the Charles family, efforts during the summer of 1974 to find their descendants in Mississippi proved unavailing. And the oldest black residents who could be located in the part of Copiah County they lived in had no memory of anyone named Charles.[16]

In the spring of 1887 Robert Charles left Copiah to work in Vicksburg, thirty miles away from his parents' cabin at Pine Bluff.

15. New York *Times*, February 9, 1888.
16. Returns, U.S. Census 1880, Miss., V, Copiah, Beat 4, pp. 18–19, in Mississippi Department of Archives and History. A letter from an uncle of Robert Charles to Ida B. Wells-Barnett is mentioned in Mrs. Barnett's pamphlet *Mob Rule in New Orleans* (Chicago: N.p., 1900), 42. Mrs. Barnett's daughter, Mrs. Alfreda M. Duster, informed me on June 13, 1974, that all of her mother's papers were burned in a house fire years ago.

He was twenty-one. Probably he was drawn to the city by urgent advertisements of the newly created Vicksburg Waterworks Company, which needed three hundred laborers (and apparently gave preference to sturdy young black males) to excavate trenches and lay pipes for the city's first unified water system. The relatively attractive pay was $1.25 a day, "with money every Saturday night." News of this offer very likely reached Robert's locale not by newspaper, but by the word-of-mouth "black telegraph," which since the era of slavery has amazed Mississippi whites with its rapidity.[17]

Robert was large and strong. Six feet tall, deep brown in complexion, he probably weighed at age twenty-one somewhat less than the 180 to 190 pounds he carried in later years. No account of him at this period of his life exists, but the blacks and whites who came into contact with him later in New Orleans would be uniformly impressed by his intelligence and the ease of expression that suggested an educated man. Robert's formal education could not have amounted to more than the two years of primary schooling which was all that either black or poor white children in Copiah were provided with. However, the schools for blacks that did exist in Copiah, one-roomed and ill-equipped though they were, reputedly had better black teachers than could be found in the majority of Mississippi counties. Copiah's superintendent of public schools during the early 1880s was surprised to find that in his county black attendance "is a good deal larger than at the white schools."[18] All his adult life, Robert would work at unskilled or semiskilled jobs; but at

17. The Warren County tax reports show that Robert Charles was working in Vicksburg in 1888 and 1889. The report for 1887 no longer exists, but I am reasonably sure, based on the fact that so many young black men from his locale were attracted to Vicksburg in 1887 to work for the waterworks company, that this is the time he arrived there. Vicksburg *Evening Post*, May 25, June 4, 1887. For comments on the "black telegraph," see S. F. Davis, *Mississippi Negro Lore* (Indianola, Miss.: McCowart-Mercer, 1914), 6.

18. New Orleans *Times-Democrat*, July 25, 1900; New Orleans *Daily States*, July 29, 1900; *Annual Report of the [Mississippi] State Superintendent of Public Education, 1874* (Jackson, Miss.: Pilot Publishing Company, 1875), 36; *Biennial*

some point he began to purchase books and writing materials. He wanted to improve his verbal and written skills, and simultaneously learn more about the world, especially about his race.

He was only one of four hundred or more black people to leave Copiah in 1887. Others would migrate from the county the following year. Many of the younger, single men went no further than Vicksburg and, like Robert Charles, labored with pick and shovel for the waterworks company, then sought other employment after the water pipes were all installed. Meanwhile, some Copiah sharecropper families were still moving to Kansas, following the route that others had taken seven and eight years earlier. But by far the majority who departed Copiah joined the thousands of blacks from other interior Mississippi counties who were relocating in the rich new farmlands being developed out of the lowland forests of the Delta region north of Vicksburg. Delta planters, having more land than labor, welcomed these newcomers and sought additional black workers from all over the South.[19]

In Copiah the departures of blacks in 1887 and 1888 provoked much the same variety of white reactions that were noticeable in earlier migrations, except that this time there seemed to be fewer prominent whites who were glad to see them go. The *Meteor* wondered why "the poor, ignorant creatures" preferred "the swamp country" over scenic Copiah.[20] (A bale of cotton to the acre instead of a half bale was one reason.) At Hazlehurst in January of 1887, leading planters met to discuss their labor's emigration, and solemnly promised to those blacks who would remain that "they [the whites of Copiah] will continue in the future to do as well by them in

---

Report of the [Mississippi] State Superintendent of Public Education, 1878–79 (Jackson, Miss.: J. L. Power, 1880), 57; *Senate Reports,* 48th Cong., 1st Sess., IV, No. 512, p. 405.

19. Hazlehurst *Signal-Copiahan,* January 6, 1887; Crystal Springs *Meteor,* January 14, May 6, 1887; Vicksburg *Evening Post,* January 12, 21, 1888.

20. Crystal Springs *Meteor,* January 14, 1887. See also, letter from "Fair Play," *ibid.,* February 4, 1887.

granting them all the privileges of citizenship as they have done in the past." These words did not measurably slow the migration. Bob Lott, an influential white man of Crystal Springs, believed there was no problem worth bothering about. "Let them go," said Lott. "We can go down in Lincoln County, or somewhere else and get as many negroes as we want. The darkies just want to go somewhere and anywhere will do."[21] Lott's analysis of black motives was incorrect; yet the emigration activity did prove statistically insignificant. In 1890 blacks still slightly outnumbered whites, as they had in 1880. Copiah's total population has dropped considerably since the late nineteenth century, but the same ratio (slightly over 50 percent black) was still reported by the census of 1970.[22]

In Vicksburg, Robert Charles found steady employment beginning in 1888 with the Louisville, New Orleans and Texas Railroad. He worked for the LNO & T as a section hand from 1888 until May of 1892. About 1890 his older brother Henry joined him with the LNO & T, and they worked together. Like other black section hands who did maintenance labor on the tracks near the city, Robert listed the Vicksburg railroad shops as his place of residence. During these years the LNO & T was the largest regular employer in Vicksburg. There were 250—more during peak seasons—on the company payroll there, not counting engineers and firemen. Locomotives needing repairs were brought to the floor of the sprawling machine shop, where lathes and drills kept up their screeching until far into the night. One hundred men kept busy in a separate building housing the great wheel lathe. Nearby, another shop specialized in building new boxcars for the company. About once a month, give or take a week, the pay car of the LNO & T

21. Hazlehurst *Signal-Copiahan*, January 6, 1887; Crystal Springs *Meteor*, January 14, 1887.

22. *Appleton's Annual Cyclopaedia and Register of Important Events for the Year 1891* (New York: Viking Press, 1892), 532; *United States Census of Population, 1970*, I, Pt. 26, *Mississippi* (Washington, D.C.: Government Printing Office, 1973), 15.

arrived at the shops on Levee Street—an event looked forward to by both the workers and the city's stores and saloons.[23]

The Vicksburg of the late 1880s and early 1890s was not a large city by the standards of most of America, but it was at that time the biggest community of predominantly rural Mississippi. Thirteen thousand people lived inside its limits; the population was about evenly divided between white and black. Situated on high bluffs overlooking the Mississippi River, it had been called the "Gibraltar" of the Confederacy during the Civil War; several hills on the eastern edge of town were literally covered with the graves of Union and Confederate dead. A river town with a sizeable Catholic population, Vicksburg to some extent was a miniature version of New Orleans, complete with rows of saloons and bawdy-houses. Disapproving Baptists looked upon it as "the Sodom of Mississippi."[24]

The railroad shops that Robert lived at were located along unpaved Levee Street, close to the river and downhill from the main business district. Dirt and noise predominated on this ugliest thoroughfare in town; the tracks of the LNO & T ran alongside warehouses, bars, and tiny wooden stores selling inexpensive goods. Blacks and whites worked on Levee Street, but the saloons were mostly for blacks. Some mornings during the spring and autumn heavy fogs blanketed this lowland area, obscuring everything more than a few yards away and causing the locomotives going in and out of the yards to shriek insistent warnings. At night, music and laughter issued from the black places of entertainment on Levee and adjoining streets, but all such establishments were required by law to shut down from 11 P.M. until after the departure of the midnight trains, so that white passengers might not be disturbed by

23. Assessment of Personal Property and Polls in Vicksburg, Warren County, 1889, in Mississippi Department of Archives and History; Vicksburg *Evening Post*, July 29, August 31, September 9, 1887, February 21, 1888.
24. A. A. Hoehling, *Vicksburg: 47 Days of Siege* (Englewood Cliffs, N.J.: Army Times Publishing Company, 1969), 1; Jackson *Baptist*, April 19, 1900.

"obscene singing, piano playing, and vociferous handclapping."[25]

During the five years he lived in Vicksburg, Robert Charles had an opportunity to learn about a more advanced black society than he had known along Bayou Pierre. A black middle class of some consequence resided in Vicksburg, where two weekly newspapers—the *Delta Beacon* and the *Labor Bee*—were published by and for blacks. One of the ablest lawyers in town (he sometimes had white clients) was the light-skinned Negro W. E. Mollison; the Vicksburg *Evening Post*, not able to dignify him with the "Mr." reserved for white men but wishing to recognize his worth, compromised by always referring to him as "W. E. Mollison, Esq." Even rank-and-file black workingmen had an opportunity for organization and self-expression not commonly found in Mississippi; for the national Knights of Labor, largest union of its day, had two lodges in Vicksburg—of which the Crown Assembly was for blacks. Some recognition of mutual class interest existed between these two labor lodges in the city, which together had an estimated 1,300 members. One Vicksburg conservative warned that white supremacy was being unintentionally undermined by this cooperation.[26] While working for the LNO & T, Robert Charles may have joined the Knights of Labor, but it was a policy of the order not to reveal the names of its members.[27]

Robert received little or no notice from the white people of Vicksburg. He was just another "darkey." He probably avoided whites whenever possible. The surviving files of the Vicksburg

25. Vicksburg *Evening Post*, October 29, 1887, August 6, 1891, August 29, 1896.

26. Vicksburg *Evening Post*, May 31, August 11, 1887, October 31, 1890, July 15, 1891, November 11, 1893; *The Leading Afro-Americans of Vicksburg, Mississippi* (Vicksburg: Biographica Publishing Company, 1908), 15; H. S. Fulkerson, *The Negro: As He Was; As He Is; As He Will Be* (Vicksburg: Commerical Herald Printer, 1887), 96–97.

27. After 1886, the Knights of Labor did not even report membership figures, except for the entire nation. Frederic Meyers, "The Knights of Labor in the South," *Southern Economic Journal*, VI (April, 1940), 484.

newspapers for 1887–1892 (white papers; no copies of the black weeklies are extant) do not once mention his name; but black laborers almost never got their names in white journals except when in trouble with the police.[28] Robert Charles is reported on the Warren County tax rolls as living at the railroad shops, and that is all. Never was he in difficulty with the Vicksburg authorities. And he must have been a satisfactory worker for the LNO & T, or he would not have been employed by the railroad for so long, especially with a surplus of black labor in the city. Thus we can conclude that he was quiet (he would have had to adopt a surface politeness toward his white foremen to avoid dismissal or worse) and that he did his work.

Robert Charles would become, of course, the object of considerable attention after he commenced shooting white people in New Orleans during the last five days of his life, in July of 1900. It was then that a Vicksburg newspaper undertook to search out and interview local blacks who had once known him. "A bad coon" he was, they reportedly agreed. According to the *Herald*, "One of his companions," who knew Charles during his life in the city, said . . . that he was a desperate man and had been known to boast that no policeman would ever arrest him without a fight." Charles "generally loafed around Levee Street," continued the paper, "but never came into contact with the police."[29] When this report was published Robert was still alive, and the subject of an intensive two-state manhunt. No black person in either Louisiana or Mississippi was then in a position to utter a kind word about him.

It is more than possible Robert Charles swore that a particular law officer in Vicksburg "would [never] arrest him without a fight." Constable John Stanley was his name, and his reputation among both the criminal and the law-abiding blacks was not good. Actually,

28. For perceptive comments about southern white journals and black news, see the address of a Baton Rouge newspaperman before the National Editorial Association, as quoted in New Orleans *Daily Picayune*, May 31, 1892.

29. Vicksburg *Daily Herald*, July 25, 1900.

Stanley seldom brought in a black man or woman without some kind of violence, but it was usually the constable who inflicted the wound or bruises. "A Memorial to the Law Abiding White People of Vicksburg" was published by spokesmen of the black middle class of the town, protesting that "John E. Stanley has for a number of years exercized a most ruthless tyranny over such of our people who have been charged with misdemeanors." Two of his killings of blacks appeared so unprovoked that white grand juries indicted him for murder, but he was never convicted. On several occasions the editor of the *Evening Post* (who once shot and killed an unarmed man himself) criticized Stanley's use of the gun as "unnecessary." Before one of Stanley's trials, five of the city's lower-class blacks pooled their resources and offered Judge Loewenberg fifty dollars to convict him. The judge almost lost his breath at this attempted bribery, and ordered the five men arrested.[30] But the episode vividly showed what many blacks of Vicksburg thought of white justice.

After maintenance work all day on the railroad tracks outside Vicksburg, Robert probably did often relax in the bars along Levee Street. As a wanted notice for him in 1900 stated, he "drinks, but not to excess." Undoubtedly he knew—or at least observed—some of the well-known black characters of the street, who included "Hollering John," a demented and harmless old man, who had fought in the Union army and would one day be buried in the Vicksburg National Cemetery. He may also have met Caesar Hennington and Jack Yarborough, both from Copiah County, who would presently go back there to become leaders of a gang of outlaws. The frequenters of Levee Street also included a beggar referred to as "Can Can Jimmie" and a black homosexual nicknamed "Dick Deadeye," whose voyeur inclinations led to his receiving a load of shotgun

30. Vicksburg *Evening Post*, April 1, August 25, September 1, 1891, March 14, 1892, January 6, 1893, January 20, 22, 1894.

pellets when he was discovered in some weeds watching white
workers use a latrine.[31]

Race relations in Vicksburg at this period appear to have been
slightly better than in most southern communities, but not by
much. As elsewhere, there were numerous "good white folks" who
were personally kind to individual blacks; nevertheless, every person with discernible African ancestry must at all times remember his
"place" and be properly respectful toward all Caucasians. The only
noticeable social contact between the races was at the level of the
cheaper saloons and whorehouses, involving white men and black
women. The Negro brothels regularly serviced whites, and occasionally mixed couples were seen eating or drinking in the black bars
along Levee and Mulberry streets. Constable Stanley and his black
mistress, Daisy Sherman, once got themselves engaged in "a most
disgraceful row" in one of those places; Miss Sherman shot at him,
only to miss. Stanley would probably have lost his job because of the
adverse publicity, but the next day he had sobered up and re-
deemed himself by locating and capturing the black outlaw Caesar
Hennington, wanted for murder in Copiah County.[32]

Contact between white men and black women in whorehouses
or behind other closed doors was hardly approved of by Vicksburg's
white society, but there were few open protests against it. Like
antebellum cohabitation with female slaves, it was considered a
regrettable fact about which the less said the better. But interracial
mixing in barrooms or other public places was quite another matter,
since this gave the appearance of some kind of equality of status, or

31. New Orleans *Times-Democrat*, July 25, 1900; Vicksburg *Evening Post*, July
12, 1889, September 1, 1891, November 15, 1895, May 19, 1896, February 11, 1898.
32. The insightful study that anthropologist Hortense Powdermaker made of
Indianola, Mississippi, during the 1930s would, insofar as white attitudes toward
blacks are concerned, apply with one exception to Vicksburg during the 1890s. The
exception is that in the 1890s prominent whites were more likely to endorse the
lynching of blacks, especially if the alleged crime was rape of a white woman. *After
Freedom: A Cultural Study of the Deep South* (New York: Viking Press, 1939), 23–55;
Vicksburg *Evening Post*, February 6 and 7, 1893.

at least comradeship, between the white men and their black partners. Particularly outrageous to the *Evening Post* was a jolly scene reported in 1889 by a party of fishermen off DeSoto Island, south of Vicksburg, where five well-known white men were observed along the island shore, completely nude, in the company of eight black women, also nude. "The white men," warned the newspaper, "if they desire to see their names in print, have only to repeat their shamelessly indecent conduct."[33] A consenting sexual relationship between white women and black men was considered virtually unthinkable, but a few cases were known, even in Mississippi.[34]

Black crime against whites occurred almost nightly in Vicksburg, but it usually amounted to petty theft and very rarely involved violence. The most frequently reported offense was chicken-stealing. A large proportion of the white residents raised chickens in their backyards, and sometimes the entire coop would be missing in the morning. The two most noted specialists in this activity were Shep Harris and William Darby, the latter reputedly being "a silent partner in a successful colored eating house in this city." Occasionally, Negro holdup men appeared in Vicksburg stores; "Black Hawk" and "Black Diamond" were two men accused of several stickups and burglaries. Many black lawbreakers evaded capture, even though they were known to the police and remained in Vicksburg, by taking refuge during the day in cabins next to a lowland, wooded area known as the American Bottoms. During the early 1890s a gang of thieves made this their headquarters, where they had a system of hilltop signals "given by colored women and small boys." The women dropped their sunbonnets whenever an officer approached, while the children commenced a "low, continu-

33. Vicksburg *Evening Post*, May 24, 1889, January 7, 1892, February 6, 1893.
34. West Point (Miss.) *New Era*, quoted in Hazlehurst *Copiahan*, April 19, 1884; Vicksburg *Evening Post*, June 24, 1892; Summit (Miss.) *Sentinel*, quoted in Wesson *Mirror*, August 29, 1891.

ous whistle"—whereupon the wanted men vanished downward into the thickets of the American Bottoms, and not even Constable Stanley dared pursue them there.[35]

Whether the crime was major or minor, lawbreakers of any color apprehended in Vicksburg faced highly unpleasant prospects. Those unable to pay fines for misdemeanors in city court worked off their debt by cleaning animal excrement and debris from the city streets. The escape-prone were shackled with the traditional ball and chain. At night, city convicts were kept awake (as were nearby residents) by frequent screams from about a dozen insane black people who were housed in the City Workhouse (jail) because there was no room for them in the Mississippi State Asylum. Obstreperous prisoners were apt to be hung up by their thumbs for "disobedience of the Workhouse rules." City and county prisoners worked off their fines at seventeen cents per day; but worse off than these inmates were the more serious offenders leased by Warren County to labor at Idlewilde plantation, owned by a fell taskmaster named Charles Smith. Six months at Idlewilde, however, was vastly preferable to a felony sentence to Mississippi's state penal system, where convicts were leased for long terms to private plantations and lumber camps. The death rate of black prisoners under the state lease varied during the 1880s from ten to sixteen percent a year. The white-convict death rate was also high, but only half that of the blacks. Seven-eights of the state's convicts were black, and of these a substantial number had been sentenced to prison for "stealing a pig of the value of one dollar."[36]

Wherever large numbers of blacks lived, lynching represented

35. Vicksburg *Evening Post*, July 18, 1887, October 14, December 18, 1891, May 26, June 25, 1892, September 28, December 16, 1893, February 6, 1894.

36. Vicksburg *Evening Post*, August 10, 1887, February 22, 1888, July 30, 1889, April 14, 1891, April 8, 21, 1892, August 26, 1896; New Orleans *Daily Picayune*, October 3, 1887; C. Vann Woodward, *Origins of the New South: 1877–1913* (Baton Rouge: Louisiana State University Press, 1951), 214; Hazlehurst *Signal*, January 14, 1886.

the most dramatic and brutal method of race control. No black person—man, woman or child—could ever feel entirely safe, and no white lynchers (at least, not in Mississippi) were convicted. The state of Mississippi statistically ranked toward the bottom of American commonwealths in most categories, but in percentage of black population, and in the number of lynchings, it stood at the very pinnacle. Between 1882 and 1903, there were 334 lynchings reported in the state, of which all but 40 of the victims were black. The record year was 1891, with 20 lynchings. These figures, however, do not include the black or white fatalities which occurred during local race riots, of which the grisliest was the LeFlore County "war" of 1889. One account of this bloodletting read simply: "Twenty-two negroes have been killed since Monday, and forty more are dead in the Tallahatchie swamps. The negroes threaten to burn every house in LeFlore County."[37]

Lynchings became so commonplace by 1890 that some Mississippi newspapers, even ones which disapproved of the practice, occasionally reported them with droll touches: "He offered to lead the mob to a railroad trestle under which the money lay buried. John and the money have now exchanged locations." Another lynching account read: "When the midnight train left Elizabeth, a large crowd [went] with Robinson to the trestle, and... Robinson remained at the trestle after the other parties had left."[38] Visiting northerners, however, were not supposed to make jokes about these events. In Copiah County a group of Chicago tomato buyers who happened to witness a lynching hurt local feelings by sending humorous telegrams about it to their home offices. One message

37. George M. Fredrickson, *The Black Image in the White Mind: The Debate on Afro-American Character and Destiny, 1817–1914* (New York: Harper & Row, 1971), 272; James Elbert Cutler, *Lynch-Law: An Investigation into the History of Lynching in the United States* (New York: Longman's Green and Company, 1905), 179, 183; Vicksburg *Evening Post*, September 6, 1889.

38 Port Gibson *Reveille*, March 1, 1892; Vicksburg *Evening Post*, February 26, 1892.

read: "NO TOMATOES CAN BE BOUGHT TODAY. BUSY ENGAGED HANGING NIGGERS." The Port Gibson *Reveille* complained that such insensitive Yankee levity "gives to death in the case of lynching an air which robs it of gravity and gives familiarity instead."[39]

While Robert Charles lived at Vicksburg no lynchings took place inside the city, although several occurred within a twenty-mile radius. A band of white "regulators" operated in town for a brief time in 1891, flogging one black man for leading an "irregular" life and threatening a number of whites with the same treatment. Curiously, of the two attempted lynchings reported in Vicksburg while Charles was there, one involved a white man in the hands of a black mob, and the other intended victim was a black man who angered this same mob. The white who was nearly lynched was an insane Swede who had murdered a popular black midwife while she fished at the river's edge. The Swede got into an argument with her over her fishing worms, which he believed were snakes. He loved snakes and was said to keep many for pets. After he stabbed the woman, the Vicksburg police were barely able to save him from an infuriated crowd of black men and women. Later the mob turned their wrath on a black man who had assisted the authorities in rescuing the Swede.[40]

At some point during his years in Vicksburg, Robert bought a pistol. It was most likely a fairly expensive Colt .44 calibre, purchased from the Louis Hoffman Hardware Company. The .44 was the favored size pistol among black men in Vicksburg, and the Hoffman firm was by far the largest gun dealership in the city. From what is known of Charles's personality and behavior patterns, he would have viewed the pistol as a defensive weapon, but would carry it almost constantly when off work, concealed in a large coat

39. Port Gibson *Reveille*, July 8, 1897.
40. Vicksburg *Evening Post*, August 30, 1889, July 31, August 1, December 15, 17–18, 1890.

pocket. Gun carrying was a common practice among Vicksburg white and black men, as it was for southerners generally. However, the law against carrying a concealed weapon was enforced almost exclusively against blacks, and the fine was often severe.[41]

Robert probably had several reasons for thinking he needed to have a gun with him, not the least of which was the frequency of lynchings and other racial troubles that occurred near Vicksburg during the late 1880s and early 1890s. Another motive prompting both whites and blacks to wear pistols concerned dogs. Great numbers of half-wild canines ran in packs across the Mississippi countryside as well as in the towns. It was estimated that over four thousand curs were loose in the Vicksburg environs; one large pack lived around the city cemetery, where they carried cow bones and offal from the nearby slaughterhouse and buried this mess in the loose earth of grave mounds. Some of these animals were apt to attack people at any time, and rabies outbreaks were not uncommon during the summer months. The problem extended beyond Mississippi. A Louisiana daily once suggested that "nothing has so much contributed to the habit . . . of the people moving about the countryside armed, as the presence of these dogs."[42]

Shortly after one o'clock on the hot Monday afternoon of May 23, 1892, Robert and his brother, Henry Charles, approached the depot of the town of Rolling Fork, forty miles north of Vicksburg. Both men had been doing maintenance work on a local section of the LNO & T tracks. And both were at this moment carrying rifles. Henry had a Winchester and Robert was armed with an old needle gun. For two black men to walk boldly into a Mississippi Delta town — especially Rolling Fork — in the middle of the day with rifles

41. Vicksburg *Evening Post*, December 14, 20, 27, 1887, March 7, 1893, December 22, 1896.

42. Hazlehurst *Copiah Signal*, November 10, 1882; Brookhaven *Mississippi Leader*, April 17, 1894; Vicksburg *Evening Post*, April 14, August 20, 1891, August 13, 31, 1896, April 8, 1898; New Orleans *Daily Picayune*, January 17, 1893.

in their hands was, to say the least, an unusual sight. But no one tried to stop them as they approached the depot.[43]

Four days earlier one of their fellow workers, William Knight, aged seventeen and a Negro, had been executed in this town for killing a white LNO & T foreman. The execution was reminiscent of a lynching. Knight had struggled on the gallows rope for quite some time before he strangled to death, as the drop did not break his neck.[44] But Robert and Henry Charles's armed visit to Rolling Fork had nothing directly to do with Knight's death, though the two black men certainly had discussed the event, and it must have been on their minds as they approached the train station.

"They came to the depot," explained the next issue of the Rolling Fork newspaper, "bent on recovering a pistol which a negro boy on the freight train had taken from one of them a few days previous."[45] The pistol—which probably belonged to Robert—apparently had been hidden somewhere on the train when the section hands were being transported from Vicksburg to work on the tracks; the youth either had found the pistol or had been allowed to look at it, and did not put it back.

43. Rolling Fork *Deer Creek Pilot*, May 28, 1892. The only files of this newspaper for the early 1890s are in the office of the present publisher, Hal DeCell, who kindly allowed me to examine them.

44. Memphis *Appeal-Avalanche*, May 20, 1892.

45. The Rolling Fork *Deer Creek Pilot*'s account of May 28, 1892, does not give Robert's first name, but describes the two black men as "Henry Charles . . . armed with a Winchester rifle and the other, whose name could not be learned [carrying] a needle gun." Although his name was not given in the newspaper account, Robert Charles was the other black man involved in this shooting, because—as the next chapter discusses—immediately afterward he departed the Vicksburg area and reemerged in Copiah County under an assumed name, Curtis Robertson. Also, what happened at the Rolling Fork depot fits his behavior pattern perfectly; he was never known to be aggressive until he thought he had been greatly wronged or was attacked first, but once violence began he would fight anyone and seemed to disregard the consequences. Undoubtedly, Henry Charles also fled the area, but what became of him afterwards is unknown. In 1900, the Winchester rifle Robert Charles used with such deadly accuracy in New Orleans belonged, Robert told a friend, to his brother Henry. Quite likely it was the same Winchester Henry carried into Rolling Fork that day in 1892. See New Orleans *Times-Democrat*, July 25, 1900.

The northbound freight Henry and Robert were looking for was at the depot, having stopped to load or unload packages. It was soon scheduled to pull out; the locomotive's boilers were on and ready. The two brothers quickly spotted the black teenager they were seeking "and ordered him to get the pistol when the boy replied that the flagman had it." At this point the flagman, who was white, jumped out of the caboose, the pistol in hand, and ordered the two blacks to let the youth go. The reporter for the local paper tersely described what happened then:

The negroes turned upon the flagman and he began emptying his pistol at them and at the same time retreated under the car. The negroes returned his fire very hotly and the flagman had to retreat to the engine, which was only three or four car lengths away. The engineer attempted to pull out but the negroes boarded the train and covering the engineer compelled him to stop. The flagman again retreated to the caboose on the opposite [end] of the train and was hotly pursued by the negroes. Seeing that they were determined to have the pistol, the flagman threw it from the train which was then pulling out at full speed. The negroes after recovering the pistol made for the swamp west of the railroad. Nobody was hurt and no arrests have been made.[46]

The shootout at the Rolling Fork depot remained a matter of local indignation and conversation for several days. It was, headlined in the town's weekly paper, "A HIGH HANDED AFFAIR." Two black men had not only walked boldly down the middle of town carrying rifles, but had violated the old taboo which said no black person may use violence toward any white person for any reason. Moreover, a respected white resident who lived near the depot, Robert Williams, "came near getting a stray bullet as he was entering his back gate."[47]

Soon, however, the episode would be all but forgotten. When

46. Rolling Fork *Deer Creek Pilot*, May 28, 1892.
47. *Ibid.*

Robert Charles plunged into so much trouble in New Orleans in 1900, police reports from Mississippi would be sent to Louisiana saying that some eight years ago (other accounts stated it might have been two, or six, or ten years before 1900) Robert had brutally murdered a brakeman (variously reported as being black or white) who was trying to put him off a freight train at Rolling Fork.[48] There were other equally erroneous reports of his bloodthirsty doings. Actually, Robert never killed a brakeman, or anyone else, in Mississippi. But he had been in a gunfight with that white flagman. And he got his pistol back.

48. New Orleans *Daily Item*, July 25–28, 1900; Vicksburg *Daily Herald*, July 25–26, 1900; New Orleans *Times-Democrat*, July 26, 28, 1900.

4
ALIAS CURTIS
ROBERTSON

The shooting at Rolling Fork made it impossible for Robert to continue working in that part of Mississippi. Nor could he remain with the LNO & T Railroad anywhere along their Memphis to New Orleans line. If he went back to Vicksburg at all, it was only to pass through and see friends. There was no extensive manhunt for him or for Henry; after all, nobody had been hurt. Of the newspapers in the area, only the *Deer Creek Pilot* of Rolling Fork reported what he had done. But Robert assumed that all the police thereabouts would know that a six-foot "darkey" named Charles who was a section hand for the railroad had shot at a white man, which was a racial offense ranking below only rape or murder. If he gave himself up or was caught, the best he could expect was a long term as a leased convict in the dread Mississippi penitentiary system. Or he might be lynched. So he went back to Copiah County and assumed the name Curtis Robertson.[1]

Even after Robert achieved his brief national notoriety in 1900, the white people of Copiah apparently did not realize that Curtis Robertson and Robert Charles were one and the same; or, if some of them did, nobody wished to admit he had been hoodwinked or had

1. Rolling Fork *Deer Creek Pilot*, May 28, 1892; interview with Hyman Levy, in New Orleans *Sunday States*, July 29, 1900.

let a "black fiend" live around him without recognizing him for what he was. As Robert Charles he was a wanted man, beginning in May of 1892; then as Curtis Robertson he became involved in a legal difficulty in Copiah County in 1894. And there in Copiah he managed to extricate himself from that trouble in 1896.

The Copiah that Robert returned to in the early 1890s was still one of Mississippi's most troubled counties. Politically, however, racial questions had seemingly been resolved to the satisfaction of the whites. The grim lessons of 1883 had taken firm hold. Mississippi's constitution of 1890, with its "understanding clause," merely legalized across the state the de facto disfranchisement already practiced in Copiah and several other counties. Few blacks bothered anymore to go to the polls. White dissidents for some years had heeded the published warning of the local Democratic organization that any signs of activity on their part would be considered an act "against white supremacy." Nominees of the county's Democratic convention were elected without even nominal opposition. The "Copiah Plan" of repression, one resident explained, had been worth the effort because it was yielding political and social tranquillity. He added that "the colored voters are [now] sensible enough to see that the owners of Copiah County should be the masters thereof."[2]

But racial problems continued nonetheless. Expression at the ballot box might be denied, yet blacks in Copiah still revealed their hostility toward the dominant whites in various ways, from rare acts of murder to the frequent placing of African voodoo charms in white homes. An increase was also noticed in the covert selling of sacks of cotton by sharecroppers (who thereby denied the landlord his

2. "To the Democratic Voters of Copiah County," in Wesson *Mirror*, September 6, 1889; letter from "Amicus," in Vicksburg *Evening Post*, July 17, 1890. By 1892 only 170 of the 2,136 registered voters in Copiah were black. See James H. Stone, "A Note on Voter Registration under the Mississippi Understanding Clause, 1892," *Journal of Southern History*, XXXCIII, (May, 1972), 295–96; Memphis *Appeal-Avalanche*, May 26, 1892.

share); certain rural storekeepers were willing to buy this cotton, with no questions asked. Whites often wondered what blacks were privately thinking, and a Hazlehurst newspaper in 1889 suspected that most of them might be dreaming of bloodshed. Yet, when observed on Saturdays in Copiah's towns, the black people seemed more orderly and polite than before.[3]

Puzzling to some whites in Copiah was an apparent resurgence of African customs during the late 1880s and early 1890s, particularly in the use of conjure (voodoo) charms against whites, and against other blacks. "Today," reported the Crystal Springs *Meteor* in 1888, "it is as strong in their belief as when practiced upon the coasts of West Africa." Not all Copiah blacks believed in voodoo, but the poorer people were said to be absolutely convinced of its power. One white man closely examined a charm found in the bed of a relative and described it as "a very artistic arrangement of many colored feathers, coiled something like a clock spring." Others, more sinister-looking, were discovered in numerous white residences: bags of "snake skins, fangs, buzzard feathers and skunk fur . . . are found in pillows, in mattresses, sewed into the clothing, in hats and in the hearth." Not a few whites more or less believed in the potency of these charms; a woman named Harriet Bell took to her bed and died, convinced she was the victim of a deadly voodoo object hidden somewhere in her home. Interestingly, the leading witch doctor of Copiah was an aged man apparently never harassed by whites, though he was known for his activities throughout the county. His name, Paris Green, was also that of an arsenic compound. Paris Green lived along White Oak Creek, in northwestern Copiah; reputedly he once practiced the art of conjure in Africa, and he always wore a necklace of alligator teeth. Occasionally he would

3. Vicksburg *Evening Post*, October 7, 1892, February 7, May 20, 1893; Crystal Springs *Meteor*, May 28, 1886, October 26, 1888, September 11, 1891; letter from "Beat Two," in Hazlehurst *Signal*, August 27, 1885; Hazlehurst *Copiah Signal*, August 29, 1889.

be seen riding a donkey into Crystal Springs or Hazlehurst, on missions of removing—or casting—spells.[4]

Overt hostility of whites toward blacks had also undergone some modifications by the early 1890s in Copiah. No longer was there need for political terrorism, since that had accomplished its purpose years before. The more prominent whites now believed that blacks should be left unmolested, unless they committed crimes or tried to disturb the status quo of white supremacy. There were only two actual lynchings reported from Copiah during the 1890s, whereas several Mississippi counties surpassed that record. But a new form of violence toward blacks did briefly emerge, though disapproved of by leading whites. It was called whitecapping.[5]

Whitecapping, as a student of Mississippi affairs has observed, meant different things elsewhere but had a special distinction in the Magnolia State: it referred to vigilante-style efforts to drive Negroes off land they owned or rented.[6] The majority of participants in the night raids on black cabins were small white farmers who felt threatened by the presence of black farmers. But other whites sometimes went along on these raids, for no specific reason. In some places Jewish merchants were also harassed by the same night riders. An outbreak of whitecapping activity swept several southwestern Mississippi counties in 1892 and 1893; and Lincoln County, on the southern border of Copiah, was the hardest hit. Copiah had one active band of these vigilantes, supposedly led by three young men named Pet Tyson, George Shields, and Butch Young.[7]

4. Crystal Springs *Meteor*, October 26, 1888, September 11, 1891.
5. The two lynchings, one in 1895 and the other in 1897, were both of black men accused of murdering white men, and both occurred at Crystal Springs. Vicksburg *Evening Post*, November 25, 1895, July 25, 1897. For a discussion of Mississippi whitecapping (which covers a broader period than the title indicates) see William F. Holmes, "Whitecapping: Agrarian Violence in Mississippi, 1902–1906," *Journal of Southern History*, XXV (May, 1969), 165–85.
6. Holmes, "Whitecapping: Agrarian Violence in Mississippi, 1902–1906," 166.
7. Meadville (Miss.) *Franklin Advocate*, December 1, 1892; Jackson *Daily Clarion-Ledger*, April 14, 1893; Gloster (Miss.) *Valley Record*, January 12, 1894; Brookhaven *Mississippi Leader*, April 18, 25, 1893.

In Copiah, as in Lincoln, several whitecapper leaders were indicted and stood trial for whipping and otherwise terrorizing blacks. The worst episode in Copiah involved a tiny (110-pound) black farmer whom a white reporter described as "one of the humblest and most industrious in the county." He almost died from the beating he received from sixteen night riders, but lived to show his scars in court. It was unusual for white men to be tried for maltreating blacks anywhere in Mississippi, but not unheard of. What was more rare, almost unprecedented, was conviction and sentencing on such a charge. It was even physically dangerous for a judge and jury to take their duties seriously in a case of this nature. Yet in Copiah and Lincoln counties at this particular time there were prominent whites who favored some kind of legal punishment for the whitecappers, and the cases were tried by an unusually courageous judge of the circuit court, J. B. Chrisman.[8]

Judge Chrisman was no Print Matthews-type southern liberal. He had been a colonel in the Confederate army and believed in the conventional racial dogmas of his day, including the need for some legal means of disfranchising blacks. But Chrisman also believed that black people deserved the protection of law. Considered in the light of his time and place, he was a fair, sensitive, and thoroughly decent man. And a brave one. "Nothing," commented a Brookhaven newspaper, "can swerve him from the path of duty as he sees it."[9]

Ten years before the whitecapping trials, Judge Chrisman had saved the life of a black prisoner, and risked his own, by facing down a lynch mob on the steps of the Claiborne County courthouse at Port Gibson. During 1884 he had attempted, and failed, to obtain indictments against known lynchers in Franklin County; the Vicksburg *Commercial-Herald*, which along with numerous other

8. Brookhaven *Mississippi Leader*, April 18, 1893; Jackson *News*, quoted in Vicksburg *Evening Post*, May 12, 1893; Port Gibson *Reveille*, May 12, 1893.
9. Interview with Thomas B. Birdsong, in WPA Source Material, Mississippi, Copiah, Assignment No. 13, p. 1; Brookhaven *Mississippi Leader*, April 25, 1893.

Mississippi papers of that day endorsed lynching, accused Chrisman of "sentimentalism" toward Negroes and the law. In Copiah in April of 1893, his court convicted and sentenced two of the whitecap leaders, Tyson and Shields, to terms of one year in the penitentiary.[10]

Chrisman's severest test came the next month in Lincoln County's seat of Brookhaven. There, as the trial of ten accused whitecappers was about to begin, a mob of two hundred of their friends gathered outside the courthouse to demand their release. When Chrisman walked out to confront the crowd, shotguns and pistols were leveled at him and he was informed that he was about to die. The judge, producing a .44 of his own from beneath his robes, delivered what was perhaps the most unforgettable tongue-lashing ever heard in that community. He then pushed through the mob and walked, unmolested, a quarter-mile to the Brookhaven fire bell and began ringing out a call for help. Twenty-five townspeople gathered and formed a posse to assist him. The mob withdrew to the woods to consider what to do next. By afternoon, Governor John M. Stone, informed of the judge's peril, was on board the Cannon Ball Express, headed for Brookhaven with a company of militia and two thousand rounds of ammunition.[11]

Organized whitecapping was, for the time being at least, subdued in southwestern Mississippi because of the actions of Judge Chrisman and Governor Stone. Eight whitecappers were transported to the penitentiary. Those from Lincoln County got two-year terms. One observer remarked, with evident relish, that, upon receiving their sentences, the young men "cringed and whimpered like curs." The whole affair had awakened a realization among at least a few responsible-minded whites that, in the words of the Port

10. Hazlehurst *Copiah Signal*, December 6, 1883; Vicksburg *Commercial-Herald*, quoted in Hazlehurst *Weekly Copiahan*, November 22, 1884; Brookhaven *Mississippi Leader*, April 25, 1893.

11. New York *Times*, May 5, 1893; Vicksburg *Evening Post*, May 6, 1893; Natchez *Daily Democrat*, May 6, 1893; Port Gibson *Reveille*, May 12, 1893.

Gibson *Reveille,* "Mississippi has no right to exist as a separate political community unless she can make the humblest negro as secure as the most powerful white citizen in the enjoyment of life, liberty and property."[12] There was even some criticism that Chrisman had been too lenient in handing down mere one- and two-year sentences to the whitecappers. Under the circumstances, however, the judge deserved high praise. As the New Orleans *City Item* noted about the cases, "Rome was not built in a day."[13] Nor was a one- or two-year term in the dreadful Mississippi penal system a prospect to be lightly regarded.

Robert Charles and J. B. Chrisman met on two occasions, in October of 1894 and in October of 1896. Both times Robert was the defendant in a felony trial at the session of the circuit court in Hazlehurst. But the judge knew him only as Curtis Robertson, as his name is inscribed in the court records. The charge on the 1894 docket was "unlawful retailing," which, translated, meant selling whiskey in a dry county.[14]

If any Copiah newspapers or other pertinent sources for these years existed today, besides the court records, then more might be known of Robert's life in the county after he returned there following the shootout at Rolling Fork in 1892. Possibly he spent some time between May of 1892 and October of 1894 somewhere else, but it is most likely that during most of these two years he lived in either Hazlehurst or Crystal Springs, Copiah's two largest towns. Having worked for the railroad and been around Vicksburg for five years, it is doubtful that he cared to return to sharecropping. But it may be assumed that he managed to spend some time with his parents at Pine Bluff.

12. Port Gibson *Reveille,* May 12, 1893. See also Vicksburg *Evening Post,* May 8, 12, 13, 15, 1893.

13. New Orleans *City Item,* quoted in Vicksburg *Evening Post,* May 17, 1893.

14. *State of Mississippi* v. *Curtis Robertson,* Case No. 2589, October 10, 1894, p. 261, in Minutes, Circuit Court, Copiah County, Letterbook W, in Copiah County Courthouse, Hazlehurst, Mississippi.

The alias he selected, Curtis Robertson, must have been chosen with care. For his purposes a better assumed name would be difficult to imagine. It bore, obviously, enough similarity to his real name to allow him a sense of retaining his personal identity; but it also offered him an excellent protection from white suspicions about his background. For there were many white and black Robertsons in Copiah. One of the old slaveholding families along Bayou Pierre bore that name, and numerous local blacks had adopted it after Emancipation. In particular, one elderly black couple who had ten surviving offspring lived close by the Charleses at Pine Bluff.[15] They had no son named Curtis (the father's name, as inscribed in the census returns, was Cluss Robertson); but Robert could say around Hazlehurst or Crystal Springs that he was one of "Cluss Robertson's boys," and no white man would be likely to question that statement. Nor would whites wonder why he occasionally went over to visit the Pine Bluff area.

Six months before "Curtis Robertson" stood in front of Judge Chrisman, Robert's older brother Luke had been scheduled for an appearance in that same Hazlehurst courtroom. Luke was supposed to be tried in April of 1894 on two felony counts, one for "cutting and wounding" and another for "assault and battery." Luke Charles used no alias; nor, as far as the county records show, had he previously had any problems with the law. His indictment on these charges stemmed from a bloody fight he and another black share-cropper, George Giles, had engaged in some weeks earlier. Vague later references to the affair indicate that other black men partici-pated in the trouble, of which one or two were brothers of Luke Charles. What caused the fight is not revealed by the court records, and the files of local newspapers for that time have been lost. Since

15. Cluss Robertson and his ten children are listed in Population Schedule of the Tenth U.S. Census, 1880, Mississippi, Copiah County, Beat 4, in Mississippi De-partment of Archives and History. The sons nearest to Robert's age were Phill and Jesse Robertson.

no whites were involved, it might not have been reported anyway. As a Crystal Springs paper once explained, "Negro murders and negro doings and [other such] trifling little local circumstances . . . had far better be omitted."[16]

Luke Charles and George Giles were the only two participants in the fight indicted, and their trials were set for the April term of 1894. Neither ever stood trial. The Giles case was dismissed by the district attorney, and Luke Charles's cases were continued (postponed). Apparently Luke soon died, possibly from wounds received in the struggle; for his cases were never *nol-prossed*, nor was a warrant issued for his failure to appear in court. Later, in 1900, a Hazlehurst journalist, upon learning that the Robert Charles of New Orleans infamy was originally from Copiah, remembered vaguely that "several years ago a shooting scrape occurred on the Fulgham place in the western part of the county . . . in which Luke [Charles] was killed." The *Courier*'s reporter added that Robert Charles had been "involved in the trouble referred to" and "was known in this county as a desperate, bad man, and always carried a gun strapped to his person."[17]

Robert might have taken part in Luke Charles's fight on the Fulgham place. If he happened to be there at the time, he probably would have aided his brother. But the fact that he soon appeared in court under his new name of Robertson, on an unrelated charge, reduces the likelihood that he was a participant in the "shooting scrape," or whatever it was. At any rate, Luke was the only member of his family charged in the Giles matter. If one of Luke's brothers

16. *State of Mississippi* v. *Luke Charles*, Case No. 2526 and Case No. 2527, April 10–11, 1894, p. 180, 187, in Minutes, Circuit Court, Copiah County, Letterbook W; *State of Mississippi* v. *George Giles*, Case No. 2540, April 20, 1894, p. 211, *ibid.*; Hazlehurst *Courier*, quoted in Vicksburg *Daily Herald*, August 10, 1900; Crystal Springs *Monitor*, December 10, 1881.

17. *Mississippi* v. *Luke Charles*, Nos. 2526 and 2527, p. 187; *Mississippi* v. *George Giles*, No. 2540, p. 211; Hazlehurst *Courier*, quoted in Vicksburg *Daily Herald*, August 10, 1900.

was involved, it was probably John Wesley Charles. What defies rational belief, however, is the assertion that while in Copiah Robert was widely known as a "desperate, bad man." True, he probably carried a concealed pistol in his coat pocket, as he did around Vicksburg. But there would be statements made, after his death, about his "having a Winchester rifle constantly strapped to his back" during his pre–New Orleans years. This could not be true because such behavior would never have been tolerated by the whites of that area. Genuine black desperados did appear in Copiah from time to time—Caesar Hennington and Jack Yarborough were the two most notable examples—but they did not enjoy prolonged careers.[18] Above all else, the whites of Copiah were vigilant. A Mississippi historian expressed it best when he said, with meaningful emphasis, "A black man never *stayed* in trouble in Copiah County."[19]

According to available county records, the first and only problem with the law Robert ever had in Copiah began with his arrest for "unlawful retailing" of liquor, sometime prior to the October, 1894, session of Judge Chrisman's court at Hazlehurst. We cannot now discover what Robert's lawful occupation was at this time, or the circumstances of his arrest. But, on the face of the record of indictment, his wrongdoing would seem a routine matter: Curtis Robertson, a twenty-eight-year-old black man, was caught peddling alcohol in a dry county. He pled guilty to the charge and when taken before the Judge was fined forty dollars plus costs. The clerk then inscribed in the court minutes: "And that he be confined in the county jail until such fines and costs are paid for."[20] Yet here the routineness of the case ends. For the court record later reveals an odd sequel.

18. New Orleans *Times-Democrat*, July 26, 1900; *State of Mississippi* v. *Caesar Hennington*, Case No. 2294, April 19, 1893, p. 1, in Minutes, Circuit Court, Copiah County, Letterbook W; Vicksburg *Evening Post*, May 20, 1893, November 27, 1895.

19. Conversation with James H. Stone of the Mississippi Department of Archives and History, July 7, 1974.

20. *Mississippi* v. *Curtis Robertson*, No. 2589, p. 261.

Robert never paid the fine. Neither did he go to jail. Six months after the sentencing, on April 13, 1895, the circuit court issued an arrest warrant "for the defendant Curtis Robertson he having pled guilty of unlawful retailing at a former term of the court." So it is apparent that Robert, despite the October sentence of fine or confinement, had managed to persuade Judge Chrisman to let him remain free while he attempted to raise the money, which with costs probably totaled over fifty dollars. Robert had the ability to impress both blacks and whites, when he wanted to, with his sincerity and intelligence. But Robert did not show up to pay the fine; possibly he tried to raise the money and could not. Whatever the situation might have been, the result of it all was that Robert Charles left Copiah County and by the end of 1894 was in New Orleans.[21] Most of Robert's remaining six years of life would be spent in New Orleans, and there he continued to call himself Curtis Robertson, at least around the one white man he saw regularly.[22] There was no need to adopt a new alias, for the Copiah sheriff's office would scarcely bother to send a deputy to New Orleans—even if they knew where to locate "Curtis Robertson"—for the sake of forty dollars and costs. For the Rolling Fork trouble he would have been extradited, but not for the relatively minor Copiah charge.

But he must have wanted very badly to clear up the difficulty in his home county. Again, nothing is known except what appears in the circuit court docket; and the name of Curtis Robertson is again inscribed, in October of 1896. He this time pleaded innocent, and stood trial, for the charge he had admitted guilt to in 1894. The most logical explanation would be that somehow new evidence had come to light, or other witnesses agreed to come forward, whom he thought would clear him. He must have come up voluntarily from

21. *Ibid.*, 349. Both a white and a black source place Robert Charles in New Orleans, as a resident, by late 1894. Levy interview, New Orleans *Sunday States*, July 29, 1900; anonymous [name withheld by recipient] letter to Ida B. Wells-Barnett, in her *Mob Rule in New Orleans* (Chicago: N.p., 1900), 42.

22. Levy interview, New Orleans *Sunday States*, July 29, 1900.

New Orleans, but it is possible he was spotted and arrested while returning to Copiah on a visit. The result of the trial indicates that his appearance in court was voluntary, because the jury, in Judge Chrisman's court, found Curtis Robertson not guilty.[23]

After the verdict and his release Robert went back to New Orleans where, a few months earlier, in May of 1896, he had joined an organization called the International Migration Society. This society proposed to transport American Negroes back to Africa, and Robert had made his first payment on a voyage to Liberia.[24]

23. *Mississippi* v. *Curtis Robertson*, No. 2852, October 15, 1896, p. 590.
24. New Orleans *Daily States*, July 24, 1900.

5
NEW ORLEANS—
THE LAND
OF DREAMS

New Orleans in the fading years of the nineteenth century was at once the shabbiest and most alluring of American cities. With a population near 300,000, it ranked as the largest of southern communities, and its complexity of racial and ethnic groupings stood unmatched anywhere in Dixie or the nation. The reputation of New Orleans as a sporting city *comme il faut* drew pleasure-seekers from everywhere, especially during Mardi Gras season. But its politics in recent years had often been a sort of organized hoodlumism. Situated on a swampy lowland along a great crescent bend of the Mississippi one hundred miles above the river's mouth, New Orleans was at this time the only large urban center in the United States at a subtropical latitude, and was said to be the only major community anywhere in the Western world without a sewage system. "You are dirty," a plainspoken sanitation expert informed New Orleans in 1899. "Nature has not been kind to you in topography, and you have returned the compliment, and with interest."[1]

Filthy, humid, disorderly, and ill-governed though it was, New

1. Felix Baumann, *Im Dunkelsten Amerika: Sittenschilderungen aus den Vereinigten Staaten* (Dresden: Ernst Beutelspacher, 1902), 48; Joy J. Jackson, *New Orleans in the Gilded Age: Politics and Urban Progress, 1880–1896* (Baton Rouge: Louisiana State University Press, 1969), 90–96; Vicksburg *Evening Post*, March 18, 1892; New Orleans *Daily States*, March 9, 1899.

Orleans was also a place of great variety and excitement. The crushing dullness of most of rural Louisiana and Mississippi made the city all the more magnetic to those who lived within a day's train travel of its crowded streets. Country people, black and white, were drawn there either for temporary pleasure or to take up residence in hope of achieving a better life. For Mississippians, with no large towns of their own, New Orleans had special allure. White people from the stern, puritanical society of the Magnolia State viewed it as an exotic oasis of romance and forbidden delights; even country ministers and deacons, as the *Copiahan* once noted, were sometimes known to suffer moral lapses there. And for Mississippi's and Louisiana's rural blacks, the city held a reputation for racial liberality and job opportunities—relatively speaking.[2]

Twenty-seven percent of New Orleans' population by 1900 was reported as "colored races." This figure represented 77,714 persons of African ancestry and a few hundred Chinese. The *Picayune* claimed (boasted would not be the right word) that New Orleans had "the largest negro population of any city in the world . . . outside Africa." In fact, however, the federal census reported both Baltimore and Washington, D.C., as having slightly more black residents than the Crescent City, although several thousand blacks were probably missed by the census enumerators in each of these three cities, especially New Orleans. The notion was common among the poorer black New Orleanians that if their family size were fully reported it would mean "increased taxation of some kind." The Board of Health believed the city contained no less than 90,000 black people. The actual figure was probably close to 85,000.[3]

2. Hazlehurst *Weekly Copiahan*, March 15, 1884; Charles Dudley Warner, "New Orleans," *Harper's*, LXXIV (January, 1887), 186–206; Dale A. Somers, "Black and White in New Orleans: A Study in Urban Race Relations, 1865–1900," *Journal of Southern History*, XL, (February, 1974), 35–39.

3. *Abstract of the Twelfth Census of the United States, 1900* (Washington, D.C.: Government Printing Office, 1904), 104; New Orleans *Daily Picayune*, July 28, 1900;

There were wide differences in life styles and attitudes among the "colored" population of New Orleans. The "Creoles of color," mostly descendants of the ten thousand free Negroes of the city's antebellum era, ranked high on the economic ladder; most held skilled jobs or were in business or the professions. A few were quite wealthy. Nearly all the Creoles of color were of visibly mixed ancestry; many spoke French as a first language, and some could pass for white. Socially, they had little or nothing to do with the generally darker descendants of slaves. Their marked separation from the majority of the New Orleans black community was no transitory thing.[4] It is still evident today.

But the Creoles of color and the blacks had a problem in common, and that was white people. Yet Louisiana whites were not, particularly in New Orleans, of one voice on how the Creoles of color should be treated. The white Creole Joseph Leveque, publisher of the city's turn-of-the-century magazine *Harlequin*, pleaded that these "hundreds upon hundreds of... self respecting, good citizens, who claim no affinity with the colored race," be considered as special cases, apart from the blacks.[5] This view had considerable support in the city, particularly as it applied to public transportation. However, by 1900 a growing number of white New Orleanians, seemingly backed by most of the rural whites of Louisiana, demanded that racial segregation in the state's one big city be extended to encompass the major exception — streetcars — and that anyone with so much as a trace of African blood be treated as inferior, unfit to sit alongside whites.

Vicksburg *Evening Post*, July 1, 1880; New Orleans *Times-Democrat*, July 7, 1900; New Orleans *Semi-Weekly Times-Democrat*, August 2, 1901.

4. John Hope Franklin, *From Slavery to Freedom: A History of Negro Americans* (3rd ed.; New York: Random House, 1969), 217, 224–26; Charles Barthelemey Rousseve, *The Negro in Louisiana: Aspects of His History and Literature* (New Orleans: Xavier University Press, 1937), 24; *Literary Digest*, LXXII (March 18, 1922), 44. The Creoles of color are not to be confused with the white Creoles of New Orleans, who are descended entirely from European (French or Spanish) ancestors.

5. "That Star Car Bill," *Harlequin*, I (June 23, 1900), 3.

The fact that Creoles of color tended to dress better than working-class whites engendered resentment among many of the latter. "A Woman Worker," stating the feelings of many poorer whites, complained that "when one of these light colored mulatresses flounces in the car, dressed in all her finery, and almost sits down on some white woman, it does indeed make one's blood boil." More tastelessly explicit was the answer of one of the most influential of Louisiana's small-town papers to the argument that it was impractical to segregate Creoles of color because they could not always be distinguished from whites: "An experienced eye," scoffed the *Iberville South*, "can spot a coon and an experienced nose can find them every time."[6] Other statements of similar import were heard with increasing frequency. As the dawn of the twentieth century approached, the southern system of racial repression was reaching the point of allowing no exceptions, even for those who looked almost white in the easygoing, polyglot city of New Orleans.

The tragedy of the Creoles of color was of little matter to the majority of New Orleans blacks, who had concerns enough of their own. The problem of most blacks in the city was simply survival. With few exceptions their work was the lowest paying, their housing the flimsiest, their mortality rate the highest, their treatment by police the harshest, their education the most neglected, and public services for their residential areas the most inadequate of any population group in New Orleans. Nevertheless, black newcomers from the Mississippi and Louisiana countryside arrived almost daily. For the lot of blacks elsewhere was certainly no better and was frequently much worse. In a big city blacks at least enjoyed wider social contacts among themselves and often had choices among a variety of low-paying jobs, instead of being limited to sharecropping cotton—which sometimes paid nothing except the provisions fur-

6. Letter from "A Woman Worker," in New Orleans *Daily Picayune*, July 2, 1900; Plaquemine *Iberville South*, quoted in New Orleans *Times-Democrat*, June 25, 1900.

nished during the growing season. For those who had fallen into trouble (or had reason to believe trouble was coming), New Orleans—like any large city—offered a measure of anonymity. And any black or mixed-blood person from the lower Mississippi Valley would find life in New Orleans at most times relatively free of white control and its intimidating, "ever-present threat of force." [7]

Despite the growing emphasis on racial separation, New Orleans during the 1890s remained surprisingly integrated, as far as housing for the laboring class was concerned. More often than not black and white working people lived on the same block, frequently under the same roof in double-occupancy rectangular wooden cottages. Some of these dwellings were two-story structures, with families of different races alongside each other both upstairs and downstairs; they were neighbors but seldom friends, living side by side not out of preference on the part of either, but from economic necessity. Prior to 1893, when the introduction of electric trolleys offered New Orleans its first rapid transportation, ordinary laborers either walked or rode the slow mule-drawn streetcars to their jobs at the riverfront and business sections or in the homes and yards of affluent whites. The poor either lived close to work or could not work at all—in which case the alternative was, in the parlance of that era, "steal or starve." By 1900, as the expanding tracks of the electric trolley companies encouraged the building of inexpensive housing several miles away from the congested inner-city area, workers of different races were beginning to live more apart from one another. But the older and cheaper residential areas within walking distance of the business district remained racially integrated. To some whites and a great many blacks, rapid transit made no difference, since they could not afford the nickel fare. [8]

7. Somers, "Black and White in New Orleans," 20.
8. New Orleans *Daily Picayune*, October 10, 1896; A. H. Ford, "From Mule to Motor," New Orleans *Times-Democrat*, September 1, 1900; New Orleans *Daily States*, July 28, 1900.

Biracial cooperation, as well as racial conflict, had marked the path of labor organizations in New Orleans. An ambitious "Association" of thirteen white and black laboring unions had been formed in 1880, but by the 1890s it no longer existed, having fallen victim to economic hard times and employers' refusals to grant concessions. Meanwhile the Knights of Labor had tried to unite white and black workers under one organization and had foundered upon the same shoals that wrecked the Association. The primary difficulty that faced such efforts was not innate racial hostility—as some suggested—but rather the surplus of labor in the city, of which the most willing to work at low wages were the penniless blacks who had recently arrived from the surrounding rural areas. Moreover, if a major strike threatened the riverfront shipping interests (the major employers of manual labor in New Orleans), "scab" labor, mostly black, would be brought in quickly from ports hundreds of miles away.[9]

The national depression of the 1890s further discouraged efforts by white and black laborers to present a united front. The competition for what jobs remained increased racial tensions. By 1900, most of the hostility that white laborers displayed toward blacks stemmed from the fact that the largest employers in the city were showing an increased preference for black labor and were turning whites away, because blacks would agree to work at cheaper rates.[10]

But amidst the racial and economic unrest of the nineteenth century's last decade, something was taking shape in New Orleans which would within a generation profoundly influence the cultural

9. Arthur R. Pearce, "The Rise and Decline of Labor in New Orleans" (M.A. thesis, Tulane University, 1938), 25; New Orleans *Weekly Louisianian*, August 13, September 17, 1881; Roger W. Shugg, *Origins of Class Struggle in Louisiana: A Social History of White Farmers and Laborers During Slavery and After, 1840–1875* (Baton Rouge: Louisiana State University Press, 1939), 302–305; Somers, "Black and White in New Orleans," 30–32.

10. *Harlequin*, II (August 18, 1900), 2; New Orleans *Daily States*, August 17, 1900; New Orleans *Sunday States*, August 26, 1900.

life of the United States. The new syncopated music first known as jass—latter called jazz—began to pierce the muggy night air from dozens of locales in New Orleans, but especially out of the crowded black dance halls and saloons on Franklin Street, just west of Basin. An amalgam of African rhythms and the more Europeanized musicianship of the Creoles of color, jazz was a more complex art form than the other "hot" music of that era, ragtime.[11] And it was too good not to spread.

Jazz was born in New Orleans, but no one can say precisely when or where. Some of the earliest jazz groups were heard along Franklin Street inside such places as the Twenty Eight Club and the Pig Ankle Cabaret. By 1900 its polyrhythmic notes echoed from black and white nightspots alike; street youngsters of both races formed "spasm bands" with homemade instruments and played on street corners, hoping for pennies in return; the sound of Buddy Bolden's powerful cornet rang out from Lincoln Park, a favorite gathering place for blacks; and the more gaudy whorehouses of Storyville, New Orleans' famed red-light district, hired musicians to play jazz numbers for their patrons. Blacks and Creoles of color (who otherwise were seldom seen together) comprised most of the early jazz bands, although several all-white ensembles played in Storyville and elsewhere. Of course not all New Orleans accepted jazz immediately; conservative white and Creole-of-color families dismissed it as "bawdyhouse music."[12] Yet it would in time become Louisiana's distinctive musical contribution to America, and in turn to the world.

11. Al Rose and Edmond Souchon, *New Orleans Jazz: A Family Album* (Baton Rouge: Louisiana State University Press, 1967), 199–200; Alan Lomax, *Mister Jelly Roll* (New York: Duell, Sloan and Pearce, 1950), xiv–xvi; Jackson, *New Orleans in the Gilded Age*, 274–82.

12. Jack V. Buerkle and Danny Barker, *Bourbon Street Black: The New Orleans Black Jazzman* (New York: Oxford University Press, 1973), 19–21; Jackson, *New Orleans in the Gilded Age*, 279–81; Sidney Bechet, *Treat It Gentle* (New York: Hill and Wang, 1960), 53–54.

Black night life during the birth time of jazz partook of more than music. The best-known places that Negro laborers frequented were rambling, barracks-like structures offering a variety of services: food, drink, drugs, crap games, and dancing. On Franklin Street were the three biggest such establishments: the Hot Cat, the Honky Tonk, and the Pig Ankle. These were patronized primarily by roustabouts from the riverboats, but received additional income from slumming white tourists. Catfish and fried pig's feet were the principal foods served. The long bars adjoining the dance halls inside these places sold whiskey at five cents a shot. For those so inclined, another drink was served for a dime: a mixture of California claret, water, and cocaine. "A pint of the stuff," asserted the disapproving *Times-Democrat*, "will transfer [sic] a stupid, good natured negro into a howling maniac. It is the popular beverage of the section."[13]

Alcohol had always been copiously available in New Orleans, but beginning in 1898 a relatively new drug, cocaine, exploded in popularity among certain groups of whites and blacks. Louisiana blacks referred to the crystalline South American import as "coke," and this has been its usual nickname since. There was at the turn of the century no Louisiana law against using cocaine, only a statute against selling it. Even so, the law requiring a prescription was seldom enforced in New Orleans. Certain drugstores were known to sell it to anyone, and one brand of cheap patent medicine that was purchasable almost anywhere had cocaine as its active ingredient. "Those days," jazz musician Jelly Roll Morton recalled a half-century later, "you could buy all the dope you wanted in the drugstore. Just ask for it and you got it." Morphine was still favored by some addicts, while others smoked opium; one bar near the French Market apparently stirred either morphine or opium into fusel oil and whiskey, creating a drink that produced, it was claimed,

13. New Orleans *Times-Democrat*, October 31, 1900.

"an effect that is peculiarly its own." Yet by 1900 cocaine had become by far the most common hard drug taken by poorer blacks and the prostitutes, black and white, who worked in or around Storyville.[14]

For such people, the *States* observed with an understanding rarely found in its columns, cocaine was "a merciful friend," for it temporarily "spread[s] a golden cloud over a wretched past and hopeless future and evoke[s] visions of wealth, contentment and happiness." Cocaine was also reported to be widely used by one group of well-paid laborers, the brawny roustabouts of the river. Some roustabouts drank it with wine and water, a la Franklin Street, or dropped a five-cent pinch of the stuff in a glass of cold beer. Other users were known as "snuffers"—for they inhaled powdered cocaine through their nostrils. A few New Orleans physicians and their affluent white patients were suspected of being cocaine addicts; these individuals, according to the *Times-Democrat*, usually injected it with hypodermic needles. But since abuse of the drug was primarily confined to the poorest blacks, along with roustabouts and prostitutes, there was no serious effort to curb its sale. It was noticed that Negro servants worked more energetically while under its stimulating influence. One New Orleans official even implied that cocaine, because of its ultimately debilitating effects, might benefit the city by killing off its surplus blacks. "I honestly believe," he said, "that the drug will go a long way toward wiping out the town darkey inside the next five years." This prospect seemed not to upset him.[15]

Among the thousands of unskilled laborers of both colors, the only men who received what were considered good wages in New

14. New Orleans *Daily Item*, May 28, July 3, 1900; New Orleans *Times-Democrat*, June 15, July 15, October 31, 1900; Lomax, *Mister Jelly Roll*, 50; New Orleans *Daily Picayune*, December 8, 1900.

15. New Orleans *Daily States*, August 8, 1900; New Orleans *Times-Democrat*, April 26, 28, 1900; "A New Orleans Official," quoted in New Orleans *Times-Democrat*, June 15, 1900.

Orleans were the five or six hundred black roustabouts. They truly earned their $60 to $120 per month. It took big, extraordinarily muscular men to handle the cotton bales, molasses barrels, and other heavy freight on the river packets that steamed to and from New Orleans. Whites could be found who were physically strong enough, but almost no Caucasian proved able to long endure the on-board living and working conditions that the packet captains insisted upon. While on the three- or four-day trips, roustabouts were seldom able to sleep more than an hour or so without being awakened to load or unload freight at the next stop. One captain, asked why he did not employ whites, explained that "a negro will sleep under . . . the boilers," and thus required none of the boat's valuable cargo space; "when you want him all you have to do is throw a chunk of coal under there after him, and the trick is done." The roustabouts received huge servings of coarse food four or five times during each twenty-four-hour period: an unvarying diet of fat pork, cornbread, peas, and molasses, washed down with strong coffee. When not on the river, most roustabouts were said to spend all their time and pay in the Franklin Street nightspots, where upstairs sleeping cubicles were provided for them free of charge.[16]

Black and Creole-of-color women comprised at least half of the two to three thousand full-time prostitutes who made New Orleans the red-light capital of America, a distinction the city had possessed since the 1850s. But since male tastes in females varied considerably, so did the selection offered—from African ebony to Swedish blonde. Copulation for pay had long been a major part of the economy of the city, and owners of the larger establishments exercised a persuasive influence on most city administrations. By the 1890s two tabloid publications, the *Mascot* and the *Sunday Sun*, gave considerable space to prurient stories about people and hap-

16. Julian Ralph, "The Old Way to Dixie," *Harper's*, LXXVI (January, 1893), 168, 174–75; New Orleans *Daily Picayune*, October 30, November 2, 1900; New Orleans *Times-Democrat*, February 16, October 28–30, November 2, 1900.

penings within the city's "scarlet world." During Mardi Gras season the strumpets were at their busiest; in February of 1895 twenty thousand copies of guidebooks to the whorehouses were distributed to tourists.[17]

Church and reform groups in New Orleans realized that outright abolition of prostitution was an impossible ideal. They worked instead to confine such activity to a particular district of the city. In 1897 the reform administration of Mayor Walter C. Flower passed an ordinance decreeing that, beginning the first of October of that year, "it shall be unlawful for any prostitute or woman notoriously abandoned to lewdness, to occupy, inhabit, live or sleep in any house, room or closet, situated [outside] the following limits. . . ." This municipal ordinance, sponsored by Alderman Sidney Story, set aside—as finally amended—an area of approximately thirty blocks near the old (French) quarter of the city, devoted entirely to houses of prostitution and cabarets and saloons that catered to the red-light trade. Alderman Story could hardly have been amused when the district adopted the name of Storyville. This was a neighborhood already considerably given over to prostitution and the rowdier forms of merrymaking for both blacks and whites; but the actual move by most of the city's prostitutes was delayed until serious enforcement of the ordinance began in July of 1900.[18] Only then did Storyville become a place distinctive from other parts of the city.

The women of Storyville varied as much in age and price as in shade of skin. Young octoroons of great beauty expected a recom-

17. Phil Johnson, "Good Time Town," in Hodding Carter (ed.), *The Past as Prelude: New Orleans, 1718–1968* (New Orleans: Tulane University Press, 1968), 236; Herbert Asbury, *The French Quarter: An Informal History of the New Orleans Underworld* (New York: Alfred A. Knopf, 1936), 424–55; Buerkle and Barker, *Bourbon Street Black*, 18–19; New Orleans *Mascot*, February 2, 1895.

18. Al Rose, *Storyville, New Orleans: Being an Authentic, Illustrated Account of the Notorious Red-Light District* (University, Ala.: University of Alabama Press, 1974), 37–39, 192–93; Jackson, *New Orleans in the Gilded Age*, 254; New Orleans *Daily Picayune*, June 19, 28, 1900.

pense of five dollars, as did the prettiest of the white prostitutes. The most lavish brothels, such as Josie Arlington's and "Countess" Willie V. Piazza's, domiciled only women of this type. At these places only white customers were allowed in. Rooms with mirrors in the ceilings or by the beds were offered at special rates. A sample advertisement in the district's guide book promised that "if you have the 'blues,' the Countess and her girls can cure them. She has, without doubt, the handsomest and most intelligent octoroons in the United States." Lulu White was the only madam of a top-rated house who was herself of African blood; the nude "circus" with its leapfrog acts performed nightly at her establishment was considered one of the great sights of the district. But Storyville was not all gilded mirrors, sex circuses, and five-dollar whores. From Arlington's and Lulu White's the houses and personnel sank considerably in appearance and price. At the lowest level were the dilapidated cottages and "cribs," which rented by the day to ugly or superannuated whores, white and black, who charged as little as twenty-five cents. Along this part of Storyville, one observer wrote, "a horrible succession of wolfish faces peer and leer at the passerby." Near the cheapest houses were located the cabarets frequented by black roustabouts, and whores in this area, regardless of race, were available to any man who had the money, regardless of race.[19]

Storyville had a boss. The "mayor" of the district was Tom Anderson, owner of the biggest white saloon in the area and overall regulator of activities. He was also an important man in city affairs. A biographical sketch of Anderson appeared in *Who's Who in Louisiana Politics*; he was elected to the state legislature in 1900,

19. Buerkle and Barker, *Bourbon Street Black*, 18–19; Lomax, *Mister Jelly Roll*, 50; Asbury, *The French Quarter*, 436–47; *Blue Book* (N.p., *ca.* 1900), 4; New Orleans *Times-Democrat*, October 31, 1900; New Orleans *Daily Picayune*, May 7, 1901. *Blue Book*, cited above, was a guidebook to the whorehouses of New Orleans, the first issue of which appeared in 1900. Four other editions were released between 1902 and 1915. Copies are now hard to find, but a xeroxed one is available in the Louisiana Room of the Louisiana State University Library.

representing the city ward which included Storyville. Under Anderson's regime (which lasted until federal authorities forced Storyville's closure during World War I) the district was relatively free of crime, with a "businesslike atmosphere" reportedly prevailing on most of its blocks. However, at the turn of the century, those customers who became victims of crime, if they told the police their troubles, would receive embarrassing publicity in the papers the next day. A typical item of this sort read: "Henry Richardson reports to the police that while he was under the influence of liquor and in the disreputable house no. 214 N. Franklin Street, he was robbed of a gold watch, valued at $30, by Liza Lee, aided by Mary Jones and Daisy Stevens." The police would usually arrest women against whom complaints were made, but as a rule the poorly paid officers and the inhabitants of Storyville were on good terms and looked after each other's interests.[20]

The New Orleans Police Department was the worst paid and, on paper at least, the most overworked of any force among the nation's major cities. In 1900 the NOPD numbered a mere 315 men, and of these only 193 were patrolmen. This meant that, even with twelve-hour shifts of duty, a city of 300,000 had not quite 100 men available for full-time street duty during the day, nor were 100 available for the night shift. The lack of personnel was only slightly eased by the 38 "supernumerary patrolmen" who worked part time and received tiny salaries. Regular patrolmen got only $50 per month (less than the black roustabouts on the river boats); the 15 sergeants each got $70 monthly and the 5 captains received $83 per month. No ranks had enjoyed a pay raise for at least six years. "A few"—number unspecified but probably less than a dozen—patrolmen were black or Creoles of color.[21]

20. *Blue Book*, 3, 99; *Harlequin*, I (April 21, 1900), 4; Dave H. Brown (comp.), *A History of Who's Who in Louisiana Politics in 1916* (N.p., 1916), 82; New Orleans *Times-Democrat*, October 7, 31, 1900; Baumann, *Im Dunkelsten Amerika*, 69–70.
21. *Annual Report of the Board of Police Commissioners, Superintendent of*

Despite miserable pay, long hours, and much danger, applications poured in for the NOPD. And most supernumerary patrolmen apparently hoped to become full-time officers. Some who applied probably did so because of the scarcity of better paying jobs; others likely supposed that a badge and a gun in a place like New Orleans offered opportunities for augmenting income. The fact was, however, that almost every conceivable form of vice was already protected by the city council, and whatever graft might be available to ordinary patrolmen consisted of small payoffs from such people as petty tradesmen operating in violation of city ordinances, or immoral women who worked outside the protection of Tom Anderson. And it was generally conceded that, whatever the shortcomings of the force might be, the New Orleans Police Department by the late 1890s had vastly improved over what it had been ten or fifteen years earlier, when its personnel was so disreputable that the city probably would have been better off without police at all.[22]

It is a fair statement that New Orleans enjoyed a better police force and a lower crime rate than the city deserved for having so long neglected the vital problem of public safety. Street robberies and burglaries of homes or stores occurred quite regularly, yet few victims of these crimes were murdered or seriously wounded. Violent street muggings of respectable citizens were quite rare, and the murder of whites by blacks rarer still. The homicide rate, it is true, was high; but nearly all killings grew out of personal or family quarrels, and a remarkably large number involved persons of status in the professions or in politics. In 1899, a very typical crime year for

Police, and Police Surgeon of the City of New Orleans, 1894, p. 4; *Annual Report of the Superintendent of Police of the City of New Orleans, 1899*, p. 40; *Harlequin,* II (February 7, 1901), 1; New Orleans *Times-Democrat,* November 1, 1900.

22. New Orleans *Daily States,* October 9, 1897; *Annual Report of the Board of Police Commissioners, Superintendent of Police and Police Surgeon of the City of New Orleans, 1896,* p. 8; L. A. Thornback to D. S. Gaster, May 18, 1900, in Mayor's Office Correspondence, City Archives Department, New Orleans *Daily Picayune,* January 17, April 1, October 27, 1881, November 6, 1896, May 19, 1901.

the period, 10,785 arrests of whites were made, and 6,824 of blacks—which meant, considering the racial proportions of New Orleans' population, that the black arrest rate was not much higher than that of whites. Moreover, blacks were more likely to be arrested on "suspicion." No attempt was made to hide the fact that black suspects, as a rule, were more harshly treated by the police and were the most apt to be locked up for the vaguest suggestion of any wrongdoing. The authorities and the city press assumed as self-evident truths the notions that most blacks would view any leniency toward them as a sign of weakness and that a relaxation of official sternness would result in a black crime wave of major proportions.[23]

While a quasi-official policy of racial intimidation did appear to hold black violence in check, the primary physical danger that police and white New Orleanians of all occupations had reason to fear came from a violence-prone class of white ruffians. As one resident observed, "The average hoodlum will shoot a policeman quicker than will the average negro criminal." The city had helped breed this class for years by the inadequacies of its institutional care for homeless youngsters. Gangs of ragged street waifs, mostly white, were a common sight on the city's downtown streets; they begged or did "all kinds of mischief" until late at night, when they lay down in doorways or protected alleys to sleep until dawn. These boys, after reaching their late teens, tended to join the ranks of the city's distinctive and long-established hoodlum element of young white adults. Frequently arrested for fighting or for larceny, the typical hoodlum would spend a few months in Orleans Parish Prison and then return to the streets and saloons for more unpleasantness.

23. *Annual Report of the Superintendent of Police of the City of New Orleans, 1899*, pp. 36–39; Parkash Kaur Bains, "The New Orleans Race Riot of 1900" (M.A. thesis, Louisiana State University in New Orleans, 1970), 33; New Orleans *Daily Picayune*, July 25–26, 1900; New Orleans *Daily States*, June 3, 1883, July 5, 25, August 7, 1900; New Orleans *Sunday States*, August 26, 1900; New Orleans *Daily Item*, July 24, 1900.

Up to 1896, many hoodlums were more or less protected from the law because they performed a political function for the city's Democratic machine, an enormously corrupt organization then known simply as "the Ring." For most of the late nineteenth century, the Ring occupied the mayor's office and a majority of the city council seats, and this machine relied on selected hoodlums to appear at the polls whenever reformers ran candidates in opposition, in order to frighten or harass those citizens thought to be anti-Ring voters. But the Australian (secret) ballot system which Louisiana adopted beginning with the presidential election of 1896 did much to spoil the usefulness of rowdies at the polls, and thus diminished their value to the Ring.[24]

Whenever New Orleans papers of this era noted that a "notorious hoodlum" had been hauled in again, the name on the arrest sheet more often than not was Irish. McGittigan, Behan, Donovan, Foley, Gillen, Flanagan, McSheen, Doyle, Ryan (especially one "Dusty" Ryan)—these were names that all the busier police precincts knew well. Sometimes such people picked on Negroes; and once in 1899, at the corner of St. Andrews and Liberty, a street brawl erupted between hoodlums and some "tough" blacks, with serious injuries resulting on both sides. But a fracas of this type was an unusual event.[25] The hoodlums mostly fought among themselves or stole from other whites, while Negro toughs seldom bothered anyone not black.

Flim-flam operators likewise, as a rule, victimized members of their own race. Illiterate blacks from rural areas particularly fell prey to Negro confidence men in New Orleans, who, as late as the turn of the century, were still passing Confederate money on what a Missis-

24. New Orleans *Times-Democrat*, June 25, August 8, 1900; Jackson, *New Orleans in the Gilded Age*, 90–91; *Harlequin*, II (August 4, 1900), 6; New Orleans *Daily States*, February 23, 1899; New Orleans *Daily Picayune*, November 4, 1896.

25. New Orleans *Daily States*, May 25, 1898, February 28, 1899, July 2, 13, 23, 1900; New Orleans *Daily Item*, July 23, 1900; New Orleans *Times-Democrat*, February 4, June 22, 1900; New Orleans *Daily Picayune*, July 23, August 4, 1900.

sippi paper referred to as "the unsuspecting country darkey." This hoary but still effective "Confederate bill racket," as it was termed, also was used by white bunco men. One white victim in the summer of 1900 was Isaac D. Moreau from the southern Louisiana town of Thibodaux. While making his complaint to the police, Moreau happened to mention that he was a schoolteacher.[26]

Mardi Gras was consistently the peak time for certain types of crime, notably pickpocketing and flim-flam operations. By the late nineteenth century the pre-Lenten carnival had grown to the point of attracting not only tens of thousands of tourists, but dozens if not hundreds of hustlers from all across the nation. (During the carnival season of 1900, two who were arrested gave their names as Patsy Hustler and James P. Hell.) As the *States* headlined, "CROOKS OF HIGH AND LOW DEGREE FLOCK SOUTH WITH THE TIDE OF VISITING STRANGERS." The undermanned NOPD scarcely made a dent in Mardi Gras illegalities, but the department was increasingly assisted by detectives from various parts of the country who came to carnival looking for individuals wanted back home; they often found them. But one who eluded capture in New Orleans, though she came there several times during the 1890s, was Minnie Williams, known in the nation's larger cities as the Queen of Pickpockets. Minnie loved crowds, and reputedly had been present at Queen Victoria's Diamond Jubilee celebration in London, as well as at the crowning of Czar Nicholas II in Russia.[27]

White Mississippians at this time usually outnumbered visitors from any other state outside Louisiana during the Mardi Gras celebration. Those from Mississippi's more rural counties provided

26. Hazlehurst *Copiah Signal*, August 30, 1895; New Orleans *Daily Picayune*, January 12, 1902; New Orleans *Times-Democrat*, July 19, 1900.

27. Dale A. Somers, *The Rise of Sports in New Orleans: 1850–1900* (Baton Rouge: Louisiana State University Press, 1972), 9; New Orleans *Times-Democrat*, January 10, February 16, 23, 1900; New Orleans *Daily States*, February 26, 1900, February 18, 1901; New Orleans *Daily Picayune*, March 2, 1897, February 20, 1901; Boston *Morning Journal*, August 7, 1900.

choice material for pickpockets and confidence men. Although many Mississippians as well as Louisianians probably agreed with the Port Gibson *Reveille* that Mardi Gras was "childish and clownish tomfoolery," thousands from that nearby state continued to take in carnival each year. The most frequent complaint of the visiting Mississippians, however, did not concern outright criminality during Mardi Gras, but rather the seasonal price gouging by the city's cabmen and hotels. Nevertheless, Mardi Gras often had sights that compensated for being robbed or cheated. This was especially true for a Mississippian from Hazlehurst who had the opportunity to observe the pastor of his church cavorting at "a sporting people's ball," with a woman clinging to him "with a dress that was simply awful in its short skirts and worse in low neck."[28]

Few if any black people in those years came to New Orleans specifically for the Mardi Gras celebration. But the blacks and Creoles of color who lived in the city seemed to enjoy carnival about as much as did the whites. Nonwhites had their own parades and revels to mark the occasion. Since Mardi Gras was a time of illusion and pretending to be what you were not, it is revealing of both races that at the turn of the century the "greatest number" of local people who masked for the event put on disguises that caricatured another race, and adopted mannerisms accordingly. White revelers tended to mask as blacks, "under the impression, perhaps," mused the *Picayune*, "that they could enjoy more license disguised as negroes than in any other character." Black celebrants usually donned war paint and costumes depicting American Indians.[29] Who, if anybody,

28. Port Gibson *Reveille*, quoted in Hazlehurst *Copiah Monitor*, November 20, 1879; Crystal Springs *Crystal Mirror*, March 4, 1876; Vicksburg *Evening Post*, February 16, 1893, January 30, 1894; New Orleans *Chronicle*, quoted in Hazlehurst *Weekly Copiahan*, March 15, 1884.

29. Grace King, *New Orleans: The Place and the People* (New York: Macmillan Company, 1895), 392–96; "The New Orleans Carnival and Its Origin," *Harlequin*, I (February 14, 1900), 3, 15; New Orleans *Southern Republican*, February 15, 1900; New Orleans *Daily Picayune*, February 15, 1899, February 20, 1901.

the four hundred residents of New Orleans' Chinatown imitated was not reported.

Next to race relations the most aggravating problem facing New Orleans was that of sanitation. Topography and human shortsightedness had combined to make the city an hygenic nightmare. Indeed, it is surprising that the high death rate was not worse. Built on marshy ground—some of it below sea level—with the Mississippi to its front and Lake Pontchartrain to its rear, the city had a drainage problem that was compounded by frequent torrential downpours, plus the fact that in many parts of town muck and water were found just a foot or so beneath the surface. (At one fire in an outlying district where no hydrants were near, firemen simply dug a hole in the yard and got sufficient water from it.) New Orleans remained without a sewage system until the early twentieth century. Reeking privy and cesspool "vaults" at each residence had to do instead. Drainage from the rainstorms was provided by a series of open gutters and canals which carried water from the major business and residential areas toward Lake Pontchartrain. But the lake area was only a few inches lower than where the water drained from, and it took an acute eye to discern movement in the canals.[30]

Nor could New Orleans boast a decent water supply until 1909. Some parts of the city had water piped in from the muddy river, without filtration, and this was considered undrinkable by most whites and blacks. People who bathed with the piped source customarily splashed a pitcher of filtered or cistern water over themselves afterwards, to clear the grit off. Most homes used cistern water for drinking, but this frequently turned sour or became

30. "Address of Mayor Paul Capdevielle to the Council of the City of New Orleans," May 7, 1900, (MS in Mayor's Office Correspondence); Walter Parker, "New Orleans Reminiscences, 1894–1940" (Bound clippings from New Orleans *Official Daily Court Reporter,* January 22–May 19, 1941, in Special Collections Division, Tulane University Library), 44; Vicksburg *Evening Post,* October 16, 1891, March 18, 1892.

infested with "wiggletails"—mosquito larvae. Wealthier residents and the better hotels installed their own filters for what came out of the river pipes, or purchased bottled water for drinking purposes. At the other extreme, some of the poorer whites and blacks were reduced to using filthy gutter liquid, or to drinking directly from the turbid river. For those so inclined, tin receptacles hung on strings from the wharves.[31]

Twice every year all the city's 65,000 privy and cesspool vaults were supposed to be emptied by a private firm, the Louisiana Excavating Company. Several times each week wagon loads of human excrement were hauled from various parts of the city to the riverfront, where the company's tugboat *Flora* (goddess of flowers) was supposed to take it on barges downriver, there to be released below the city limits. The same dumping procedure was required by law of the garbage and dead-animal tugboats, the *Napoleon* and the *Belle of Baton Rouge*. Public garbage bins were placed at various points in New Orleans, and city workers were expected to empty these regularly and transport the contents, along with all animal cadavers—from rats to mules—found in the streets, to the privately owned *Napoleon* and *Belle of Baton Rouge*. However, all three tugboat captains had decided that the trip downriver was a foolish waste of time and fuel; consequently, all habitually dumped their noisome loads at midstream, directly facing the downtown area. Much of the material—particularly the bloated, gas-filled dead animals—drifted over to the pilings along the wharves and ferry dock. Captain Charles Strend of the ordure boat *Flora*, interviewed by a reporter, blandly explained that he had been dumping what he called "the stuff" in front of the city regularly for ten years,

31. Jackson, *New Orleans in the Gilded Age*, 156; Frank Putnam, "New Orleans in Transition," *New England Magazine*, XXXVI (April, 1907), 228–29; Julian Ralph, "New Orleans, Our Southern Capital," *Harper's*, LXXXVI (February, 1893), 370; Clifton Johnson, *Highways and Biways of the Mississippi Valley* (New York: Macmillan Company, 1906), 2.

but conceded that he "sometimes worried about crews in passing vessels who drank from the river at that point."[32]

Sanitation was no exception to the rule that anything of importance in New Orleans must, some way or the other, have racial overtones. The poorer areas of town where blacks were located had the least in sanitation services, and in this respect the poor whites who lived next to blacks were no better off. There is no specific documentation, but, given the racial climate of the time and place, it is reasonable to assume that those city blocks with the highest proportion of Negroes received the fewest visits from garbage collectors, cesspool cleaners, or the street-sweeping gangs. The New Orleans *States* decided that the extremely high death rate of New Orleans blacks was primarily due to "their vicious habits," but the fact that black residents on the average had a worse water and sewage system pointed to a more logical explanation. Between 1890 and 1900 the death rate in New Orleans dropped from 25.41 to 23.80 per thousand for white people; but the Negro death rate meanwhile climbed from 36.61 to 42.40—almost twice that of the whites.[33]

Race relations in New Orleans, for all the city's reputation for liberality, had never really been much better than in other southern communities. Virtually all whites in the South, including New Orleanians, were absolutely convinced that the mass of Negroes were innately inferior mentally and morally to most whites, and were perhaps even more certain that wherever two disparate races occupied the same soil one race must rule the other. Antebellum traditions and attitudes survived to the new century almost unchanged. A black newspaper had warned in 1865 that "the sting of the serpent of slavery is in the hearts of the people," and thirty-five

32. New Orleans *Daily States*, March 9, 1899; New Orleans *Times-Democrat*, May 21–23, 1900.

33. New Orleans *Daily States*, October 2, 1897; Jackson, *New Orleans in the Gilded Age*, 183.

years later another black publication in New Orleans noted that the venom showed no signs of abating.[34]

There were some exceptions. The novelist and essayist George W. Cable, a former Confederate soldier, returned to New Orleans after the war and gradually became a strong defender of black civil rights and capabilities, but in 1885 he moved to Massachusetts, largely because of the hostile reactions his writings had provoked in his home city. A few other white New Orleanians who privately shared his views also made plans to move away because, as one of them wrote Cable, they were sick of the "nightmare" of living in a "melancholy atmosphere of slavery and criminal prejudice."[35] But of the city's many educated whites who were reflective enough to examine their own assumptions about blacks, most seemed always to arrive back at essentially the same conclusions as before. What appears to have been representative of the thinking of this class was the statement of Joseph Leveque, publisher of *Harlequin* magazine, who acknowledged "distress" over "the wall between humanity in this part of the globe," but who saw no practical answer other than going along, for the most part, with the rising tide of racial repression. For race antagonism was part of the "law of nature"; Leveque "felt" this, knew it instinctively—and he was, after all, a white man. The only people of African ancestry he could truly sympathize with were the near-white Creoles of color. But Leveque realized too that disfranchisement and segregation of the blacks were only the makeshift expedients of his generation. He did not believe that blacks would always submit to these forms of race control. He had

34. New Orleans *Black Republican*, April 15, 1865; New Orleans *Republican Courier*, January 27, 1900. For a valuable analysis of racial attitudes among whites and blacks in the city during the Civil War–Reconstruction period, see John W. Blassingame, *Black New Orleans: 1860–1880* (Chicago: University of Chicago Press, 1973), particularly pages 173–210.

35. *Dictionary of American Biography*, III, 392–93; George H. Clements to George W. Cable, November 17, ca. 1890, in George Washington Cable Papers, Special Collections Division, Tulane University Library.

no final solution to offer and in fact dreaded to consider what the future might hold.[36]

There was one man in New Orleans who did not shrink from proposing a lasting answer to the race question. His name was Henry J. Hearsey. For twenty years Hearsey edited and published the powerful *States*, official journal of the city government and Louisiana's leading afternoon newspaper. Known to all as "Major" Hearsey, he indeed had been a major in the Confederate army. Wherever he went, an ever-present little rebel flag shined in his coat lapel. And he sincerely hated Negroes. Once, in what may still stand as a journalistic record of sorts, he used the epithet *nigger* twenty-eight times in one editorial. For years he had hinted in the columns of the *States* that something drastic might be necessary to resolve "the negro problem" (as he referred to the black race in his calmer moments); and in the summer of 1900 an editorial headline announced that Hearsey had reached a decision upon "THE NEGRO PROBLEM AND ITS FINAL SOLUTION."[37]

Extermination was the key word Hearsey used in outlining his solution. If, the Major explained, Negroes continue to show by words and deeds dissatisfaction with white rule, and "if they listen to the screeds of agitators in the North . . . the result will be a race war, and race war means extermination." Bloody as this might be, and though the whites would suffer some casualties in the conflict, there was—in Hearsey's view—this consolation: "Then the negro problem of Louisiana at least will be solved—and that by extermination." Later, on a less vitriolic note, Hearsey suggested that a war of genocide might yet be avoided and a more "humane" solution

36. "New Troubles Abrew," *Harlequin*, I (January 3, 1900), 5.

37. *National Cyclopaedia of American Biography* (New York: James T. White & Company, 1907), IX, 499; Compiled Service Records of Confederate Soldiers, Mississippi, Company K, 16th Miss. Regt., in Mississippi Department of Archives and History; New Orleans *Sunday States*, February 11, 1900; New Orleans *Daily States*, August 7, 1900.

achieved, but only if Negroes completely submitted to a more thorough "repression." "That is to say," explained the Major, "the negro must be ruled down with an iron hand." If Negroes would only accept the fact of innate black inferiority, then the South would know peace and Negroes could even be "happy" in the lowly position that Providence had ordained for them.[38]

Actually, Hearsey and his *States* did not exercise all the power to mold white opinion that they were sometimes credited with; if they had, Louisiana and Mississippi (the paper circulated in both states) would have undergone some kind of racial climacteric long before the Major's career ended. But he was for a generation the most influential newspaperman in New Orleans. While he lived, Hearsey and the *States* were synonymous. He was its founder (in 1880) and continued as editor long after others had purchased controlling shares of the paper; it was almost eerie, a fellow journalist observed, how the old man's spirit "seemed to pervade" everything about the *States*.[39]

Hearsey's newspaper career went back to 1860, when he edited the Woodville (Mississippi) *Republican*, before joining the Confederate army when the Civil War began. He fought Yankeedom with a gun until Appomattox, and afterwards with his acid pen. Disliking the general run of northerners almost as much as Negroes, he ranked Massachusetts as the most despicable place in America, with Connecticut a close second. "The Major," an old acquaintance explained, "never became reconciled to General Lee's defeat."[40]

38. New Orleans *Daily States*, August 7, 12, 16, 1900. See also the quotation from Hearsey's paper in the Abbeville *Meridional*, September 1, 1900.
39. Henry Rightor, *Standard History of New Orleans, Louisiana* (Chicago: Lewis Publishing Company, 1900), 279–81; Plaquemine *Iberville South*, May 23, 1896; *Harlequin*, II (November 3, 1900), 6–7.
40. New Orleans *Daily States*, February 25, 1883, May 5, 1898, February 27, 1899, October 30, 1900; Woodville (Miss.) *Republican*, November 3, 1900; Parker, "New Orleans Reminiscences," 28. Before moving to Mississippi, Hearsey had attempted (earlier in 1860) to found a newspaper in West Feliciana Parish, which was his birthplace; but his newspaper career really began when he accepted the editorship of the Woodville *Republican*.

Nor did Hearsey ever accept the northern-imposed Thirteenth Amendment. As late as 1900 he was still denouncing the emancipation of slaves as "a crime." Aging, weakened by Bright's disease and far too much whiskey, he was fiercely proud that his opinions on race and politics had changed not one whit since the night Fort Sumter was fired upon. The dead Confederacy was his great, lost love; to change himself would be to dishonor her. Hearsey's old friend, the Reverend B. M. Palmer of the First Presbyterian Church of New Orleans, would declare at the Major's funeral that "a beautiful consistency pervaded his whole career from its beginning to its close . . . the power of his influence remains."[41]

Insofar as race relations were concerned, Hearsey's influence was never greater than in the summer of 1900, when both he and the nineteenth century were close to dying. He who had witnessed and welcomed so much turmoil and hatred in his sixty years lived long enough to play a role in one more bloody tragedy, which began late on a sweltering July night when three New Orleans policemen came upon a big black man, Robert Charles, seated on a doorstep along Dryades Street.

41. New Orleans *Daily States*, June 19, 1900; Parker, "New Orleans Reminiscences," 28; New Orleans *Times-Democrat*, February 20, November 1, 1900.

⑥
WAITING FOR
A FRIEND

Robert Charles was only one of two thousand or more Mississippi blacks who moved to New Orleans during the 1890s. Copiah, along with nearby Lincoln and Pike counties, furnished a large share of this migration. Because of whitecapping and similar activities these three counties had become the most notorious of what the *Southwestern Christian Advocate*, a black New Orleans publication, referred to as the "terror stricken districts." Thousands of additional blacks from the Louisiana countryside also arrived during that decade. Yet fear of racial violence was probably not the fundamental reason for their migration to the city. New Orleans enjoyed a reputation as a place where black people could find paying work.[1]

From the time he arrived in the city in 1894, Robert was usually able to find some kind of employment. But never would he have a steady, year-in-and-year-out job such as he had once known at Vicksburg with the LNO & T. During his six years in New Orleans he found work, sometimes with tools and at other times as a manual laborer, at a variety of places in and around the city: with the contracting firm of Wolf and Seeman; on the docks at Port Chal-

---

1. New Orleans *Southwestern Christian Advocate*, August 16, 1900; "Anent the Riot and the Millennium," *Harlequin*, II (August 18, 1900), 2–3; New Orleans *Daily Item*, August 12, 1900.

mette, downriver from New Orleans; at the St. Charles Hotel, where he helped lay pipes and cables and later shoveled coal in the hotel's boiler room; as a streetcleaner for the city; and occasionally as a labor contractor for sugar planters. In the early summer of 1900 he was stacking lumber at the Pelican Sawmill Company. "He was a quiet nigger," several of his employers would recall. They added that he did his work well enough, but seemed to pay little attention to anyone around him.[2]

He was twenty-eight when he first came to New Orleans, using the same alias, "Curtis Robertson," that he had assumed in Copiah County after leaving the Vicksburg area in 1892. As time went on he appeared to use the alias less and less, having decided that the Rolling Fork trouble was now forgotten by Mississippi authorities. He was—by 1900 at any rate—know as Robert Charles among those with whom he associated in the black community, though a number of them were aware that he had previously used the alias Robertson. As early as 1895 he gave his real name while working for the Wolf and Seeman Company; in May of the following year a white supervisor for that firm wrote him a letter of recommendation, certifying that "R. Charles has been in my employ for some time, and any person in need of a good man will find the bearer a good, honest and reliable man."[3]

Only one white person in New Orleans ever knew him and talked with him over an extended period of time. Hyman Levy, a salesman in a clothing store at 829 Poydras Street, met Robert when the black man walked into the store one day in 1894. Having just arrived from Mississippi, Robert introduced himself as Curtis Robertson. For the next six years he traded at this store and appar-

2. New Orleans *Daily States*, July 24, 1900; New Orleans *Daily Picayune*, July 26, 1900; New Orleans *Times-Democrat*, July 25, 1900; Parkash Kaur Bains, "The New Orleans Race Riot of 1900" (M.A. thesis, Louisiana State University in New Orleans, 1970), 23.

3. New Orleans *Times-Democrat*, July 25–26, 1900; New Orleans *Daily States*, July 24, 1900.

ently would not purchase his clothing from anyone except Hyman Levy. Since he had used an assumed name in the beginning, Robert continued to call himself Curtis Robertson whenever in that store, and he told Levy that his nickname was "Buster." Levy's later description of their dealings clearly indicates that the two men, although they seldom met outside the store, came to like and respect each other. Levy lived for some time not far from where Robert often stayed, and they would sometimes greet each other on the streets.[4]

Levy thought highly of Charles and said so even after the black man was described across the United States as a fiend and a desperado. The salesman was impressed by the fact that "Buster" always paid cash, and also by his taste in clothes. "He was," remembered Levy, "what you call a stylish negro and was above the average darkey in intelligence. In fact he struck me as being fairly well educated." Levy contradicted several newspaper accounts that appeared during the time of Robert's great trouble; the papers claimed Robert's hometown was Vicksburg. "His home," asserted the salesman, "was either in Hazlehurst or Summit, Mississippi. I am certain of that because I have forwarded clothes to him on different occasions at both places." Summit was in Pike County, about thirty miles south of Copiah, and a family named Jackson, who were friends and possibly relatives of Robert's and with whom he frequently lived in New Orleans, were originally from there.[5]

But Levy was puzzled as to what Curtis Robertson did for a living most of the year. For some reason the black man never told Levy about the work he did with his hands, and the salesman knew only that for a few weeks each autumn Robertson was a labor contractor, receiving a fee for hiring city blacks as extra hands to

4. Levy interview, New Orleans *Sunday States*, July 29, 1900.

5. *Ibid.*; New Orleans *Daily Picayune*, July 28, August 1, 4, 1900; H. N. Crawford and others to W. W. Handlin, December 3, 1900, in Case No. 30, 086 File, Clerk's Office, Criminal District Court, Parish of Orleans, Louisiana.

harvest sugarcane on the plantations near New Orleans. Levy realized that this work alone could not provide the man with enough money to live the year round and buy nice clothes at the Poydras Street store. Yet Robert never mentioned his other jobs and always came to the store in clean attire. Levy was confident, however, that whatever else "Buster" did, he was no criminal. "He seemed to be so honest and upright," said Levy, "that it hardly seemed possible to me that any thing was wrong with him."[6]

By the time he was thirty-four, in 1900, Robert's physical appearance had of course changed somewhat since his time in Vicksburg ten or twelve years earlier. There was now more flesh on his six-foot frame; he weighed between 180 and 190 pounds—sufficient to earn him the description "burly" (as in "burly brute," a popular term of the time for any large, muscular Negro who was suspected of committing any act of violence toward whites). Between medium and dark brown in skin color, he wore his hair closely cropped. One of Robert's most noticeable features was the long, drooping moustache he had grown after coming to New Orleans. Either because he was proud of the moustache, or out of nervous habit, he often curled it with his fingers. When out of doors he usually wore a hat; and, like most New Orleans men of that era, he wore a coat even in the most hot and humid months.[7]

The drawings of him that would appear in the New Orleans press during late July of 1900 are not especially helpful in trying to visualize his actual appearance. The *Times-Democrat* presented him as a surly-looking mulatto with small, baleful eyes, and the *States* ran a similar drawing. The *Picayune* first drew him as more of

6. Levy interview, New Orleans *Sunday States,* July 29, 1900.

7. This and subsequent descriptions of Robert Charles's appearance are based on the interviews of black men and women who knew him, as published in the New Orleans dailies from July 24 to August 1 of 1900. The fullest descriptions are found in the *Times-Democrat* of July 25. See also, Vicksburg *Daily Herald,* July 26, 1900.

an African type, but with large, expressive eyes and a benign countenance—then in the next issue depicted him as very dark and ferocious-looking. The *Item* and the French-language *L'Abeille* used the same woodcut, which showed neither the moustache nor much ability on the part of the artist. The only other daily whose files are extant, the German *Deutsche Zeitung,* ran no picture of him at all—nor did the only black New Orleans paper whose files for that period have survived, the weekly *Southwestern Christian Advocate.* The police managed to acquire a photograph of Robert Charles from a woman he went with, but like his rifle and pistol and other artifacts associated with him, it seems to have been taken as a souvenir and has been lost.[8]

Because of an old ankle injury Robert walked with an almost imperceptible limp. Two of his upper front teeth were discolored and showed signs of decay. He drank rather often, but none who knew him remembered his ever showing any sign of intoxication. He may have occasionally taken cocaine. As in Vicksburg, he often carried a big Colt revolver—probably the same one that caused the fight at Rolling Fork—inside his left coat pocket. At his lodgings he kept a Winchester rifle. Not gregarious but not sullen either, Robert was always silent while working and at no time cared to talk about himself. Yet there were some subjects he liked to discuss and on these he would converse at length in his usual low-toned voice, but with the words tumbling out in quick, decisive sentences.[9]

Robert came to know a large number of black people in New Orleans, but he seems to have made few close friends. Naturally, once he began shooting policemen and other whites, no black person could be discovered who cared to admit to the police or the press that he had been a regular associate of Robert's. Those who

8. New Orleans *Daily Picayune,* July 25–26, 1900; interview with Major Henry M. Morris, Chief of Detectives, New Orleans Police Department, June 19, 1974.
9. Vicksburg *Daily Herald,* July 26, 1900; New Orleans *Times-Democrat,* July 25, 1900.

could not avoid saying they knew him endeavored, when questioned, to put as much distance between themselves and him as possible. This was particularly necessary because of the widespread assumption, or at least suspicion, among whites that Charles was part of some kind of armed racial plot; Major Hearsey was only one of many who jumped to the conclusion that "he was unquestionably busy in an effort to stir up a sort of servile war that would have inflicted great damage on the city."[10]

However, of the many statements made by blacks about Robert Charles at this time, there were some assertions that, when matched with other information about him, had the ring of truth. And on these points all were agreed: he was quiet and unobtrusive, but somehow gave the distinct impression of being a man with whom it would be best not to trifle. And everyone who met him described him as intelligent. Lenard Pierce, who had the misfortune to room with him when Charles's New Orleans trouble began, said that he "never talked of himself" and especially avoided mentioning his past life in Mississippi. Pierce further stated that Robert often grumbled about the wrongs inflicted on the black race in America and said that emigration to Africa was the best solution; Pierce also told the police that Charles talked about the right of self-defense, but "he never told me to go against the white people." The police themselves conceded that as far as they knew Charles was never involved in any kind of crime or disturbance in New Orleans, at least not until the evening of July 23, 1900. He was in the city six years and the authorities had never heard of him until then.[11]

Shortly after Robert Charles died, a prominent black woman in Chicago, Ida B. Wells-Barnett, received a letter postmarked New Orleans from a black man who had known Robert for some time.

10. New Orleans *Daily States,* July 28, 1900.
11. New Orleans *Times-Democrat,* July 25–26, 1900; New Orleans *Daily Picayune,* July 26, 1900.

Mrs. Wells-Barnett, a civil-rights activist who earlier had to leave Tennessee because of the outspokenness of a newspaper she had edited at Memphis, reprinted the letter from Charles's friend in a pamphlet she published about events in New Orleans. To protect the person who wrote her she did not give his name. The letter read:

New Orleans, Aug. 23, 1900

Mrs. Ida B. Wells Barnett:

Dear Madam—It affords me great pleasure to inform you as far as I know of Robert Charles. I have been acquainted with him about six years in this city. He never has, as I know, given any trouble to anyone. He was quiet and a peaceful man and was very frank in speaking. He was too much of a hero to die; few can be found to equal him. I am very sorry to say that I do not know anything of his birthplace, nor his parents, but enclosed find letter from his uncle, from which you may find more information. You will also find one of the circulars in which Charles was in possession of which was styled as a crazy document. Let me say, until our preachers preach this document we will always be slaves. If you can help circulate this "crazy" doctrine I would be glad to have you do so, for I shall never rest until I get to that heaven on earth; that is, the west coast of Africa, in Liberia.

With best wishes to you I still remain, as always, for the good of the race,

_____12

During the last year of his life Robert became increasingly involved in promoting the cause of black emigration to Africa. He would have first listened to talk of returning to the black homeland as a youngster in Copiah County, but it was most probably while in the Vicksburg area, from 1887 to 1892, that he became deeply

12. Anonymous [name withheld by recipient] letter to Ida B. Wells-Barnett, in her *Mob Rule in New Orleans* (Chicago: N.p., 1900), 42. This pamphlet has been reprinted with other writings of Mrs. Wells-Barnett under the title *On Lynchings* (New York: Arno Press, 1969), and with a new preface by August Meier. As mentioned previously, the letter from Robert Charles's uncle referred to, along with the original copy of this letter, apparently was destroyed in a fire at Mrs. Wells-Barnett's home.

interested in the subject. An acute observer of Vicksburg life expressed astonishment in 1889 at the tenacity with which blacks in the little city "hold to the belief that they will ultimately return to that county, and . . . this opinion is believed to prevail among them to a great extent." The short-lived African Emigration Society of 1887–88 (in which a certain George Charles of Mississippi was active) apparently played no significant role in promoting the idea. It was simply a deeply rooted conviction among rank-and-file blacks in the area, probably handed down from previous generations. And black religious lecturers, some of them returned missionaries, occasionally came to Vicksburg during those years, speaking on Africa and its history. Their lectures were held in black Methodist and Baptists churches, and it is quite likely that young Robert Charles attended some of these gatherings.[13]

Vicksburg's interest in Africa and black migration was not entirely confined to the black community. Late in 1887 one of the city's most respected white men, Horace S. Fulkerson, published a booklet titled *The Negro: As He Was; As He Is; As He Will Be,* which stirred much comment in the area and was probably read by more than a few blacks. The booklet contained the customary panegyric to southern whites as "the most perfect race of people existing on the globe" and discussed at length the "undeniable proposition" of black inferiority; it also endorsed some of the current white folklore about blacks, such as the beliefs that the bite of a Negro with blue gums was poisonous and that mulattoes were more criminally inclined than either whites or pure blacks. However, Fulkerson also made a strong plea for a government-financed resettlement of the entire American Negro population, either in Africa or in some other tropical land. He proposed this not only as a guaranteed means of ending racial tensions in the United States, but also as an obligation which the white race owed to the blacks for having uprooted them

13. Vicksburg *Evening Post,* June 14, August 31, 1887, March 19, 1889. See also New York *Times,* February 9, 1888.

from their natural home. "Give the negro a country which he can call *his own*," Fulkerson urged, "and he will have a fair opportunity to develop his highest capacities. . . . We at least owe it to him to give him this chance. It is the only hope for him." And, the author suggested, this was also the only chance for future peace in the South, because he refused to believe that black people, being human, would forever submit to the humiliations of disfranchisement and segregation.[14]

Another booklet which circulated among blacks in Mississippi at this time had been published in the North in 1884 under the title *Liberia As It Is.* Written by a black missionary, W. E. De Claybrook, it did not openly advocate a mass return of American Negroes to Africa, but by its positive description of Liberia would have encouraged the idea. Claybrook made a point of stressing the "independent and self-possessed appearance of the natives." Being free from white domination, "there is nothing slavish or cringing in their manner." He also emphasized the need for black Christians to bring the gospel of Christ to Africa, a work he believed white missionaries could not properly perform.[15]

Whatever the influence that back-to-Africa talk and writings may have had on Robert Charles in Mississippi, there is no hard evidence that he became personally active in this cause until two years after he first arrived in New Orleans. Among his effects would be found a certificate from the International Migration Society, dated May 22, 1896, acknowledging that Robert Charles had joined the organization and had paid his first dues "for the purpose of going with a party of 1,500 to Liberia." The certificate was signed by the

14. H. S. Fulkerson, *The Negro: As He Was; As He Is; As He Will Be* (Vicksburg: Commercial Herald Printer, 1887), 57, 73–74, 87–89, 107, 117–18; Vicksburg *Evening Post,* January 2, February 15, 1888. For more on Fulkerson, see P. L. Rainwater (ed.), "Notes on Southern Personalities," *Journal of Southern History,* IV (May, 1938), 210–11.

15. W. E. De Claybrook, *Liberia As It Is* (Boston: N.p., 1884), 53, 128, copy in Alfred Holt Stone Collection, Mississippi Department of Archives and History.

president, Daniel J. Flummer, at the society's home office in Birmingham, Alabama. Robert would have learned of the organization and its purpose from promotional literature distributed by the society's New Orleans agent, an itinerant black minister named William Royal.[16]

The International Migration Society that Robert joined in 1896 had been formed two years earlier by four Birmingham white men, of whom Flummer was one. It existed under that name until its collapse in 1899, but was presently reorganized by Flummer under the name Liberia Colonization Society. The organization existed more for profit than humanitarian reasons. Each black person who joined was to pay one dollar per month for forty months; in return the society pledged to thereupon ship the individual to Liberia, along with provisions to last three months. Those who did not keep up their dues forfeited whatever they had invested. Obviously, the society's white promoters figured on making their profits from the forfeited payments.[17]

Nothing more than a crooked scheme "to beguile money from poor ignorance," was the way a New Orleans magazine described Flummer's project. Various black leaders across the South castigated it in similar language. Yet the International Migration Society, as a careful study of back-to-Africa movements points out, "apparently acted in good faith with most of the people who purchased tickets," though Flummer's motives and methods were questionable. The society did charter two voyages: the ship *Horsa* in 1895 took 197 southern blacks to Liberia and the *Laurada* sailed with 321 more the next year. On the other hand, these emigrants had not been adequately prepared or supplied for a new life in a

16. New Orleans *Daily States*, July 24, 1900; New Orleans *Times-Democrat*, August 4, 1900.
17. "Direct Communication with Africa Established," *Voice of Missions*, II (March, 1894), 2; Edwin S. Redkey, *Black Exodus: Black Nationalist and Back-to-Africa Movements, 1890–1910* (New Haven: Yale University Press, 1969), 195–97.

strange country. Many died shortly after their arrival and most of
the others reportedly became unhappy and were anxious to return.[18] The society's well-advertised activities had aroused the
hopes of many thousands of poor blacks across the South, but its
meagre results clearly demonstrated that any such project, to suc-
ceed at all, would require dedicated organization and funding on a
massive scale.

The date on which Robert Charles became a member of the
International Migration Society — May of 1896 — is probably significant. Something had just happened locally which heightened
black resentment and feelings of futility. Louisiana, in April of that
year, had experienced its most crucial election since Reconstruction, with a fusion ticket of Populists and white and black Republicans making a strong bid to unseat the ultraconservative Democratic
state administration. Whether Robert was registered as a Louisiana
voter at this time is unknown, but he probably was, since he took an
interest in politics and in that year would not have encountered
difficulty in registering in New Orleans. The "Mississippi Plan" of
legal disfranchisement had not yet been adopted by the Pelican
State, but Louisiana blacks realized that their future citizenship
rights probably depended on the outcome of this election and so
almost to a man they supported — wherever allowed to cast a free
ballot — the fusion ticket. In the April election the Populist-
Republican coalition won a majority of the votes actually cast but
was counted out by fabulously doctored returns from certain
Democratic-controlled plantation parishes. This 1896 election engendered more racial feeling and violence than the state had known
in any campaign since Reconstruction. Fusion candidates contested
the returns, but early in May the legislature refused to investigate
what everyone knew had been a stolen election. Also, there were

18. "The Times-Democrat's Liberian Expose," *Harlequin*, II (August 11, 1900),
3; Redkey, *Black Exodus*, 195–269.

twenty-one reported lynchings in Louisiana that year, which topped the previous annual record for any state, even Mississippi.[19]

Robert never sailed for Africa and whether he kept up his dues in the International Migration Society was not disclosed. But he continued a fairly regular correspondence with the society's president, whom he may or may not have known was a white man. Charles became, according to Flummer, one of the local subagents of the society and "set about faithfully distributing the literature that we issued from time to time." Flummer added that "he always appeared to be mild but earnest in his advocacy of emigration, and never to my knowledge used any method or means that would in the least appear unreasonable, and had always kept within the bounds of law and order in advocating emigration." Robert did not receive or ask for any pay for what he did. He occasionally went back into Mississippi, and while there probably did some of his gratis work for the society.[20]

Late in July of 1900, two days before the violent series of events began in New Orleans, Flummer received what would be his last communication from Charles. The society's president subsequently sent the letter to Mrs. Wells-Barnett in Chicago, who had requested from him more information about the obscure black man who had died under such remarkable circumstances. Charles's letter was brief:

Mr. D. J. Flummer:
Dear Sir - I received your last pamphlets and they are all given out. I want you to send me some more, and I enclose you the

19. William Ivy Hair, *Bourbonism and Agrarian Protest: Louisiana Politics, 1877–1900* (Baton Rouge: Louisiana State University Press, 1969), 234–67. See also New Orleans *Daily Picayune*, April 29–30, 1896; Natchitoches *Louisiana Populist*, March 6, April 10, May 1, 1896; James Elbert Cutler, *Lynch-Law: An Investigation into the History of Lynching in the United States* (New York: Longman's Green and Company, 1905), 183.

20. D. J. Flummer to Mrs. Ida B. Wells-Barnett, quoted in Wells-Barnett, *Mob Rule in New Orleans*, 41. The New Orleans press believed Charles had been a

stamps. I think I will go over to Greenville, Miss., and give my
people some pamphlets over there. Yours truly,

                                             Robert Charles[21]

Between 1896 and 1900, while Robert worked at various jobs
and handed out migration literature during his spare time, Louisiana's Democratic government, having survived the crisis of the
recent gubernatorial election, set about by quasilegal processes to
effectively disfranchise the black race. For this purpose complex
registration and ballot box laws were enacted, to be augmented by
the even more decisive suffrage provisions of the Constitution of
1898. This new organic law set literacy or property requirements for
voting but allowed a "grandfather clause" loophole (at least in
theory) for poor, illiterate whites who had voted, or whose ancestors
had voted, prior to Reconstruction. Solemnly, the presiding officer
of the constitutional convention informed that assembly that disfranchisement was an act not of hostility toward Negroes, but of
kindness. "We owe it to the ignorant," he continued, "we owe it to
the weak, to protect them just as we would protect a little child and
prevent it from injuring itself with sharp edged tools. . . ." Major
Hearsey of the *States*, who was awarded the printing contract for the
convention, grumbled because the same kindness was not shown
poor whites. But Hearsey cheered up when he remembered that
"after 1900 the [new] poll tax will knock out most of them."[22]

Black voters in many Louisiana parishes had seldom, since
Reconstruction, been able to cast a free ballot anyway, but the

---

subagent for the International Migration Society only since 1899, but Flummer
indicated that his "business connection" with the society went back several years.

21. Robert Charles to D. J. Flummer, quoted *ibid.*

22. *Official Journal of the Constitutional Convention of the State of Louisiana,
1898* (New Orleans: H. J. Hearsey Convention Printer, 1898), Art. 197, p. 10; New
Orleans *Daily States,* May 31, 1898. See also Perry H. Howard, *Political Tendencies
in Louisiana* (Rev. ed.; Baton Rouge: Louisiana State University Press, 1971), 188–
91; and J. Morgan Kousser, *The Shaping of Southern Politics: Suffrage Restriction
and the Establishment of the One-Party South, 1880–1910* (New Haven: Yale University Press, 1974), 164–65.

Consitution of 1898 and attendant legislation gave the force of law to what he been outright fraud. After 1896, especially after 1898, the decline in black registration statewide was phenomenal. Within four years (by 1900) it fell from 130,444 (44 percent of the total) to 5,320 (4 percent of the total), and later plummeted to an all-time low of 598 by 1922.[23] Robert Charles had lived in Mississippi when outright disfranchisement took place there in 1890. Now, a few years later, he saw it happen again in the state to which he had moved. Those who knew Charles said it visibly affected him, that "he deeply resented the disfranchisement of his race in Louisiana."[24]

Another event, this one in April of 1899, further alienated Robert Charles from American society and prompted him to devote more of his time to his back-to-Africa activities. He must have read about it in the papers, for it happened four hundred miles away, near Newnan, Georgia. Sam Hose (or Holt), black, was on April 23, 1899, lynched on suspicion of rape and murder. A lynching under these circumstances was scarcely unusual; this was only one of 107 reported mob murders in the nation that year. But Sam Hose died in particularly horrible fashion. He was slowly tortured and then burned alive, before a huge crowd which included women and young boys. Indeed, special trains had been run from Atlanta that Sunday so more people could witness the event. Afterward, his half-consumed body was pulled from the fire, he was cut open, and slices of his heart and liver were sold as souvenirs. One enthusiast took a heart slice to Atlanta, hoping to present it to the governor.[25]

23. *Report of the Secretary of State to His Excellency W. W. Heard, Governor of the State of Louisiana, 1902* (Baton Rouge: News Publishing Company, 1902), 554–57; Howard, *Political Tendencies in Louisiana*, 190; Riley E. Baker, "Negro Voter Registration in Louisiana, 1879–1964," *Louisiana Studies*, IV (Winter, 1965), 338–39.

24. "Race Riots in New Orleans," *Independent*, LII (August 2, 1900), 1822.

25. Monroe N. Work (ed.), *Negro Year Book: An Annual Encyclopedia of the Negro, 1931–1932* (Tuskeegee, Ala.: Negro Yearbook Publishing Company, 1931),

Reading of this atrocity, knowing that no one would ever be prosecuted for what happened, Robert Charles went into a rage. It was the only time, according to his acquaintances, that they had ever seen anger get a complete hold on him. He was, said one, "beside himself with fury."

Robert was also reported to have exclaimed "that the time had come for every black man to prepare to defend himself." One black levee worker who knew him, William Butts, said that Robert, upon reading about the Hose lynching, had declared "it was the duty of every negro to buy a rifle and keep it ready against the time they might be called upon to act in unison." Butts also maintained that Charles had talked vaguely about "an uprising" and had hinted that "some kind of organization [was] being formed."[26] This assertion was, however, the sole report that indicated Robert ever spoke approvingly of any sort of violence, except in self-defense.

Soon after the Sam Hose lynching, Robert Charles contacted the Atlanta offices of Bishop Henry M. Turner of the African Methodist Episcopal Church. He wanted to become a subscription agent for Bishop Turner's monthly magazine, *Voice of Missions,* and his application was accepted. Turner had long been a champion of the back-to-Africa cause, had visited Liberia several times, and had endorsed—although he was not directly associated with—Daniel Flummer's International Migration Society. The Bishop was a blunt and forceful man; he had been a chaplain in the Union army during the Civil War and was a Republican legislator in Georgia during Reconstruction. His speeches and writings on the subject of black grievances in America were bitter, but he was correctly civil when

293; New York *Times,* April 24–25, 1899. Presumably, Georgia Governor Allen D. Candler did not accept the slice of Sam Hose's heart, but he did criticize some black leaders who came to him to protest the lynching. Said Governer Candler, speaking of the angered Negroes: "They are blinded by race prejudice, and can see but one side of the question. This is unfortunate. They must learn to look at both sides." See Atlanta *Constitution,* April 24, 1899.

26. New Orleans *Times-Democrat,* July 29, 1900.

dealing with whites. Turner's *Voice of Missions* had begun publication in 1893 as a personal vehicle for his religious and emigrationist philosophy.[27]

In the summer of 1899 Robert began regular visits to black homes and gathering places in New Orleans, peddling the *Voice of Missions*. Most of the poverty-stricken blacks whom he approached could not afford to purchase long-term subscriptions, so Robert personally delivered and collected for the monthly issues, receiving for this a small commission. He made his rounds when off duty from whatever job he currently had. Each month bundles of the periodical were shipped from Atlanta to wherever his residence happened to be; like so many unmarried workingmen in New Orleans, white and black, he changed lodgings rather frequently.[28]

Some of Robert's acquaintances, seeking to discredit him and thereby deflect from themselves any imputation of guilt by association with him, claimed that he bragged of getting "a big commission" for his work in the back-to-Africa movement. It is doubtful that he said any such thing, which at any rate was not true, since the *Voice of Missions* sold for only five cents per copy. Robert also continued his activity in distributing free pamphlets for Flummer's International Migration Society and at the same time encouraged blacks to begin, or continue, the monthly payments of one dollar for the society's proposed voyage to Liberia. For this he was paid nothing.[29]

Charles's low-key promotion of African emigration never attracted the attention of the New Orleans police and it is unlikely that they would have bothered him had they known everything about his

27. *Voice of Missions,* I (January, 1893), 2–3; New Orleans *Times-Democrat,* July 25, 29, 1900; Mungo M. Ponton, *Life and Times of Henry M. Turner* (Atlanta: A. B. Caldwell Publishing Company, 1917), 51–60; See also Redkey, *Black Exodus.*

28. New Orleans *Times-Democrat,* July 25, 29, 1900; New Orleans *Daily Picayune,* July 25, 1900.

29. New Orleans *Times-Democrat,* July 29, 1900; Flummer to Wells-Barnett, quoted in *Mob Rule in New Orleans,* 41.

work for Turner and Flummer. What he did was not illegal and the majority of New Orleans whites would hardly have opposed the idea of black departures for Africa, or for anywhere. In rural Louisiana or Mississippi, where multitudinous black workers were still desired, Robert might well have been stopped for being an "agitator" if he had been caught distributing such literature, but not in a big city where whites and blacks bitterly competed for the available jobs. (As a prominent sugar planter, speaking of an effort to recruit southern blacks for Hawaiian plantations, remarked in 1900: "Louisiana needs her good [agricultural] niggers." However, he smilingly added, "here in New Orleans you have a lot of nigger dudes you can spare." And this appeared to be the general view of the city's white population.)[30] The violent confrontation that Robert Charles eventually had with the New Orleans Police Department would not be directly related to his back-to-Africa endeavors.

Voice of Missions was the most plainspoken nonpolitical black publication of that era. Bishop Turner had long since despaired of any meaningful future for the black race in America, either in the South (where 90 percent of the nation's black people still lived) or in the North. Moreover, he was utterly convinced that "the Negro must have a nation of his own, before he is going to be a man." Yet, while condemning white racism, Turner never urged blacks to adopt an attitude of hatred or vengeance toward whites, and he was quick to point out the peril of armed collision. "What could the Negro do," he rhetorically asked, "with the whites in a war? They would exterminate him in a day." Nevertheless, the bishop was not totally an apostle of nonviolence. He maintained that individual blacks, like all members of the human race, had a natural right to fight defensively if their lives were in jeopardy.[31]

30. New Orleans *Daily Picayune*, August 7, 1900.
31. Henry M. Turner, "Races Must Separate," in *The Possibilities of the Negro in Symposium* (Atlanta, 1904), 97–98; article on Henry M. Turner in "Black Georgians in History," Atlanta *Journal*, February 4, 1974; *Voice of Missions*, V (May, 1897), 2–3; Ponton, *Life and Times of Henry M. Turner*, 60.

Major Hearsey, outspoken editor of the New Orleans *Daily States,* with the habitual rebel flag in his lapel.

Lenard Pierce, roommate and companion to Robert Charles at the time of the incident. This is probably a very accurate drawing of him, since it was done by a New Orleans *Daily Picayune* artist who sketched Pierce while he sat in a cell.

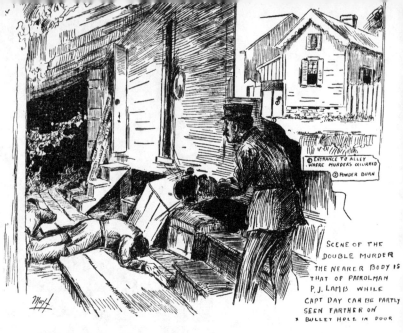

Within the image: ① ENTRANCE TO ALLEY WHERE MURDERS OCCURRED ② POWDER BURN

SCENE OF THE
DOUBLE MURDER
THE NEARER BODY IS
THAT OF PATROLMAN
P. J. LAMB WHILE
CAPT DAY CAN BE PARTLY
SEEN FARTHER ON
× BULLET HOLE IN DOOR

"Scene of Double Murder." This sketch of the slain Captain Day and Patrolman Lamb appeared in the New Orleans *Times-Democrat,* July 25, 1900.

The House on Saratoga Street, scene of the final shootout. The building shown is the annex of 1208–1210 Saratoga. It appeared in the *Daily Picayune* and was sketched from a photograph taken shortly after the shootout.

Closeup of Saratoga Street Annex, from which Robert Charles defied the besiegers. This drawing appeared in the *Daily Picayune*.

1. Captain John T. Day

2. Patrolman Peter J. Lamb

3. Sergeant Gabriel Porteous

4. Corporal John F. Lally

Officers Killed by Charles

Patrolman August T. Mora, whose clash with Charles on Dryades Street was the beginning of the train of events.

Corporal Ernest J. Trenchard, tried and convicted of cowardice for his performance against Charles.

A HEROIC (?) CORPORAL.

"*A Heroic Corporal,*" a cartoon that appeared in the New Orleans *Item,* August 2, 19 showing Trenchard and Aucoin sweating it out inside Miss Cryder's room, with Char raging about outside.

Souvenir-Hunters, going through Robert Charles's things. Sketched by a *Daily Picayune* artist on the scene.

Miss Jewett, the "Joan of Arc of the Negroes," from Boston. This appeared in the *Picayune*, probably redrawn from some Boston paper.

The Negroes Arrested on Saratoga Street, the Jacksons, Imogene Nixon, Annie G etc. This group photograph of them in Parish Prison appeared in the New Orleans *Ite* October 21, 1900.

Turner's vision of black nationalism accepted one of the old proslavery arguments of the antebellum South—that slavery had been part of God's plan for bringing Christianity to the African race. But, he hastened to add, the whites of America had failed in their obligation to God and humanity by not permitting blacks to develop their full capabilities and by not doing more missionary work in Africa itself. Consequently, American blacks were now under Almighty direction to assume the simultaneous tasks of achieving human dignity for themselves and bringing the gospel to Africa, by returning to the homeland. Turner did not believe all or even most American blacks were fit recruits for such work; he wanted only the best of the race and was quite willing for America to keep all the others. In Turner's plan the benefits to Africa would include not only Christianity but also the knowledge of Western technology which these emigrants could bring. To finance such an undertaking he proposed that the United States should, as reparation for two centuries of unpaid slave labor, finance the exodus to Africa.[32] In the meantime he endorsed Flummer's International Migration Society, which Turner clearly saw as being more a means of publicizing the black desire for emigration than as a practical organization.

In April of 1900, while Robert Charles sold the *Voice of Missions* on the poorer streets of New Orleans, Louisiana underwent another state election, the first since the massive constitutional disfranchisement of black voters. The planter-merchant oligarchy that had ruled the state since Reconstruction was never more sure of victory. Not only were blacks no longer a political threat, but white agrarian opposition had meanwhile sunk into apathy and "sullen despair," as one of their erstwhile leaders described it; the gigantic frauds of 1896 had convinced thousands of poor white farmers that "it was no use, the Democrats would count them out."[33] Thus the forlorn

32. Redkey, *Black Exodus*, 35–39; *Independent*, LI (September 7, 1899), 2430–32.

33. Natchitoches *Louisiana Populist*, November 11, 1898. See also Monroe

ticket that remnants of the old Populist-Republican coalition put forward in 1900 would not require the previous defrauding on election day. It was already beaten.

Tens of thousands of Louisiana black men, being literate or property owners, were entitled to register under the new constitution. But they did not. Apathy and resignation had gripped their ranks just as it had the poor whites; but for the blacks fear also played a role. The constant and increasing pressure to leave politics alone had largely proven successful. Many Negroes who were qualified to register refused to do so because, as they told one northern writer who visited Louisiana to investigate black disfranchisement, "We [would] only gain the ill will of the whites and run the risk of bad treatment." Even so, as late as 1900 one predominantly black parish, St. James, still had a sizable black registration, and it was to be the only parish the Democrats would lose in the April election.[34] A story from St. James carried by the New Orleans papers on April 4—two weeks before the election—made a strong impression on two quite different New Orleanians, Major Hearsey and Robert Charles.

The St. James Parish town of Lutcher had been the scene the day before of a Republican-Populist fusion rally, in which one of the speakers, Dennis Sholars, angrily proposed armed revolution against the incumbent Democratic state administration. Sholars contended that the oligarchy was planning for the upcoming 1900 election the same tactics they had used in 1896: that the fusion ticket "was to be counted out by fraud." Since the ballot box was useless against such tyranny, there was "but one recourse. . . . And that was to *oil up their Winchesters* and prepare for a fight." The representa-

Bulletin, quoted in Shreveport *Evening Journal*, April 22, 1900; New Orleans *Daily Item*, April 18, 1900.

34. Paul L. Haworth, "Negro Disfranchisement in Louisiana," *Outlook*, LXXI (May 17, 1902), 163; *Report of the Secretary of State*, 1902, pp. 557–64.

tives of the people could then be installed by force, said the speaker.[35] Sholars' audience included both whites and blacks.

Sholars' speech was widely commented upon in New Orleans and provoked another choleric outburst from Major Hearsey, whose paper was a mainstay of the office-holding class of Louisiana. Hearsey said the talk by Sholars, before a racially mixed audience, was "insane rot," and he hotly resented the fact that some of the fusionists who advocated revolution were pointing out that Major Hearsey had done the same thing when Louisiana was under a Republican government. Robert Charles, on the other hand, was in his own way impressed by reading of the speech in St. James. For he clipped out the two-column account of it in the *Times-Democrat* and carried it around with him. The clipping was found after his death in one of his pockets.[36]

Robert lived in at least a dozen shabby residences during his six years in New Orleans. And like thousands of other black people he managed to avoid being listed in *Soards' New Orleans City Directory*. The 1897 listing did name a "Robert Charles," whose occupation was "bridge builder," but the address was in a predominantly white neighborhood on Magazine Street and it is unlikely that a black laborer resided there, or would have received such a euphemistic job title. No "Curtis Robertson" appeared at all in the 1894–1900 directories. For that matter, numerous whites as well as blacks went to great lengths to avoid the directory's annual survey; bill collectors were one good reason, and another was that jury lists for Orleans Parish were drawn from Soards's directory (the voter registration rolls being so unreliable). Jury duty paid nothing.[37]

35. New Orleans *Times-Democrat*, April 4, 1900 [Italics mine].

36. New Orleans *Daily States*, April 4–5, 1900; New Orleans *Times-Democrat*, July 28, 1900.

37. *Soards' New Orleans City Directory for 1897*, XXIV, 195; Vicksburg *Even-*

Between spring and midsummer of 1900 Robert Charles changed residences three times. From 1515 Freret Street he moved to 1212 Gravier; and from there, on July 16, he carried most of his belongings to room No. 4 of a dilapidated cottage at 2023 Fourth Street, between Rampart and Saratoga. This was an even cheaper lodging than his Gravier residence, which had rented for $3.00 per month. He had reason for the strictest economy; in June he was laid off his last job, at the lumber yard of the Pelican Sawmill Company. The few pennies he made peddling the *Voice of Missions* was currently his only income. So he persuaded a nineteen-year-old friend, Lenard Pierce, to move to the Fourth Street room with him and share expenses.[38]

Out of work, Robert spent considerable time in his and Lenard's one-room lodging at 2023 Fourth Street. In a corner of the room he piled bundles of unsold copies of the *Voice of Missions,* along with pamphlets from the International Migration Society. But not all of his reading material concerned the back-to-Africa movement. Elsewhere in the room were a number of worn textbooks on various subjects, marked here and there, and with the name "Robert Charles" inscribed on the inside covers. There were some copies of the *Police Gazette* as well as a few other popular, sensationalist magazines. On the mantelpiece opposite the room's single door, Robert had placed a bullet mold and device for reloading used cartridge shells. He had a scabbard for his Colt revolver; probably the Winchester rifle was just leaned against the wall.[39]

Most puzzling of all to the police, reporters, and curious white citizens who would crowd into the little room a few days later were the contents of Robert's trunk, near his bed. Inside that trunk were a

ing *Post,* July 1, 1890. Federal census takers encountered similar difficulties in the city. See New Orleans *Times-Democrat,* June 3, 1900.

38. New Orleans *Daily States,* July 24, 1900; New Orleans *Daily Picayune,* July 25, 1900. Pierce's first name was sometimes listed as "Leonard" and at other times as "Leon," but he spelled it Lenard.

39. New Orleans *Times-Democrat,* July 25, 1900.

number of composition books, all of them filled with Charles's handwriting. Exactly what these writings were—whether they were original essays, or a diary, or copied passages from printed works—the police and the press never said. But the *Times-Democrat*'s reporter, who looked into the composition books, stated that the contents "showed that he had burnt the midnight oil, and was desirous of improving himself intellectually," in order, the reporter assumed, "that he might conquer the hated white race."[40] Soon either the police or souvenir hunters hauled away Robert's personal effects, including those composition books. Probably all were later destroyed, or they may lie forgotten in some New Orleans attic today.

"There was an air of elegance about Charles," two elderly black women told a *Picayune* reporter who came to the Fourth Street address on July 24, seeking more information about the man who had suddenly become the subject of a two-state manhunt. Old Annie Cryder and Fanny Jackson lived in the first two rooms of the house, and Robert had shown them his books and papers. They thought him "a scholar" but wondered what he did for a living. During the week he resided at 2023 Fourth Street, Robert remained in his hot little room most of the time, but he went out frequently in the evenings. For he had a girl friend, named Virginia Banks.[41]

Monday, July 23, was the usual sort of steamy, lethargic midsummer day in New Orleans. The temperature at daybreak already stood at seventy-nine degrees and it climbed to near ninety by midafternoon, when scudding clouds from the Gulf dumped a rainshower that kept the thermometer from going even higher. Afterward the declining sun broke through again. Well-to-do people found some comfort from their electric fans, while the poor

40. *Ibid.*; New Orleans *Daily Item*, July 24, 1900.
41. New Orleans *Daily Picayune*, July 25, 1900; New Orleans *Times-Democrat*, July 25–26, 1900.

endured the heat as usual. But the entire city fairly dripped from humidity.

That day five hundred white Mississippians were busy touring the city, having arrived Sunday on a chartered train from Wood-ville, in Wilkinson County (the Mississippians would leave at 10 P.M. and arrive home next morning, "completely worn out"). At noon a state Negro Baptist convention assembled in the city, with two hundred delegates from across Louisiana. The docket that Monday in New Orleans Municipal Court was lighter than ordinary, since the weekend had been relatively peaceful. Mr. and Mrs. Pasquale Giordano were both before the judge, she for threatening a neighbor and he for threatening the policeman who came to arrest her. And "Dusty" Ryan was in court again. Sunday he had been in a knife fight at the corner of Tchoupitoulas and St. James streets with James McSheen and Arthur Doyle, after battling earlier in the day with yet another hoodlum, James McLaughlin.[42]

Towards evening of this hot Monday the temperature leveled off at eighty degrees and remained at that point throughout the night. Shortly after sundown Lenard Pierce, who had spent an unsuccess-ful day looking for work, arrived back at the room he shared on Fourth Street. He found Robert seated at a little table, busily writing. Robert was dressed to go somewhere. Lenard noticed that his roommate had on a brown hat, a white shirt and black coat, and dark striped trousers. He also observed the bulge of Robert's pistol from one of the inside coat pockets.[43]

Robert looked up presently and asked if Lenard would like to go with him and meet two women. Lenard, tired and somewhat dubi-ous, asked if there was "anything in it." Robert assured him that the

42. Woodville (Miss.) *Republican*, July 28, 1900; New Orleans *Daily States*, July 23, 1900; New Orleans *Daily Picayune*, July 24, 1900.
43. Interview with Lenard Pierce, in New Orleans *Times-Democrat*, July 25, 1900.

visit would be worthwhile. Pierce quickly washed up from the pitcher and basin in the room and put on his best clothes. And, emulating the older man whom he obviously admired, he placed a pistol of his own, a .38 Colt revolver, into his waistband where the coat would conceal it. He and Robert then walked down Fourth Street in the direction of St. Charles Avenue and the river.[44]

The two black women Robert had in mind were Virginia Banks and Ernestine Goldstein, who together rented a back room at the residence of a white woman, a Mrs. Cooley, at 2849 Dryades Street. Robert had known Virginia Banks for about three years, and there were conflicting reports as to whether they had lived together at one of his previous addresses. Described by the *Picayune* as "a rather neat looking woman of the usual servant type," she currently worked at the home of a white family on Louisiana Avenue. She later declared—it was manifestly in her interest to do so—that Charles often abused her and that she went with him out of fear instead of love.[45] Whatever the truth of their relationship was, it would die with him, and with her.

Robert and Lenard did not go directly to the Dryades Street address. Pierce would later relate (and at this point his story became what police suspected was "a tangle of truth and fiction") that once they set foot on Fourth Street, Robert informed him that "it would be late before they could meet the women," because the two were coming in from a railroad excursion that had gone to Baton Rouge. Robert suggested they spend some time at another address about twelve blocks away, visiting someone named Alice Pitkin. Lenard seemed reluctant to say anything about this woman, and neither the police nor the press would be concerned with her. But subsequent evidence indicates that the woman Pierce called Mrs. Alice "Pitkin"

44. *Ibid.*
45. New Orleans *Daily Picayune*, July 25, 1900; New Orleans *Times-Democrat*, July 25, 1900.

was actually named Pittman and was the former Alice Charles, Robert's younger sister.[46]

About 10 P.M. Robert and Lenard, having left Alice Pittman's residence, walked to the corner of Dryades and Washington, at the opposite end of the block from Mrs. Cooley's house, where Virginia Banks and her roommate were staying. The two men were now within four blocks of their own lodgings on Fourth Street. They waited on the corner for half an hour. Pierce began to grow nervous and told his companion that a policeman might spot them and "think that they were up to mischief." Robert and he then walked a short distance down Dryades and sat on some box steps along the sidewalk. The steps led to the front door of 2815 Dryades, the home of a white family named Schwartz. Robert and Lenard waited there about fifteen minutes, but once or twice they walked down the block toward the address they were interested in, 2849 Dryades. Each time they returned to the Schwartz doorstep. It was then close to 11 P.M.[47]

Virginia and Ernestine were, all the while, inside Mrs. Cooley's home; there was no excursion to Baton Rouge. The Dryades Street neighborhood, like many in that part of New Orleans, was racially mixed. Three middle-aged black women stood talking in front of the residence of one of them, Kate Clark; she lived not thirty yards away from the Schwartz home. The three wondered what two black men were doing sitting on the doorstep of a white family. Although Pierce never said so, the most likely explanation for his and Robert's behavior was that they were simply waiting for the appropriate time to seek admittance to the Cooley house. Virginia Banks and Ernestine Goldstein had been there all evening. They claimed to be asleep at this time, and Ernestine had taken a front room in the

46. *Ibid.* The police would later find a two-year-old letter to Robert Charles from his sister, Alice Pittman, who was then living in Natchez. Apparently she had moved to New Orleans in 1899 or early 1900. See also Baines, "The New Orleans Race Riot of 1900," 22.

47. New Orleans *Times-Democrat*, July 25, 1900.

house that night. Both would deny they were expecting visitors.[48]
Robert and Lenard were, it appears, planning to tap on the windows
in the expectation—or hope—of being admitted. They had some
good reason for delaying; perhaps a light was still on in the room
where Mrs. Cooley lived. After all, a white woman would not be
likely to appreciate having black men admitted to her house in the
middle of the night.

Sergeant Jules C. Aucoin of the New Orleans Police Department was in charge of the night shift at the Sixth Precinct that
evening. While making his rounds in the vicinity of Dryades Street,
about 11 P.M., someone—he said a black man—told him that "two
suspicious looking negroes" were sitting on a doorstep down the
next block. Aucoin then summoned Patrolman August T. Mora and
Supernumerary Patrolman Joseph D. Cantrelle, who were standing
nearby on Washington Street, to come and help him investigate.
Mora and Cantrelle had just remarked to each other "how remarkably dull it was," when they heard Sergeant Aucoin's whistle.[49]

But apparently Robert Charles and Lenard Pierce did not hear
the whistle, or did not think it concerned them; for they were still on
the doorstep of 2815 Dryades Street when the three officers approached.

What happened then, at this seemingly trivial encounter, commenced one of the bloodiest, most anarchic weeks in New Orleans'
history. And precisely what occurred on Dryades Street can never
be known, since each participant told a somewhat different story.
Moreover, some of the versions would change to suit future events.
The most believable and generally consistent account was that of
Patrolman Mora, who was the first to make contact with Charles.
When interviewed later that night at the hospital, Mora related that
he and the other two officers stepped in front of the doorstep and

48. *Ibid.*; New Orleans *Daily Item*, July 24–25, 1900.
49. "Official Report, Sgt. Jules C. Aucoin," in New Orleans *Daily Picayune*, July
24, 1900; New Orleans *Times-Democrat*, July 24, 1900.

demanded to know what the two black men "were doing and how long they had been here." Mora said they gave some vague answer about working for someone and having been in town for only three days. Another officer remembered that either Charles or Pierce had added "they were waiting for a friend."[50]

"At this stage," Patrolman Mora recalled, "the larger of the two negroes [Charles] got up." Mora must have interpreted this as a menacing gesture—for Charles was larger than Mora, and he was black.

After Charles "got up," Mora continued, "I grabbed him. The negro pulled, but I held fast, and he finally pulled me into the street. *Here I began using my billet* and the negro jerked from my grasp and ran. He then pulled a gun and fired. I pulled my gun and returned the fire, each of us firing about three shots." In a later version, Mora admitted that he—*not* Charles—had drawn his pistol first, and that "a moment later Charles drew his weapon." Cantrelle added that he too aimed several shots at the black man.[51]

Charles stumbled and momentarily fell, but got up and ran off, zigzag fashion, down the dark street. One of Robert's bullets had struck Mora in the right thigh, and another had grazed the patrolman's fingers. Cantrelle and Aucoin were uninjured. Recovering days later in a bed at Charity Hospital, Patrolman Mora lamented that his wooden billet had seemed to have no effect on the big Negro, and suggested that if he had possessed something bigger to whack heads with the gunfight might never have occurred. "For a nigger such as Charles is," Mora added, "a club is the only effective weapon."[52]

50 Interview with August T. Mora, in New Orleans *Daily Picayune*, July 24, 1900; New Orleans *Times-Democrat*, July 24, 1900.

51. New Orleans *Times-Democrat*, July 24, 1900 [Italics mine]; interviews with August T. Mora in New Orleans *Times-Democrat* and New Orleans *Daily Picayune*, both for July 27, 1900. See also, letter from the Reverend D. A. Graham, in Indianapolis *Freeman*, August 18, 1900.

52. Mora interview, New Orleans *Times-Democrat*, July 27, 1900.

7
THE YELLOW
HOUSE
While Robert Charles made his escape, Lenard
Pierce sat transfixed by the pistol that Sergeant
Aucoin held aimed at his face. The youth had never risen from the
steps. He heard the firing as Robert Charles exchanged shots with
officers Mora and Cantrelle, but all he said he could see "was the big
Colt's revolver" leveled at his eyes. Lenard was still quietly sitting
there when a passing white resident of the neighborhood, attracted
by the shooting, had the presence of mind to reach under the young
black man's coat and find the hidden .38. Sergeant Aucoin, in his
excitement, had neglected to search the prisoner.[1]

Robert was by now several blocks away, still running. But he had
been hit and was bleeding considerably. One of either Mora's or
Cantrelle's bullets had gone through the upper portion of his right
leg. Cantrelle followed him for a block or so but Robert easily
outdistanced him, fleeing down the darkness of Sixth Street in the
direction of St. Charles Avenue. Cantrelle went back to where the
shooting had occurred and he saw Sergeant Aucoin still standing
there with his gun aimed on Lenard Pierce. Mora lay bleeding in
the street. Cantrelle then hurried to Stendel's Drugstore at the

1. "Reports of Arrests," New Orleans Department of Police, Sixth Precinct, July
25, 1900, in Central Records and Identification Section, New Orleans Police Department; New Orleans *Times-Democrat*, August 25, 1900.

corner of Dryades and Third to telephone for an ambulance and a patrol wagon. Drawn by horses, these vehicles took some time in arriving; but by midnight Mora was in a Charity Hospital bed and Pierce was being grilled at the Sixth Precinct Stationhouse.[2]

The Sixth Precinct Stationhouse on Rousseau Street was a cramped and untidy place. But Lenard Pierce was not able to notice much about his surroundings because his attention had been focused on the commanding figure of Captain John T. Day. What in police parlance was called the "sweating process" had begun. Charged with shooting at Sergeant Aucoin (which both he and Patrolman Mora firmly denied had happened), Pierce was informed that his future looked bleak. Badly frightened, he began crying and told them he was only nineteen and had never been in trouble before. In fact he had no police record. What Captain Day primarily wanted from him, of course, was information that might lead to the still unknown big Negro man who had shot Mora. Pierce told Day the person he was looking for was named "Robinson" or "Robertson," from somewhere in Mississippi. Other than that he at first had little to say. A *Picayune* reporter who came into the stationhouse wrote that "while Pierce does not present the appearance of a negro of much sense, he is just shrewd enough to keep his mouth shut."[3]

Towards 1 A.M. Captain Day ordered several patrolmen, including Cantrelle, back to the 2800 block of Dryades with orders to try to pick up "Robinson's" trail from there. Day remained at the stationhouse to continue sweating Pierce. The officers, taking a horse-drawn patrol wagon, traced bloodstains from the corner of Dryades and Sixth to Baronne Street, near St. Charles Avenue.

2. "Record of Inquests," Coroner's Office, Parish of Orleans, July 27, 1900, p. 322, in City Archives Department, New Orleans Public Library; New Orleans *Times-Democrat*, August 25, 1900.

3. *Report of the Board of Commissioners of Prisons and Asylums of New Orleans, November 1, 1900*, pp. 6–7, in City Archives Department, New Orleans Public Library; New Orleans *Daily Picayune*, July 25, 1900.

They found that Robert had turned right on Baronne (which parallels St. Charles) and had crossed Louisiana Avenue. The officers, arriving there, heard a report that the stains extended as far as General Taylor and Carondelet streets.[4] At this point Robert would have been over a dozen blocks from where the shooting occurred, and further than that from his Fourth Street residence.

Somewhere around General Taylor and Carondelet the bleeding from his leg wound nearly stopped, and Robert must have decided to double back. By 2:30 A.M. he had returned to his room on Fourth Street. The patrol wagon, meanwhile, had given up the search and returned to the stationhouse. Before the tired officers could climb down, Captain Day came out the front door, smiling. "I know," he announced, "where I can get that nigger now."[5]

Robert had gone back to his room to do something about his wound, and to get the Winchester. He must have approached the place very carefully, and finding the area quiet, slipped in. The rifle, later described as "an ordinary weapon," was a breech-loading, lever-action repeater of .38 calibre. Of some age, and showing several nicks and dents, it was probably an 1886 "take-down" (easily disassembled) model—one of the cheapest and most popular ever produced by the Winchester company. The rifle belonged, Robert once told Lenard Pierce, to his brother Henry Charles. Robert had borrowed it from Henry some months earlier. Very likely it was the same weapon Henry had used at the Rolling Fork depot in 1892.[6] (If Robert ever told Lenard where Henry now lived, the young man never revealed it to the police.)

4. "Official Report, Officer Caspar Pincon," in New Orleans *Daily Picayune,* July 25, 1900.
5. *Ibid.*; New Orleans *Daily Item,* July 24, 1900.
6. For descriptions of the Winchester rifle Charles possessed, see New Orleans *Daily Picayune,* July 28, 1900; New Orleans *Times-Democrat,* July 28, 1900. An illustration and description of this model rifle is found in Harold F. Williamson, *Winchester: The Gun That Won the West* (Washington: Combat Forces Press, 1952), 100–101, 429. This model was sold in various calibres, the .38 being first produced in 1887.

There were no appropriate medical supplies in Robert's room. By the light of his kerosene lamp he searched around for something to use. Finally he dressed the wounded leg with vaseline and wrapped it with a green gauze.[7] Knowing that sooner or later the police would discover from Pierce where he lived, Robert must have been about ready to depart when he began to hear noises and saw the flash of lanterns.

Captain Day was in the patrol wagon when it drove up Fourth Street. The time was close to 3 A.M. A big, handsome man of thirty-seven, Day loved excitement and was deservedly considered one of the bravest men on the force. His efforts in saving the lives of fourteen people from the St. Charles Hotel fire of 1894 had helped promote him from police sergeant to captain the following year. The more dangerous an assignment, the more likely he was to accompany his men. Day and the six officers with him halted the wagon at the corner of South Rampart and Fourth, then walked up the block to the 2023 address. Two white bystanders, who since 11 P.M. had been aiding in the search for Charles, saw Day and his men approach the house and heard them say the fugitive might be in there. One of the civilians warned Captain Day to be careful. "Oh pshaw," Day replied. "I'll go and take that nigger myself."[8]

Charles's room was the fourth one down the side of this long and oddly fashioned little cottage. No doors fronted Fourth Street proper, but to the left a tiny gate opened into a dank, roof-covered alley, where planks had been laid to form a walkway for the six separate compartments of the building. Small steps led from the planking to each door. All the tenants were black. Room No. 1 was occupied by aged Fanny Jackson; her slightly younger friend Annie Cryder lived

7. "Record of Inquests," Coroner's Office, July 27, 1900, p. 322.
8. *Annual Report of the Board of Police Commissioners, Superintendent of Police, and Police Surgeon of the City of New Orleans, 1894*, p. 9; *ibid., 1900*, p. 28; New Orleans *Daily Picayune*, July 25, September 27, 1900.

in No. 2. An old couple named Cole resided in room 3; next was the room that Lenard and Robert shared; and an unidentified woman and her daughter lived in Nos. 5 and 6. In the light of the kerosene lanterns some of his men carried, Captain Day could see that the house was painted a dark yellow.[9]

The Captain detailed his men. He told Corporal Honore Perrier to remain on the street, along with Patrolman Caspar Pincon and Supernumerary Cantrelle. Day motioned to Sergeant Aucoin, Corporal Ernest J. Trenchard, and Patrolman Peter J. Lamb to come with him. William Schmidt, an interested civilian who had been helping search the neighborhood, walked up and volunteered to go in with them; Schmidt was accepted, or at least Day did not prevent him. Three of these five men were carrying kerosene lanterns. Prior to leaving the precinct station, Captain Day had taken a fancy to Lenard Pierce's .38, and since it was much better than his own revolver, decided to take it with him. Day was holding Pierce's .38 in one hand as he pushed open the gate.[10]

Day entered the alleyway first, followed by Schmidt, Aucoin, Trenchard, and Lamb. The captain knocked on the door of room No. 1, where Fanny Jackson was sleeping. "Where do those men live?" one of the officers demanded to know. "In room No. 4," she replied, after some hesitation. They then walked down the creaking planks in that direction, the lanterns guiding their path. The door of the room they were looking for was slightly ajar. Corporal Trenchard shouted: "Open up there!" The door opened, suddenly. In the dim lantern's glow stood Robert Charles, with his Winchester leveled at Captain Day, who was standing not ten feet from him. Before Day could aim the .38, a rifle bullet tore directly into his

9. New Orleans *Times-Democrat*, July 25, 1900; New Orleans *Daily Picayune*, July 25, 1900.

10. New Orleans *Daily Item*, July 24, 1900; New Orleans *Times-Democrat*, July 25, September 27, 1900.

heart. The captain wheeled about, made what Trenchard described as "an awful moaning cry," and fell dead on the plank walkway.[11]

For about fifteen seconds everybody, including Charles, stood as if mesmerized by what had happened. The first to move was Schmidt, who ran out of the alley and dropped his lantern on the sidewalk. "My God," he told another civilian standing outside, "I think they have killed Captain Day." Inside the alley, Sergeant Aucoin turned to Corporal Trenchard and said—as Trenchard described it—"My God, Corporal, our Captain has been killed. Look what that negro has done." Charles thereupon fired several more shots into Day's body. Trenchard and Patrolman Lamb, both standing against the side of the house, continued to stare at the body in disbelief. Trenchard and Lamb began to say something to each other when they heard the black man in the doorway shout: "You ———— I will give you all some!" One second later Patrolman Lamb's head exploded. A Winchester bullet had entered his right eye and shattered through the back of his skull.[12]

Then Sergeant Aucoin, as if coming out of a trance, fired a shot or two at Charles but missed, the bullets striking the half-open door of the Negro's room. Corporal Trenchard aimed and attempted to shoot, but the cylinders of his cheap regulation .32 would not work. Charles closed his door and they heard him reloading the Winchester. At this moment Annie Cryder opened the door of room No. 2 and called : "Come in officers! Come in here!" Aucoin and Trenchard hurried into Miss Cryder's room just as Charles, his rifle ready again, stepped out onto the plank walkway. With more presence of mind than her guests, Annie Cryder blew out her lamp and

11. New Orleans *Daily Picayune*, July 25, 1900; "Official Report, Sgt. Jules C. Aucoin," *ibid.*, July 24, 1900; interview with Ernest J. Trenchard, in New Orleans *Times-Democrat*, July 26, 1900; "Record of Inquests," Coroner's Office, July 24, 1900, pp. 305–306.

12. Interviews with Ernest J. Trenchard, in New Orleans *Times-Democrat*, July 25, 26, 1900; New Orleans *Times-Democrat*, September 27, 1900; "Record of Inquests," Coroner's Office, July 24, 1900, p. 307.

the three of them remained quietly there in her room, listening to Robert Charles cursing the police and daring them to come outside. "Those white men was scared," Miss Cryder told a reporter the next day. "And I don't know who was the worst. The old man sat by the door and the other officer kept at the window."[13]

The "old man" referred to was Sergeant Jules C. Aucoin. He was indeed much too old for active police work, being sixty-six years of age. Aucoin had been a law officer for thirty years, first in Jefferson Parish and then in New Orleans. Once he was considered "a terror to the hoodlum element" of his precinct, but that was long ago. In one respect he seems to have kept his vigor; at age sixty-two he had been fined ten day's pay on charges of being "a constant visitor" to a house of ill fame. But as a policeman he was, by 1900, living proof that the NOPD to some extent really was, as one citizen claimed, "a sort of haven for aged and infirm."[14]

The "other officer" in Annie Cryder's room, Corporal Ernest J. Trenchard, was about forty years old. He had been on the force nine years. Prior to this night Trenchard had stood accused of various shortcomings, but never of cowardice, and once (in 1893) the mayor had presented him with a medal for rescuing a little girl from drowning in the New Basin Canal. But more than once he had been charged with petty extortion or bribery. He was dismissed from the force in 1897 for attempted extortion of a saloonkeeper. Shortly thereafter, as if to dramatize his dedication to the NOPD, Trenchard applied for a job as stableman for the patrol wagon horses; meanwhile he had assisted the police in killing a black murder suspect who had taken refuge in a barn. In January of 1898 he was reinstated, but in May of 1900 the superintendent of police had

13. New Orleans *Daily Picayune*, July 25, 1900; interview with Annie Cryder, in New Orleans *Times-Democrat*, July 26, 1900.
14. *Annual Report of the Board of Police Commissioners and Superintendent of Police of the City of New Orleans, 1893*, p. 20; ibid., 1900, p. 24; New Orleans *Daily Picayune*, November 6, 1896; New Orleans *Times-Democrat*, July 28, October 4, 1900; New Orleans *Daily Item*, November 4, 1912.

received another complaint about Trenchard's dealings with a shop-keeper.[15]

For about two hours, until daybreak, Aucoin and Trenchard remained in room No. 2, not venturing out or—more inexplicably—ever blowing their police whistles for assistance. The old couple who lived in room No. 3, having been awakened by the shooting, remained awake the rest of the night but decided to remain incurious as to exactly what was happening. Outside, on the street, Corporal Perrier, Patrolman Pincon, and Supernumerary Cantrelle also displayed during those two hours a seeming absence of curiosity about the gunfire and cursing they had heard in the dark alley. Perrier had ordered Pincon to the corner of Fourth and Saratoga (at the opposite end of the block), while he and Cantrelle remained at Fourth and South Rampart. About 3:30 A.M., thirty minutes after the shooting, Patrolman Pincon walked over to the gate of the yellow house and shouted "Do you need any assistance in there?" There was no reply, but he thought he might have heard groans. Pincon went back to the street corner. More time passed, but none of the three officers on the street either ventured inside the gate or went for help. At about 4:30 A.M., shortly before dawn, Robert Charles walked to the front of the plank alley and looked out the gate. By the glow of a streetlight he saw Perrier and Cantrelle, seventy-five yards away. Robert raised the Winchester and fired at Corporal Perrier. The ball grazed the corporal's cap and buried itself in a gallery post.[16]

Perrier and Cantrelle both immediately ran away. They were

15. *Annual Report of the Board of Police Commissioners, 1893*, p. 4; *ibid.*, 1897, p. 14; *ibid.*, 1900, p. 24; New Orleans *Daily States*, October 9, 1897, May 6, June 9, July 21, 1898; Thornback to Gaster, May 18, 1900, in Mayor's Office Correspondence. Corporal Trenchard was sometimes confused with Patrolman Henry J. Trinchard of the mounted force of the NOPD because of the similarity in their names, which must have caused Patrolman Trinchard discomfort on several occasions.

16. New Orleans *Daily Picayune*, July 25, 1900; New Orleans *Times-Democrat*, July 25–26, August 8, 1900.

seeking, they would later insist, not safety but a telephone. Cantrelle bolted down South Rampart and turned on Third Street, down which he ran to the all-night drugstore at the corner of Dryades, from where he had called about Officer Mora over five hours earlier. (This telephone at Stendel's Drugstore, being the only available one in the neighborhood, had been so often resorted to by patrolmen that Stendel's establishment was popularly known thereabouts as "the police station.") Cantrelle now informed his precinct that there had been "considerable firing" at the Fourth Street address. Corporal Perrier, meanwhile, was running all the way across St. Charles Avenue to Prytania Street—six blocks away from the shooting. He explained later that he could not find a phone. Cantrelle, having made his call at Stendel's, ran some more and overtook his superior officer at the corner of Prytania and Washington. All this time Patrolman Pincon remained in the vicinity of his post at Fourth and Saratoga, but obviously he had decided long before not to play any conspicuous role in the murky drama.[17]

At 5 A.M. the dawning of Tuesday, July 24, began to lift the darkness around the yellow house on Fourth Street. Observing the light filtering in from the dingy window of their refuge, Sergeant Aucoin and Corporal Trenchard slowly, very cautiously, opened the door. There was no indication of Charles's presence. The two officers stepped out on the planking, near the stiffening bodies of Day and Lamb, and then dashed through the gate and onto Fourth Street. Here they saw several units of police hurrying towards them. Two city detectives had already arrived. Immediately a thorough search of the area began; but, in the words of a New Orleans black minister, "the tiger was gone."[18]

17. New Orleans Times-Democrat, July 25–26, August 8, 1900; New Orleans *Daily Item,* July 24–25, 1900.
18. New Orleans *Times-Democrat,* July 25–26, 1900; letter from the Reverend D. A. Graham, in Indianapolis *Freeman,* August 18, 1900.

By 6 A.M. the police and a growing throng of white spectators were literally tearing room No. 4 apart, looking for anything that might aid in the search for the big Negro they knew now, from his letters and papers, was really named Robert Charles. Virtually the entire police force of New Orleans converged on the area by 7 A.M., the day shift having been informed of the tragedy by the night shift. One after another the officers filed through the little alley to gaze upon the bloody remains of Captain Day and Patrolman Lamb.[19]

All kinds of rumors swept through the excited crowd on the street outside. Suddenly the word was passed that Charles was still in the square block; that somebody had seen him taking refuge inside the backyard privy vault of a cottage next to the yellow house. "In a moment," related the *Item*'s reporter, "a hundred or more infuriated men had run into the yard . . . quicker than word could tell they had torn up the floor of the vault and a veritable hail of lead . . . was being poured into the dark hole." After more than nine dozen bullets were fired, the privy was ripped from its foundations and the odorous mass below was then dragged. They found nothing there but excrement and bits of paper.[20]

Superintendent of Police Dexter Gaster's workday usually did not begin until 10 A.M. On arrival at headquarters he always first checked dispatches from the chief telegrapher and then had a brief conference with the chief of detectives. After that he would invariably go to his office, light a fresh cigar, and read through the morning papers. Shortly before noon the sergeants from the city's eleven precincts would come in to make their reports. The remainder of his day was ordinarily taken up by a procession of citizens who came to see him with grievances against their neighbors, members of their families, or the police.[21] But Tuesday, July 24, was not to be

19. Boston *Morning Journal*, July 25, 1900; New Orleans *Daily Item*, July 24, 1900.

20. New Orleans *Daily Item*, July 24, 1900.

21. A description of Superintendent Gaster's life and habits is found in the New Orleans *Daily Picayune*, August 14, 1901.

one of Superintendent Gaster's routine days. In fact it would be some time before his schedule could go back to normal.

At daybreak on July 24 the telephone in Gaster's house on Baronne Street began to jangle and the superintendent, roused from bed, was told of the bloody events on Fourth Street. Presently a man from headquarters arrived with a buggy and Gaster went directly to the yellow house. It was Gaster who ordered the door of room No. 4 broken down, for Robert Charles had locked it on his way out. Later, outside, Gaster told the police and spectators that he "wanted that man badly," and informed his officers that if they found him "not to hesitate in shooting the villain if he showed the slightest attempt to fight." [22]

By 8 A.M. it was obvious that Charles was nowhere in the immediate neighborhood of the yellow house, and Gaster waited fretfully for the arrival of a bloodhound which Patrolman Sam Exnicios was supposed to be bringing to the scene. But Exnicios had encountered problems with the conductors of the electric trolleys, who firmly refused to let the animal ride in the cars—police business or not. Finally the dog got to Fourth Street in a borrowed delivery wagon and was given Robert's scent from some clothing left in the room. The bloodhound picked up the trail for about twenty yards, then commenced baying at a shed-like closet. When opened, it was found that Robert had changed his clothes there. At this time a light morning shower began to fall and the dog was of no further use. [23]

The *Voice of Missions* and other publications that Superintendent Gaster and his officers found in Charles's room first puzzled and then outraged them. Although Gaster was an Ohioan who first came to Louisiana as a Union soldier in the army of occupation, he had settled in New Orleans after the war and soon embraced the

22. New Orleans *Daily Item*, July 24, 1900; New Orleans *Daily Picayune*, July 25, 1900.
23. New Orleans *Daily States*, July 24, 1900; New Orleans *Daily Picayune*, July 25, 1900.

politics and racial attitudes of his adopted state. Examining Charles's belongings, Gaster decided that some of the written material "gave an insight into the character of the negro and [showed] that his intention in life was one of evil toward the white man." Actually, the nearest to an inflammatory statement that could be found was a passage in one of the International Migration Society pamphlets: "In sheer desperation, the negro turns like a hunted beast and defends himself as best he can, while the white man, who brooks no interference from the weaker race, resorts to more desperate means to force an humble submission." A reporter from one of the two most race-minded of the city's dailies, upon reading this pamphlet, was reminded of the old adage that "a little learning is a dangerous thing."[24]

Every object in the room was examined with keen interest. Even the cooking pots by the fireplace were looked into. Next to the bullet mold on the mantlepiece was discovered a small amount of a substance which the police never publicly identified but which the *Times-Democrat* claimed was "a bottle of cocaine." The *States* described it as a "box" of cocaine. The *Picayune* reporter thought it was morphine. "Nothing was found in his room that could lead to the belief that he was a thief," observed the *Times-Democrat*, "except fifty or more small bits of soap." This paper's reporter, entering the room after much trampling around and hauling off had occurred, wrote that "his wearing apparel was little more than rags" (which would have surprised Hyman Levy of the Poydras Street store) and that "his bedding and clothing were nasty and filthy beyond belief." The reporter concluded that this "'philosopher of the garret' was a dirty wretch."[25]

24. Parkash Kaur Bains, "The New Orleans Race Riot of 1900" (M.A. thesis, Louisiana State University in New Orleans, 1970), 30–31; "Report of Superintendent D. S. Gaster to the Board of Police Commissioners," in New Orleans *Daily Picayune*, August 31, 1900; New Orleans *Times-Democrat*, July 25, 1900.

25. New Orleans *Daily States*, July 24, 1900; New Orleans *Daily Picayune*, July 25, 1900; New Orleans *Times-Democrat*, July 25, 1900.

By midmorning of the twenty-fourth, the police had learned from Lenard Pierce, or someone, that Robert Charles's girlfriend was named Virginia Banks and that she lived at 2849 Dryades Street. During the shooting the night before Miss Banks had remained inside her room at Mrs. Cooley's. She claimed to have slept through the trouble that erupted down the street at 11 P.M., insisted that she had not been expecting Charles that night, and knew nothing about anything that had happened until she learned of it this morning. A white interviewer described her as "a young, brown-skinned woman . . . possessed of more than average intelligence."[26] Certainly she was quick to understand that she was in a highly dangerous situation, and she proceeded immediately to extricate herself from it.

At noon Virginia was taken to the yellow house on Fourth Street and from there to police headquarters where she was grilled for some time. Later in the day reporters from the various daily papers interviewed her at length. She told the same story to all. She had known Robert Charles for three years, having met him at a black social club "of which we were both members." He "seemed to immediately take a fancy to me, and although I showed him that I did not like him, he persisted and began to give me trouble at once." This brutal man, Virginia declared to the police and reporters, made her go with him by threatening her life. "I escaped him many times," she added, but "he would always find me and beat me for having run away from him."[27]

Seeing that her audience was buying it, Miss Banks then began to embellish her account of how Charles had victimized her. Once he almost threw her into the New Basin Canal to drown, but the drawbridge nearby began to open and Robert became "frightened" and ran away. Another time he took her to Douglas Park, pulled off

26. New Orleans *Times-Democrat*, July 25, 1900.
27. New Orleans *Daily Item*, July 24–25, 1900; New Orleans *Daily Picayune*, July 25, 1900; New Orleans *Times-Democrat*, July 25, 1900.

her clothes, and "beat me into insensibility." Finally, on July 2 of this year he acted as if he might kill her on the street but she escaped by running into the house of some white people. It was then, she said, that she made an affidavit against him in city court. Because she had finally reported him to the authorities, Virginia was positive that he was seeking revenge when he came to Dryades Street on Monday night. "I know," she concluded, "that he was waiting to kill me when he shot Officer Mora."[28]

Virginia Banks said what she had to say in order to protect herself. Possibly her relationship with Robert Charles had not always been smooth, but her narration of a three-year reign of terror at his hands was obviously given for effect. Whether the police really accepted all this is uncertain; the press swallowed every word. At any rate she was released before nightfall, with no charges. Others of Charles's friends would not be so fortunate. Her claim that she had signed an affidavit against him earlier that month was never confirmed (or denied) by the police or municipal court. The records of Charity Hospital, where most black people in the city went if injured, do not show a Virginia Banks as ever having been admitted.[29]

Only once during the long hours she spent telling her story in Superintendent Gaster's office did Virginia Banks give any hint of love or loyalty toward Robert Charles. A black man whose last name happened to be Charles was brought in to headquarters by a patrol wagon. The man lived in nearby St. Bernard Parish; he worked as a coal-shoveler at the American Sugar Refinery, and he vaguely

28. Interview with Virginia Banks, in New Orleans *Times-Democrat*, July 25, 1900.
29. The clerk of the New Orleans Municipal Court Record Room informed me on June 19, 1974, that it has long been the practice there to destroy affidavits after five years. And the New Orleans Charity Hospital records for the period concerned are now at the Louisiana State Archives in Baton Rouge. Dr. A. Otis Hebert, who was then the Archivist, informed me by letter, July 16, 1974, that the admission cards of Charity Hospital do not show a Virginia Banks. However, he added that there are no records of simple emergency treatments.

matched the description of Robert Charles. So he was taken into the superintendent's office to be confronted by Miss Banks. She looked "at the man steadily for a time, seemingly a bit puzzled and uncertain." After a delay which may have been agonizing for her and certainly was for the trembling refinery worker who stood in front of her, she declared that the man in custody was not Robert Charles.[30]

By the time Virginia Banks was allowed to go home, late in the afternoon of the twenty-fourth, the largest manhunt New Orleans ever witnessed had been underway for some hours. Each boxcar on every train leaving the city was searched. So were the ferryboats and river craft of all kinds. Citizens' posses patrolled all roads leading out of town. Reports were beginning to come to police headquarters that Robert Charles was lurking in the marshes at the rear of the city, near Lake Pontchartrain; that he had fled to St. Bernard Parish; that he was seen in the suburban town of Kenner; that he had been cornered inside a vacant lot at Gretna, across the river. Up in Vicksburg the police began looking for him there.[31]

No longer was Robert Charles underestimated. His days of being just another "darkey" were finished. He had already gotten the best of eight policemen who were considered among the top men on the force, and had killed two of them. That he would kill others before he could be taken was freely predicted. Speaking of his exploits the previous night, the *Times-Democrat* marveled at his marksmanship and said "his coolness must have been something phenomenal." This combination of deadly talents, the paper concluded, "makes him one of the most formidable monsters that has ever been loose upon the community."[32]

What Robert was actually thinking during the night of July 23 will never be known. Perhaps he regretted that he did not meekly

30. New Orleans *Times-Democrat*, July 25, 1900.
31. New Orleans *Daily Picayune*, July 25, 1900; New Orleans *Times-Democrat*, July 25, 1900; Vicksburg *Daily Herald*, July 26, 1900.
32. New Orleans *Times-Democrat*, July 25–26, 1900.

submit to being hit over the head by Officer Mora; perhaps he looked back on his actions with exultant pride; very likely he alternated between these two conflicting emotions. But, once he had fired his gun at a New Orleans policeman, a sense of desperation unquestionably took possession of him. His lifetime in Mississippi and Louisiana had taught him that a black man who shoots a law officer would probably be better off dead than in custody, and that one who actually kills a policeman—much less two—was liable to die in some terrible fashion at the hands of a mob. No doubt occasionally during that night, and later, Robert thought of what had happened to Sam Hose, of Georgia. That was a fate he was utterly determined would not be his.

All the while, as the widening manhunt for him continued, Robert Charles remained inside New Orleans. He was not in the marshes back of town, nor in any of the suburban parishes, and certainly not in Mississippi. From the yellow house on Fourth Street he had gone, probably directly, to a ramshackle two-story dwelling just fourteen blocks away. He asked refuge from people he knew at this house, 1208 Saratoga Street. They let him in. And there he would remain from Tuesday morning until Friday afternoon.

RACE RIOT

If Robert Charles had remained all his life in that remote sharecropper's cabin along Bayou Pierre, New Orleans might still have had a race riot before the summer of 1900 was over. Hostility between whites and blacks in the city had been mounting for some time, and all the ingredients for an outbreak of racial terror were already present.[1] For several weeks prior to July 24, any trifling episode, of which there were many, could have provided the spark for an explosion. But the apparently successful escape of a "black fiend" who had killed two of the most popular officers of the NOPD, wounded another, and humiliated several others, furnished not a spark but a flame.

Much of the racial tension was of economic origin. New Orleans had not yet pulled out of the depression of the 1890s and the unemployment rate remained high. But by all accounts the problem of finding work was most acute among the white poor. Many of the city's larger employers showed a marked preference for black laborers, who seemed to grumble less about lower wages and harsher working conditions. Often white men lost their jobs to blacks.

---

1. Parkash Kaur Bains, "The New Orleans Race Riot of 1900" (M.A. thesis, Louisiana State University in New Orleans, 1970), 52–53; "The 'Race Riot' Episode," *Harlequin*, II (July 28, 1900), 8; New Orleans *Daily States*, July 5, 8, 1900.

"Today hundreds of whites," noted *Harlequin* magazine, "are crowded out of work they formerly fed and clothed their little ones upon, by the negro." The continuing influx of unskilled rural blacks from the plantations of Louisiana and Mississippi further depressed the job market and thereby aggravated racial feelings among the white poor.[2]

Leaders among the black and Creole of color communities, on the other hand, were becoming alarmed and angry over the attempted introduction of more thorough practices of racial segregation in the city. Hitherto New Orleans had shown considerable ambivalence about segregation. Discrimination had usually been the custom in the city's hotels, restaurants, and places of recreation (whorehouses excepted), although for a time during Reconstruction Orleans Parish did have a racially mixed school system. But residential segregation was as yet unknown by law, nor did custom decree it; there were no large all-black ghettos, for on almost every block where poor blacks lived, some poor whites lived also. And the presence of so many Creoles of color had long served to discourage efforts for a more comprehensive system of segregation. The Creoles of color held enough economic power to be of some influence on city affairs, while the light skin texture of many of them convinced the owners of the streetcar companies, among others, that additional segregation would cause more confusion and trouble than it was worth.[3]

Streetcars were, in 1900, the one notable exception remaining

2. Dale A. Somers, "Black and White in New Orleans: A Study in Urban Race Relations, 1865–1900," *Journal of Southern History*, XL, (February, 1974), 38–39; *Harlequin*, II (August 18, 1900), 2; "The New Orleans Mob," *Outlook*, LXV (August 4, 1900), 760–61.

3. John W. Blassingame, *Black New Orleans 1860–1880* (Chicago: University of Chicago Press, 1973), 117–22, 184–98; Louis R. Harlan, "Desegregation in New Orleans Public Schools During Reconstruction," *American Historical Review*, LXVII (April, 1962), 663–75; Somers, "Black and White in New Orleans," 22–38; *Harlequin*, I (June 23, 1900), 3; New Orleans *Times-Democrat*, October 20, 1900.

to the rule of Jim Crow in New Orleans. They had been integrated since 1867, after blacks and Creoles of color vigorously protested—with some violence—against the custom of forcing all nonwhites to ride in separate cars. Four different companies owned and operated the fast electric trolleys that had been installed during the 1890s; in a city famed for charm but not efficiency, the trolley service had become one of the few modern conveniences about which the Crescent City was able to boast. Actually, the trolleys served a predominantly white clientele even without segregation. Most black New Orleanians could not afford to ride on a regular basis. Two of the four companies reported virtually no black passengers.[4]

But when the state legislature met at Baton Rouge in the late spring and early summer of 1900, the demand for streetcar Jim Crow in New Orleans was loudly voiced by a number of representatives from the rural parishes. A bill which would require separate cars for white and all "colored" passengers in cities of over 50,000 (of which New Orleans was the only one in the state) was introduced by Representative Harry D. Wilson of Tangipahoa Parish. Wilson later pointed out that the major purpose of his bill was not the physical separation of the races. "The demonstration of the superiority of the white man over the negro is the greater thing," he remarked. In New Orleans, white opinion seemed confused and divided by the issue. Support for segregation came from the Central Trades and Labor Council, a federation of the city's white unions. But of New Orleans' daily papers, only Hearsey's *States* endorsed Wilson's bill. The streetcar companies fought it mightily; one company president explained when a similar proposal appeared before the city council later that year: "Our conductors are men of intelligence, but the

4. Roger A. Fischer, "A Pioneer Protest: The New Orleans Street-Car Controversy of 1867," *Journal of Negro History*, LIII (July, 1968), 219–33; New Orleans *Times-Democrat*, September 1, October 20, 1900.

greatest ethnologist the world ever saw would be at a loss to classify street car passengers in this city."[5]

The separate-streetcar bill passed the lower house of the legislature in June but, largely through the influence of the trolley companies, it was quietly buried by a Senate committee early in July. Representative Wilson later asserted that if Robert Charles had begun using his guns a few weeks earlier the bill "would have passed overwhelmingly." A modified version of the Wilson bill did indeed become law at the next legislative session, in 1902.[6] But for New Orleans in the summer of 1900, the introduction and near-passage of the bill had the effect of opening up an old racial wound in the city and thereby indirectly contributed to the riot of late July.

Signs of increasing animosity between the races were to be seen almost daily in New Orleans during June and July of 1900. Both the police and the press received an unprecedented number of complaints about the behavior of certain black youths in the city's parks. In Morris Park young blacks were said to be making "questionable if not indecent remarks" within the hearing of white girls, while other reports said the youths "lie in the grass, evidently waiting for the young [white] maidens to pass near them." Similar complaints came from Beauregard Square.[7] The streetcar controversy and the alleged black misbehavior in the public parks offered additional ammunition to those who for years had urged even greater repression as the answer to New Orleans' race problems.

Of the city's three largest daily papers, all except the *States* were

5. *Official Journal of the Proceedings of the House of Representatives of the State of Louisiana*, May 14, 1900, pp. 81, 308; New Orleans *Daily Picayune*, October 15, 1900; New Orleans *Daily States*, July 2, 1900; New Orleans *Times-Democrat*, October 20, 1900.

6. New Orleans *Times-Democrat*, July 8–9, 1900; New Orleans *Daily Picayune*, October 15, 1900; *Official Journal of the Proceedings of the Senate of the State of Louisiana*, May 12, 1902, p. 220.

7. New Orleans *Times-Democrat*, July 3–4, 13, 1900; New Orleans *Daily States*, July 3, 1900.

becoming more stridently racist in their editorial columns and treatment of the news; and if Major Hearsey's paper was not, it was only because he already occupied the outermost limits in that regard. The newspaper which ranked fourth in circulation and influence, the *Item*, was independent Republican in politics and the most racially moderate in tone, but even so its editor admitted to having "about as much 'prejudice'. . . when it comes to considering the 'negro question' as the common average white man." The *Picayune*, oldest and most sedate of the dailies, had long maintained an editorial policy of relative caution and restraint on racial matters, yet by 1900 its benignity had eroded considerably. The *Times-Democrat*, which ranked second only to Hearsey's *States* in Negrophobia, on June 8 quoted approvingly from a remarkable diatribe against the black race which almost reached the level of Hearsey himself. Among other things, the article stated: "He (the negro) calls no man 'massa' unless he has been tipped a quarter. He will call you God for fifty cents; and grovel at your feet for a dollar. He never did an hour's honest work in his life save when driven at the end of a lash, and that is now unhappily against the law . . . to glorify him is like glorifying unspeakable lust and bestial cruelty."[8]

Even more to the point, the *Times-Democrat* in June and July of 1900 ran a series of articles on "The Negro Problem" by a local physician, Dr. Gustav Keitz, who announced that "the fact we are on the threshold of a race war cannot be denied." For his part, Dr. Keitz suggested the relatively humane solution of forced "deportation" to the Philippine Islands, or somewhere; but on July 17, six days before the Robert Charles troubles began, this New Orleans physician claimed that the medical men he knew "are agreed that the number of negroes should be reduced, and have discussed asexualization, a measure which should be practiced at the earliest

8. New Orleans *Daily Item*, June 11, 1900; New Orleans *Times-Democrat*, June 8, 1900.

possible period of life." Only the columns of the *States* offered a more drastic solution.[9]

All day long on July 24, as the news of Robert Charles's deeds and escape spread around the city, portents of the riot to come could be witnessed on many streets. Vengeful talk among the whites and scarcely disguised glee among the younger and poorer blacks over what Charles had done clearly pointed to a racial clash of possibly huge proportions. The *Item*, seeing and dreading what was coming, lamented that "New Orleans has had, God knows, trials enough within the past five years, but a race riot now . . . would be the cap of ruin."[10]

Minor collisions between the races occurred several times during the day near the shabby block where the yellow house was located. The square bounded by Fourth, South Rampart, Third, and Saratoga Streets was inhabited almost entirely by blacks, and the immediate neighborhood was one of the poorest in the city. But the crowd that gathered there within hours of Charles's escape on the morning of the twenty-fourth, was all white; and this crowd continued to swell until at least five thousand people were milling around the block by late afternoon. Some talked of burning the yellow house, although nobody believed Charles was still in there. On the blocks adjacent to where the whites were gathered, small groups of Negroes could be seen, watching the whites and talking among themselves. Where the two groups were closest, heated words sometimes were passed and a few scuffles developed.[11]

From early morning on, the police who were detailed near the yellow house began arresting those black men and youths who

9. Dr. Keitz also endorsed the lynching of Negroes who were accused of serious crimes, but unlike Major Hearsey he drew the line at torture. "Lynching," Keitz suggested, "should be done with as much speed and as little pain as possible." New Orleans *Times-Democrat*, June 19, 26, July 7, 17, 1900; New Orleans *Daily States*, June 11, August 7, 1900.

10. New Orleans *Daily Item*, July 25, 1900.

11. New Orleans *Times-Democrat*, July 25, 1900.

appeared to be approving Robert Charles. In one hour a dozen arrests were made and others followed during the day. It was "just like some fool niggers," grumbled the *Picayune*, to talk "too much." But in some instances on the twenty-fourth, the police were roughed up by whites when they attempted to break up interracial fights in the area. Only one white man was arrested in the yellow house neighborhood, but not for fighting. His name was Ed J. McCarthy; he was a merchant seaman from New York and considered himself broadminded on racial matters. He was also plainspoken, a quality which nearly got him killed. McCarthy suggested that Charles might simply have been defending himself and in any case he "should be given a fair show." Incredulous whites within earshot began to argue hotly with him, but McCarthy persisted. Soon the crowd surged around him, with some men shouting "Get a rope! Let's lynch the white nigger loving _____!" Police charged into the crowd and rescued McCarthy, but then arrested him and took him to the sixth precinct stationhouse, where he was placed in a cell near Lenard Pierce. The next day McCarthy was fined twenty-five dollars for making "incendiary remarks" and disturbing the peace.[12]

About 1 P.M. a "very noisy" demonstration among some black people was noticed down Fourth Street and the presumed leader, George Meyers, was arrested by two patrolmen. Since the patrol wagon (being already full of black prisoners) had just left, Meyers was walked toward the stationhouse. A large crowd of blacks followed a few paces behind. At Baronne Street, Corporal Trenchard came running toward the group, pistol in hand, threatening to shoot. Trenchard—who lived on Second Street, only five blocks from the yellow house—had remained in the vicinity all day; he was

12. "Reports of Arrests," New Orleans Department of Police, Sixth Precinct, July 25, 1900, in Central Records and Identification Section, New Orleans Police Department; New Orleans *Daily Picayune*, July 25–26, 1900; New Orleans *Times-Democrat*, July 25, 1900; "Report of Superintendent of Police D. S. Gaster, in New Orleans *Times-Democrat*, August 31, 1900.

tired and excited, and obviously aware that people were calling him a coward because of the previous night's occurrences. Trenchard began walking next to Meyers, punching him with the barrel of his worthless .32 at every step. The corporal's actions led white onlookers to believe that he had Robert Charles in custody, and cries of "lynch him! kill him!" went up. Meyers was hastily placed in an empty ice wagon and hauled to the sixth precinct stationhouse.[13]

Shortly before the ice wagon with Meyers inside arrived at the stationhouse, Lenard Pierce was transferred to the parish prison. The move was made to protect Pierce's life. A crowd had gathered outside the stationhouse and some men were saying that it "must be attacked and the negro lynched." Superintendent Gaster ordered a patrol wagon filled with officers to take Pierce away. He was placed next to the driver's seat and the wagon clattered down the streets toward the prison at Tulane Avenue. Lenard was described as being "in a terrible state of fright" as he made the journey to the grim building where he would remain for many months to come. Another unruly crowd by this time had assembled outside the morgue, where an inquest was being held on the bodies of Captain Day and Patrolman Lamb. Five hundred or more people had to be restrained by police from tearing down the doors of the building, so determined were they to look at the bodies.[14]

The crowd in front of the yellow house on Fourth Street remained there until long after nightfall, and by dark had begun to resemble a mob. Black onlookers were no longer present in the surrounding blocks. Some men in the crowd said they were sure Charles was still hiding in the area, and that the time had come to drive all "niggers" out of that part of town. Especially was there a desire to ransack the houses on the block where the killings had

13. "Reports of Arrests," Sixth Precinct, July 25, 1900; New Orleans *Times-Democrat*, July 25, 1900.

14 New Orleans *Daily Item*, July 24, 1900; New Orleans *Daily States*, July 24, 1900.

occurred. Police on duty there managed, with some difficulty, to discourage the whites from going into nearby houses; the crowd was told that all these dwellings had already been thoroughly searched. A number of patrolmen were heard to say that "if they [the police] knew where the nigger was, they would let them go ahead."[15]

Random encounters between whites and blacks continued late into the evening. Several black men and two black women were severely beaten by roving packs of young white men. The most potentially dangerous situation developed at Lee Circle, on St. Charles Avenue, where shortly after dark a crowd of excited white men, described as being "of all classes," gathered with shotguns, rifles, and other weapons. After listening to impromptu speeches about the need for avenging the deaths of the police officers, the mob moved up St. Charles in the direction of the neighborhood where the shootings had taken place. At the intersection of Jackson Avenue and St. Charles a group of prominent citizens persuaded the mob to halt. Alderman J. S. Zacharie informed the crowd that Robert Charles had been located and jailed in the town of Kenner, and that he had been positively identified. Hearing this the mob cheered and then dispersed, and the city became relatively quiet for the remainder of the night.[16]

Wednesday the twenty-fifth developed into a day of even more tension than the one preceding it. That the rumor of Charles's capture in Kenner proved false scarcely helped white tempers, and once again numerous white men were seen on the streets openly carrying weapons. No attempt was made to disarm any of them. Every police stationhouse in the city was profusely draped in mourning. That afternoon the funeral corteges of Captain Day and Patrolman Lamb drew hundreds of spectators, and the priest who spoke a eulogy at St. Michael's Church for Captain Day declared

15. New Orleans *Daily Picayune*, July 25, 1900.
16. New Orleans *Times-Democrat*, July 25, 1900; New Orleans *Daily Item*, July 25, 1900.

that Robert Charles should be made to pay with his life. "When men tell me of their scruples against capital punishment," Father Coughlin concluded, "I have no patience with them. Those who have scruples against capital punishment should be marked out and be branded on their seats. I trust that the assassin will be brought to justice."[17]

In the absence of Mayor Paul Capdevielle, who was recovering from illness forty miles away in Bay St. Louis, Mississippi, Acting Mayor William Mehle posted a $250 reward for the arrest of Charles; and, for the state, Governor W. W. Heard authorized an additional 250 dollars. (The city's reward notice was later amended to read "for the capture and delivery, dead or alive [of] the body of the negro murderer.") Acting Mayor Mehle, noting the explosive situation on his hands, issued on the afternoon of the twenty-fifth a proclamation which he hoped would help prevent a major riot:

PROCLAMATION

City Hall, July 25, 1900

Whereas, as a result of the regrettable assassination of Capt. Day and Officer Lamb and the wounding of Officer Mora, there is a disposition manifested on the part of certain of our citizens to take the law into their own hands, much to the prejudice of the good name of the City of New Orleans:

Now, therefore, I, William Mehle, Acting Mayor, call upon good citizens to aid the authorities in preserving the peace; not to assemble on the public streets and places discussing the sad events hereinabove set forth, but to let justice take its course.[18]

Each of New Orleans' four major newspapers, in their issues of July 25, contributed to some extent to the violence which would come that night. None exercised the kind of restraint in their news columns which might have helped calm white anger. Editorially,

17. New Orleans *Daily Item*, July 26, 1900; New Orleans *Daily Picayune*, July 26, 1900.

18. New Orleans *Times-Democrat*, July 26, 1900.

only the *Item* took a strong stand against mob action. Of the two morning papers, the *Picayune* was not blameless, but its guilt did not begin to approach that of the *Times-Democrat,* whose lead editorial of that day, "NEGRO CRIMINALS," would be justly accused of promoting vigilante action. The paper blamed "the negroes as a class" for the crimes committed by any members of their race. Most Negroes, this paper averred, "do nothing to help the community in punishing the outlaws of their own race, but on the contrary, they show every disposition to shield them." The same editorial further insisted that "hundreds of negroes" in the city must have known that this Robert Charles was a "dangerous agitator" who "with his fanatical hatred of the white race . . . was certain sooner or later to commit some crime as that of yesterday." Yet Robert Charles had never been reported to the police—therefore, all Negroes who knew him (or knew others like him) were guilty. The *Times-Democrat* concluded that "a vigorous course [should] be adopted now." [19]

Still it was the afternoon *States* whose temper most approximated the emotions of those who were already carrying shotguns and rifles around the downtown streets. For two decades Major Hearsey's heated editorials in the *States* had instructed (and entertained) thousands of white Louisianians of both high and low socioeconomic status. Although Hearsey was an unabashed elitist who sometimes denigrated the white "rabble," many ordinary whites—particularly Confederate veterans —faithfully read the *States*. Militant conservatives, both rich and poor, considered him a great intellectual. Even a rival editor remarked that "his fine ability to think and express great thoughts" was recognized across the state. Because he had risked prison by calling for the assassination of Republican public officials during the Reconstruction era (he then edited the Shreveport *Times*), and because since then he had so

19. *Ibid.,* July 25, 1900. See also New Orleans *Daily Item* and *Daily Picayune* for July 25, 1900.

zealously defended his state and race against what he considered to be legions of enemies both within and without, Hearsey was by 1900 looked upon as the grand old man and chief ideologist of the Louisiana Democratic party. His *States*, since the early 1880s, had been the official journal of the city government.[20]

In private life Major Hearsey was known to be a genial, very courteous man. "Fiery of pen and soft of heart" read one summation of him. He was utterly sincere and, unlike so many prominent figures in Louisiana, was personally honest. Hearsey never held or sought public office and money seemed to be no concern to him. (Since financial affairs even of his beloved newspaper bored him, the *States*'s economic survival depended mainly upon the acumen of its business manager, Robert Ewing.) Understandably, not everyone approved of Hearsey. Blacks in the city had long recognized him as an implacable enemy and many whites thought his Negrophobia too extreme. The *Item* had recently referred to him as "a toothless serpent."[21] But when the major sat down to write his editorial for July 25, his fangs appeared to be still intact.

The first edition of the *States* was on the streets at 2:30 P.M. And the major had lived up to expectations. His lead editorial, "NEGRO MURDERERS," summoned up the deepest racial fears of the New Orleans white community. "Under the dark, seething mass of humanity that surrounds us and is in our midst," he wrote, "all appears peaceful and delightful; we know not, it seems, what hellish dreams are arising underneath; we know not what schemes of hate, of arson, of murder and rape are being hatched in the dark depths. We are, and we should recognize it, under the regime of the free negro, in

20. Henry Rightor, *Standard History of New Orleans, Louisiana* (Chicago: Lewis Publishing Company, 1900), 279, 281; New Orleans *Times-Democrat*, October 31, 1900; New Orleans *Daily States*, April 5, 1900.

21. Walker Parker, "New Orleans Reminiscences, *1894–1940*" (Bound clippings from New Orleans *Official Daily Court Reporter*, January 22–May 19, 1941, in Special Collections Division, Tulane University Library), 6; Rightor, *Standard History of New Orleans*, 279; New Orleans *Daily Item*, April 5, 1900.

the midst of a dangerous element of servile uprising, not for any real cause, but from the native race hatred of the negro, inflamed continually by our Northern philanthropists." Hearsey further asserted that "the ugliest feature" of Robert Charles's bloody activity "is that it is calculated to give the worst negroes of the community a contempt for the prowess of the police and to encourage them to newer and bolder crimes." He went on in this vein at some length, and concluded with a strong implication that the manhood not only of the police force, but of all white New Orleans, had been challenged by the "extraordinary" deeds of "one bold negro." Hearsey did not specifically call for massive mob retaliation on the black community, but his words gave moral support for those on the streets who did.[22]

By nightfall word had been passed from one end of the city to the other that another meeting was to be held at the Robert E. Lee monument. And this time, it was promised, there would be action. All afternoon talk on the street corners and in the saloons had been to the effect that the blacks of New Orleans were hiding Robert Charles, and that all Negroes "were secretly glorying in the deed of the black fiend." By 8:30 P.M. about two thousand white men and youths had arrived at Lee Circle, perhaps half of them armed with either guns or clubs. After a few brief oratorical efforts by some who were present, the mob proceeded in the direction of Washington Avenue. Their ultimate objective became to take Lenard Pierce out of the parish prison and lynch him. Along the way they began assaulting any blacks they came upon.[23]

It had been nine years since New Orleans had undergone a major riot. The violence of 1900 bore more than a slight resemblance to that of 1891, when eleven Sicilians had been taken

22. New Orleans *Daily States*, July 25, 1900; New Orleans *Daily Item*, August 12, 1900.
23. *Outlook*, LXV (August 4, 1900), 760–61; New Orleans *Southwestern Christian Advocate*, August 2, 1900; New Orleans *Times-Democrat*, July 26, 1900.

from the parish prison and shot or hanged by a large throng of citizens. Ordinarily, Sicilians were not as despised or feared as were Negroes, but most native whites in the city tended to view them as also criminally inclined. The eleven men lynched in March of 1891 were accused of murdering Chief of Police David Hennessy, and were thought to be members of an underworld organization "fashioned after the Mafia of Sicily." Various prominent citizens had participated in the mob action, and a grand jury later refused to indict anyone because, stated the official report, it was "a spontaneous uprising of the people." The city's major newspapers had condoned the lynching, even though the affair led to a serious diplomatic problem between the United States and Italy.[24]

The Negro-hunting mob of the evening of July 25, 1900, did not include the more respectable types of citizens who had participated in the lynching of the Sicilians nine years earlier. This throng was composed mostly of laboring-class young white men and ragged teenagers, along with a solid admixture of chronic hoodlums. To some extent, explained *Harlequin*, "it was a 'bread riot' " by out-of-work whites who had been replaced, or could not find jobs, because of cheaper black labor. But for the most part sheer racial animus and a desire for excitement seems to have pervaded the mob. At least half its membership was made up, several reporters speculated, by people who intended no violence themselves, but simply went along to see the fun.[25]

Patrolmen in the vicinity made little effort to disperse the throng, which gathered in size as it approached Washington Avenue. There the mob halted, considering where to go next. At this point a man in his mid-thirties mounted a box and attempted to get

24. Joy J. Jackson, *New Orleans in the Gilded Age: Politics and Urban Progress 1880–1896* (Baton Rouge: Louisiana State University Press, 1969), 245–50; *Nation*, LII (May 14, 1891), 393.

25. *Harlequin*, II (August 18, 1900), 2; Chicago *Tribune*, July 26, 1900; Washington *Post*, July 31, 1900; New Orleans *Daily Picayune*, July 26, 1900.

the crowd's attention with a weighty announcement. "Gentlemen," he intoned, "I am the Mayor of Kenner." His audience seemed unimpressed, but after waving his arms for some moments he received a hearing. "I am from Kenner, gentlemen, and I have come down to New Orleans tonight to assist you in teaching the blacks a lesson. I have killed a negro before, and . . . I am willing to kill again. The only way you can teach these niggers a lesson and put them in their place is to go out and lynch a few of them as an object lesson . . . that is the only thing to do—kill them, string them up, lynch them. I will lead you if you will follow. On to the Parish Prison and lynch Pierce." The orator was, in fact, the Mayor protempore of the suburban community of Kenner. His name was S. M. Cowen and he would later be indicted on a charge of unlawful assembly.[26]

After Cowen finished speaking a young lawyer, St. Clair Adams, attempted to discourage the crowd with words about the law and the honor of New Orleans, but amidst the general shouting his words were hardly audible ten feet away. The mob now began to turn in a downtown direction, toward Tulane Avenue and the prison. Soon passing streetcars began to supply victims. The cars were stopped and searched and the few black passengers on board were either shot or beaten. One elderly black man escaped harm by crouching under a seat occupied by a formidable-looking white woman, who spread her long skirts over him and defied the mob to bother him. But on another car, two young white men were beaten up because it was mistakenly thought they had attempted to assist a black man the mob was after; the young men were reportedly not as upset over their beating as they were about being mistaken for "nigger lovers."[27]

26. New Orleans *Times-Democrat*, July 26, 1900; New Orleans *Daily Picayune*, August 4, 1900; *State of Louisiana* v. *S. M. Cowen*, Case No. 30,033, Criminal District Court, Parish of Orleans, Louisiana.
27. New Orleans *Southwestern Christian Advocate*, August 2, 1900; New Orleans *Times-Democrat*, July 26, 1900.

By 9:30 P.M. the yelling crowd, having swollen to over three thousand, arrived in front of Parish Prison. Here for the first time they met resistance from the authorities. Orleans Parish Sheriff Remy Klock had barricaded the prison door; all his deputies were on duty along with about thirty city policemen. All were armed with Winchesters. The senior officer among the city police was Sergeant Gabriel Porteous, who had long been considered by whites and blacks who knew him as the most likable and fair-minded member of the NOPD. But Porteous was not in a friendly mood tonight, and it took both shooting and pushing to convince the mob they would not be allowed to have Lenard Pierce. There appeared to be no desire among those in the street to fire upon the officers, and by 10 P.M. the mob turned away from the prison and headed toward Storyville.[28]

"The red light district was all excitement" as the mob poured into its streets, the *Picayune*'s reporter noticed. Houses that specialized in black or mixed-blood prostitutes were shut and unlighted, but from the other places numerous white women were leaning out of windows or standing on front doorsteps, and many began cheering the mob along. The mob's apparent objective now was the black area of cabarets and saloons along Franklin and Customhouse streets. But these places were closed and deserted by the time the throng arrived. Along the way, however, an incident occurred which was probably inevitable for a race riot in New Orleans; a young man whose race was uncertain was sighted and caught. There appeared to be a question as to whether he should be shot or permitted to join the mob. Wallace Sabatier was finally taken under an electric light and examined closely; it was decided he was a white man. "Sabatier was glad," wrote one observer.[29]

After midnight the size of the mob dwindled considerably, but its more determined members kept up their activities in small,

28. New Orleans *Times-Democrat*, July 26, 1900; New Orleans *Southwestern Christian Advocate*, August 2, 1900; New Orleans *Daily Item*, July 26, 1900.
29. New Orleans *Daily Picayune*, July 26, 1900.

roving bands. By this time most blacks in New Orleans were aware of what was happening and had no intention of coming into the downtown area until the trouble was over. But a few had not heard, and throughout the night additional victims were taken to Charity Hospital, or to the morgue. One of the most brutal of the killings that night occurred near the French Market about 2:30 A.M. Baptiste Philo, black and aged seventy-five, was on his way to work at the market when he was shot at from a distance and fatally wounded. The man who did the shooting, upon approaching to see if his target was dead, reportedly remarked: "Oh, he's an old negro. I'm sorry that I shot him."[30]

The early daylight hours of Thursday, the twenty-sixth, revealed several hundred disorderly people still on the downtown streets. Soon they were reinforced by others who had gone home for a few hours sleep and who hurried back at daylight. In terms of casualties, the night's violence had not been nearly as bloody as first reports indicated: three blacks were dead and six had been seriously injured. Five whites also required hospitalization, two of whom had been accidently shot by the mob; the three others were streetcar employees who had bravely tried to prevent the mob from boarding their trolleys. But at least fifty other people, mostly black, had been beaten by the mob and, after being given emergency medical treatment, had been released.[31]

For a time it seemed that the previous night's work by the mob might be only the beginning of anarchy. The understaffed, ill-trained New Orleans Police Department was clearly unable—and some of its personnel visibly unwilling—to stop further trouble. Most businesses which attempted to open in the downtown area Thursday morning discovered they had no black employees and few

30. *Ibid.*; letter from the Reverend D. A. Graham, in Indianapolis *Freeman*, August 18, 1900.
31. New Orleans *Times-Democrat*, July 26, 1900; New Orleans *Daily Item*, July 26, 1900.

customers of any color; and on the docks, where black labor was concentrated and most depended upon, virtually nobody showed up for work. In fairness to the businessmen of New Orleans, it should be supposed they would have wanted the violence against innocent blacks to cease in any case; but this severe disruption of the city's economic life made it imperative to them that order be restored as quickly as possible.[32]

Mayor Capdevielle returned to the city early Thursday morning; before leaving Bay St. Louis he had heard about Robert Charles but knew nothing of the rioting until his arrival. Capdevielle, realizing his police force was totally inadequate to meet this continuing emergency, and aware that a real bloodbath threatened, issued a call for five hundred citizens to act as a "special" police force in quelling the rioters. By afternoon, with disorders continuing, he increased the call to fifteen hundred. Hundreds of the most prominent men in the city responded, as well as clerks and laborers; within an hour of each call the Mayor had all the men he requested. On this same day Louisiana Governor Heard ordered to active duty all state militia units in the New Orleans area and placed them at the disposal of the mayor. Capdevielle also received an unwanted offer of assistance from the president of a "Citizens Improvement League" of Tangipahoa Parish, across Lake Pontchartrain; the head of this organization promised to send the mayor, if desired, enough armed and able-bodied white men to "annihilate the negroes of New Orleans."[33]

By nightfall of the twenty-sixth the special police and the state

32. *Ibid.*; New Orleans *Southwestern Christian Advocate*, August 2, 1900; Atlanta *Constitution*, July 27, 1900.

33. "Report of the Operations of the Special Police Force from July 26th to 30th," in Mayor's Office Correspondence; New Orleans *Times-Democrat*, July 27, 1900; New York *Times*, July 29, 1900. Other members of the "Citizens Improvement League," however, informed Mayor Capdevielle that they did not endorse President J. P. Holt's offer. F. M. Brish and others to Paul Capdevielle, *ca.* July 28, 1900, in Mayor's Office Correspondence.

militia were organized, armed, and being posted at known trouble spots throughout the city, particularly in the downtown area. In the meantime, New Orleans had undergone yet another twelve hours of sporadic, mindless violence. Two more black men were fatally injured and fifteen others shot or severely beaten by white rioters. There were scattered reports of looting. During the coming night an elderly black woman, Hanna Mabry, would be shot and killed in her home by the last of the roving bands of troublemakers.[34]

But once stationed, the special police and militia were able to establish a reasonable semblance of order throughout the city. By daylight of Friday the twenty-seventh New Orleans was quieter than it had been since the Dryades Street shooting episode of the previous Monday night. If the restored order could be maintained, the leadership of New Orleans was prepared to congratulate itself in so rapidly pulling away from the edge of anarchy, and with so few casualties. Yet Robert Charles was still at large. And on this day, shortly before noon, Superintendent of Police Gaster would receive a tip from a black informer that the wanted man possibly was being hidden by a family named Jackson at a house on Saratoga Street.[35]

34. "Report of the Operations of the Special Police Force," Mayor's Office Correspondence; New York *Times*, July 27, 1900; New Orleans *Daily States*, July 27, 1900.

35. Letter from John C. Wicliffe, in Boston *Morning Journal*, August 18, 1900; "Report of the Operations of the Special Police Force," Mayor's Office Correspondence; Jules Dreyfous to Paul Capdevielle, July 27, 1900, in Mayor's Office Correspondence; New Orleans *Times-Democrat*, August 30, September 1, 1900.

9
1208 SARATOGA STREET

Throughout the rioting, and while the frantic manhunt for him continued, Robert Charles quietly remained inside his refuge at 1208 Saratoga Street, within the square block bounded on its other sides by Clio, South Rampart, and Erato streets. It was not an ideal hiding place, since many blacks and at least one white man had noticed him going in and out of the residence on numerous occasions during the past three years. But he was wounded and had nowhere else to go. NOPD detectives were convinced that Charles was still somewhere inside the city, probably being protected by some black family; yet they feared that unless they obtained a definite lead on his whereabouts he might remain hidden long enough for his leg to heal and then manage an escape.[1]

Robert was in the rear annex of dwelling 1208. Both the front and rear buildings were frail wooden structures, and each was part of a duplex arrangement. The left half of both the front and rear structures constituted dwelling 1210. Both buildings were two-story affairs painted a light shade of green; the front structure, which abutted Saratoga Street, was larger than the annex and had two

1. New Orleans *Times-Democrat*, July 28–29, 1900; Parkash Kaur Bains, "The New Orleans Race Riot of 1900" (M.A. thesis, Louisiana State University in New Orleans, 1970), 34.

rooms upstairs and two downstairs in both its 1208 and 1210 residences. The annex, however, had only one room upstairs and one downstairs for each half of the duplex. Between the front building and the annex was a little yard, twenty feet wide—actually two tiny yards, since a flimsy partition divided it in the familiar duplex style.[2]

The rear building, where Charles was hidden, was almost back-to-back with a one-story duplex which faced South Rampart Street. Little space existed between any of the dwellings on that square and the only entrances to the yards between the annex and the main building of duplex 1208–1210 were two narrow alleys—one on the Clio Street (residence 1208) side, and the other on the Erato Street (residence 1210) side. As a place of defense, the rear building had certain advantages. The upper windows looked down upon the alleys and yard through which any attackers would have to come.[3]

Both buildings within the duplex arrangement were owned by a white man, John Joyce. An electrician by trade, Joyce lived with his family in the four rooms of the front building of 1210, and used one of the ground floor rooms of the annex as a kitchen; but Joyce rented out 1208, as well as the upper annex portion of 1210, to a black laborer named Silas Jackson. Silas and Martha Jackson, and their two children, used as their living quarters only the upper rooms of the annex; Mr. and Mrs. Jackson slept in the upstairs room of the 1208 annex and their children in the upstairs room of the 1210 annex. As was the practice of many black renters in New Orleans of that day, Silas Jackson subrented to other blacks. In the downstairs room of the 1208 side of the annex lived his cousin Burke Jackson, and Silas rented to several people in the 1208 side of the larger main building: Annie Gant and her common-law husband Albert Jackson

2. See the diagram of 1208 and 1210 Saratoga Street in New Orleans *Times-Democrat*, July 30, 1900. But this needs supplementation with the statement of John Joyce, who described exactly where the various black occupants lived, in New Orleans *Daily Picayune*, May 15, 1901.

3. New York *Times*, July 28, 1900; New Orleans *Daily States*, July 28, 1900; New Orleans *Times-Democrat*, July 28–30, 1900.

(no relation to Silas) lived in the downstairs front room; Boss Nixon and his wife Imogene had the downstairs back room; upstairs, the front room was rented to Silas' cousin Isaac Jackson and the rear room to Silas' brother Charles Jackson. Silas had resided here for about eight years and some of his subtenants had lived in their rooms for almost that long.[4]

Robert Charles had known the Jacksons for at least three years and probably longer. The white salesman of the Poydras Street store, Hyman Levy, had seen him coming and going from 1208 Saratoga on many occasions since 1897, and some of Robert's books and other belongings were stored there. Silas Jackson was from Pike County, Mississippi, but his wife Martha, a tall and angular woman, appears to have been from Copiah County. Three of her sisters were still living there in 1900. Indeed, all of the black renters at the 1208 address were former Mississippians, and at least two of them, Boss and Imogene Nixon, were from the Crystal Springs vicinity of northern Copiah County.[5] It is more than probable that Robert either was related to some of these people or had known them years before in Mississippi. Certainly he trusted them above any other residents of New Orleans, since it was there he sought refuge. And they at great peril granted it to him.

There must have been a number of other New Orleans blacks who knew that 1208 Saratoga was Robert Charles's most likely hiding place in the city. But for the police that piece of information proved hard to get. In addition to the reward posted by the city and state, the NOPD also offered money for any leads on where Charles's associates or relatives might be living in New Orleans. Yet the blacks, complained the *Picayune*, "were holding what informa-

4. "Testimony of John Joyce," in New Orleans *Daily Picayune*, May 15, 1901. See also New Orleans *Times-Democrat*, July 28, 30, August 4, 1900.
5. Levy interview, New Orleans *Sunday States*, July 29, 1900; Crawford and others to Handlin, December 2, 1900, in Case No. 30,086 file in Criminal District Court, Parish of Orleans, Louisiana; New Orleans *Times-Democrat*, August 1, 4, 1900.

tion they had, and price could not tempt them."[6] There was, however, one exception.

Fred Clark lived at 1129 South Rampart Street, about three blocks from Silas Jackson's residence. Clark was considered by whites "a good negro, ready to help the police at all times." He had furnished valuable leads in the past, and on late Friday morning, July 27, he did again. Superintendent of Police Gaster's office at that time received word from Clark that Robert Charles had a relative or relatives (Clark thought a brother) named Jackson, who lived somewhere near the intersection of Saratoga and Erato streets. Clark also related that the person in the Jackson household most likely to harbor Charles was a woman named Martha.[7]

Superintendent Gaster had received many tips during the past three days, and so far all had proven worthless. But all possibilities were being checked out. Shortly before 3 P.M. Gaster sent two memos to the commanding sergeant of the second precinct, Gabriel Porteous. The superintendent had learned from an unnamed source (later revealed to be Clark) not only about the possible relationship between Charles and the Jacksons, but that Lenard Pierce's mother was now living at an address on Freret Street, and it was thought Charles might be hiding there. Porteous, receiving the memos, decided to check out the Jackson possibility first. To assist him he selected the three best available men at the second precinct: Corporal John F. Lally, Patrolman Andrew Zeigel, and Supernumerary Patrolman Rudolph Esser.[8]

There was no better man in the NOPD than Sergeant Gabriel Porteous. He was one of the few policemen who treated whites and blacks alike and was considered, a local black publication reported, "a liberal-minded high-toned gentleman [who] was esteemed by the

6. New Orleans *Daily Picayune*, July 28, 1900.

7. *Ibid.*, September 3, 1900; "Report of Superintendent D. S. Gaster," in New Orleans *Times-Democrat*, August 1, 4, 1900.

8. New Orleans *Daily Item*, July 28, 1900; "Report of Superintendent D. S. Gaster," in New Orleans *Times-Democrat*, August 31, 1900.

colored people of this city who knew him." His reputation for
bravery was equally well established; Porteous had received com-
plimentary mention in the Board of Police Commissioner's *Annual
Report* many times. Forty-seven, he had lived in New Orleans all
his life and had been on the force since 1889. At one time or the
other he had served in every precinct in the city.[9]

Sergeant Porteous and his three men took a patrol wagon up
Erato Street. Arriving at the corner of Erato and Saratoga, they
began to ask passersby about a black woman named Martha. They
were first directed to the residence of a Martha Williams, one block
away from the Jacksons, at 1305 Saratoga. Mrs. Williams, quite old,
was ironing when Porteous came to her door. When interviewed
later she said that she told the "white folks" to come on in and search
her house if they wanted to. Porteous wanted to. "They went
through every place," even the garret, Mrs. Williams recalled, "and
then [one of them] asked me if I knew a Si Jackson or Martha Jackson
and I said yes, they live down there in that green house near the
corner of Clio." A few minutes later she heard some shooting and
she knew that Robert Charles had been found.[10]

Robert had been told or had seen that a patrol wagon was in the
neighborhood and he had hidden himself in a closet on the bottom
floor of the 1208 annex, in Burke Jackson's room. The closet,
beneath a rickety staircase, was rather large and Robert had obviously spent much time in it during the past three days. Inside was a

　9. New Orleans *Southwestern Christian Advocate*, August 2, 1900; "Record of
Inquests," Coroner's Office, Parish of Orleans, July 27, 1900, pp. 317–18, in City
Archives Department, New Orleans Public Library; *Annual Report of Board of Police
Commissioners, Superintendent of Police and Police Surgeon of the City of New
Orleans, 1900*, p. 28; New Orleans *Daily States*, July 28, 1900.
　10. New Orleans *Daily States*, August 4, 1900. Mrs. Williams knew Robert
Charles and believed, as did several other people, that Silas Jackson was his brother.
However, several white residents of Pike County, Mississippi, positively stated that
Silas and Charles Jackson had lived there all their lives, before coming to New
Orleans. Robert may have been distantly related to Silas and Charles Jackson, but it is
more likely he was a nephew or cousin of Silas' wife Martha, who was from Copiah.

chair, about eight pounds of lead pipe from which he had been making bullets, and a miniature charcoal furnace, in which some of the lead pipe was already melted down. (Martha Jackson later testified that the little furnace had been left there some time earlier "by a girl" whom she did not know.) Two pieces of steel pipe lay near the furnace; the diameter of this was the same as the calibre of Robert's Winchester, so he had been using it to mold his homemade bullets. The closet, with its door slightly ajar, gave the man inside a direct view of the front doorway of the 1208 side of the annex. Burke Jackson was away; there was nobody in the room when Robert seated himself in the closet, with the Winchester across his lap.[11]

Silas Jackson, weary from his day's work at the Illinois Central Roundhouse, had come home about 3 P.M., gone to his upstairs room in the annex, and immediately fallen asleep. About 3:20 he was awakened by the shouting of Imogene Nixon, from her downstairs rear room in the main building. Sergeant Porteous and Corporal Lally were standing in the alley next to her window, and they had wanted to know where Si and Martha Jackson lived. She told Porteous that Silas Jackson was upstairs in the annex and the sergeant asked her to call him out. Imogene had to yell twice before Silas woke up. Looking down from his window, Jackson saw the policemen and quickly he descended the stairway above the closet where Robert Charles sat hidden. Porteous and Lally were the only officers in the yard, for the sergeant had stationed Zeigel and Esser on Saratoga Street.[12]

In the middle of the little yard Jackson and the two officers met. Porteous asked Silas "where his brother Robert Charles was." Silas replied that he "had a brother named Charles Jackson, but Robert Charles was no relation of his." Porteous and Lally insisted that the

11. *Ibid.*, July 28, 1900; New Orleans *Daily Picayune*, July 28–29, 1900.

12. *State of Louisiana* v. *Silas Jackson et al.*, Case No. 30,085, Criminal District Court, Parish of Orleans, Louisiana; "Testimony of Imogene Nixon," in New Orleans *Daily Picayune*, May 16, 1901.

killer was his brother; then, placing Silas Jackson under arrest, they told him to lead them through the rear building. Porteous and Lally, following Jackson, entered the doorway of the 1208 side of the annex. Directly across the room was the closet where Robert Charles waited, absolutely still.

Seeing a water bucket and a dipper atop a little stand next to the closet, Sergeant Porteous remarked that he was thirsty and walked toward it. Now Robert Charles thrust the barrel of his Winchester out the crack in the closet door and fired. First he shot at Porteous and then at Lally. Like Captain Day, Porteous was struck in the heart and died almost immediately. Lally, hit in the abdomen, would die at Charity Hospital the next day.[13]

Frantically, Silas Jackson bolted from the room, ran through the yard and narrow alleyway and into Saratoga Street. "Oh, Lordy," he began to shout. "Oh, Lordy. Oh, Lordy." Then, not knowing what else to do, he dashed back into the yard of 1208 Saratoga. He was still standing there when Officer Peter Fenney, who lived at the corner of Saratoga and Erato and had been awakened by the shooting, came into the yard and arrested him. Officer Fenney then learned about Porteous and Lally and went into the room to see about them.[14]

Officers Zeigel and Esser were meanwhile busy catching a black man named John Willis who upon hearing the shots went running down Saratoga Street. Willis lived at 1204 Saratoga, and, as he was of a nervous, fearful disposition (he probably knew of Charles's presence and thus realized what those shots meant), his only thought was to flee the neighborhood at once. "There he goes! There he goes over the fence!" several white men shouted at Zeigel and Esser; and the two patrolmen, thinking Willis was Robert

13. "Testimony of Silas Jackson," in New Orleans *Daily Picayune*, May 15, 1901; *Louisiana* v. *Silas Jackson et al.*, No. 30,085; "Record of Inquests," Coroner's Office, July 27, 1900, pp. 317–18, and July 28, 1900, pp. 313–14.
14. *Louisiana* v. *Silas Jackson et al.*, No. 30,085; "Testimony of Officer Fenney," in New Orleans *Daily Picayune*, May 15, 1901.

Charles, ran him down a few blocks away on Clio Street. But they quickly realized by his demeanor that he could not be the wanted man. Described as being "insane from fright," Willis literally groveled at the feet of his captors. "Boss," he sobbed, "I'm an innocent nigger."[15]

By the time Officer Fenney discovered Porteous and Lally, Robert Charles was gone from the bottom floor of the annex. Taking his Winchester and Colt pistol, along with most of the ammunition he had been making during the past three days, Robert had run up the stairs to Silas and Martha Jackson's room, immediately above where Porteous and Lally had been shot. Hastily he went to the wall separating this room from the other half of the duplex arrangement; on the other side was the Jackson children's room. Using his feet, Robert began pounding a large hole through the plaster and timber. Soon he was able to pass to and fro in the two upstairs rooms, and the windows on the 1210 side gave him added visibility on the yards and alleyways below. Neither of the Jackson children was home. Outside, Silas and Martha were being led away to police headquarters, and white people were beginning to gather along Saratoga Street.[16]

With the exception of Robert Charles, everybody inside residences 1208 and 1210 fled the buildings at some time or another after the shooting commenced; and with the exception of John Joyce, the white landlord, those away at the time decided not to go home when news of what was happening there reached them. Inside the main building, fronting Saratoga Street, John Joyce's wife grabbed up her two baby daughters as soon as the gunfire began and ran across the street to a neighbor's house; Mrs. Joyce's sister and elderly mother, who were in 1210 at the time, also wasted no time in getting out.[17] Since they were the only white occupants in the two

15. New Orleans *Daily Picayune*, July 28, 1900; "Testimony of Officer Esser," *ibid.*, May 15, 1901.

16. New Orleans *Times-Democrat*, July 28–29, 1900; New York *Times*, July 28, 1900.

17. New Orleans *Daily States*, July 28, 1900.

buildings, the Joyces were thus the only residents assumed by the police not to have known of Charles's presence.

Charles Jackson, Silas' brother, was upstairs in the main building when he heard the shots, and he immediately fled to a nearby house; Burke Jackson was coming home from work when two white women stopped him and warned him that a mob was gathering in his neighborhood and he, thinking the trouble probably involved Robert Charles, departed that day for his parents' home in Mississippi. Isaac Jackson, another cousin of Silas, was out of town at the time and was therefore the only one of the black residents of 1208 not arrested later. Boss Nixon, who had a job with a New Orleans veterinarian, was nursing some sick horses that afternoon and remained at the stable overnight. His wife Imogene took flight at the first shots and hid in or under a nearby grocery store that night; the following day Nixon's employer gave him some money along with advice to get himself and his wife out of town. The Nixon couple on the morning of Saturday, the twenty-eighth, took the train to Crystal Springs. Albert Jackson, who lived with Annie Gant, sat on the front steps for a minute or so after the first shots, considering what to do; presently he crawled under the annex building where Robert was located and remained there most of the time from Friday afternoon until the following Wednesday night, August 1, when he emerged to seek water and was arrested. Annie Gant stayed in her room for over an hour after the shooting started. Eventually some white men burst into her room and one of them told her: "You better get out of here you damned old fool." She then ran into the street, where the police placed her under arrest.[18]

Most bizarre of all the stories told by the blacks who were in the duplex when Charles shot Porteous and Lally was that of George Ford. He was visiting Boss Nixon's wife Imogene. They both fled

18. New Orleans *Times-Democrat*, July 28, 29, August 1, 4, 1900; New Orleans *Daily Picayune*, August 1, 3, 1900; New Orleans *Daily Item*, July 28, 1900.

upon hearing the gunfire, but Ford was confused by the excitement and remained too long in the little yard. Someone in the crowd of white men now gathering on nearby streets and rooftops shot at Ford, the bullet grazing his back. Although the wound was superficial, it convinced Ford that he had best not remain where he was, so he ran into the 1210 portion of the annex, going upstairs into the room of the Jackson children. Robert Charles must have been in the other upper room at the time, or at least Ford insisted later on that he had not seen him. Ford then hid under a bed, pulling the mattress and sheets down so that he was totally concealed. He remained there during the siege that followed and was not discovered until 8:30 that evening, when some police officers pulled him out by his legs.[19]

When Patrolman Fenney entered the lower right room of the annex, he saw that Sergeant Porteous was already dead but Corporal Lally was sitting up in the midst of a spreading pool of blood, which kept flowing from the wound in his stomach. Lally spoke first: "I am fatally wounded. I'd like to see a priest. Please go and get me one, quick." A priest was already on the way, attracted like hundreds of other people by the shooting. Father Fitzgerald of St. John's Church was stopped by Fenney on Clio Street and told that he was needed to administer the Last Sacrament to a dying policeman. The priest was shown the way to the room behind the little yard.[20]

As yet Robert Charles had given no indication of his continued presence in the building, and for a time it was assumed by the police and the growing crowd outside that he had fled. White spectators were now coming through the alleys and into the partitioned yard of the duplex, unaware of danger. A policeman went to the door of the

19. New Orleans *Daily Picayune*, July 28, 1900; New Orleans *Times-Democrat*, July 28, August 1, 1900.

20. New Orleans *Times-Democrat*, July 28, 1900; "Testimony of Rev. Father Fitzgerald," in New Orleans *Daily Picayune*, May 15, 1901.

room where Porteous and Lally were, then came out and told those in the yard not to make any noise as Father Fitzgerald was giving the Last Sacrament. At this point—it was now close to 3:45 P.M.—Robert Charles, upstairs, decided it was time to clear the yard below. He selected as a target a nineteen-year-old white youth named Arthur Brumfield. Oddly, Brumfield only two weeks earlier had been arrested for "unlawful retailing" of whiskey in Copiah County, Mississippi.[21]

An eyewitness to Brumfield's death said he heard the unmistakable crack of a Winchester and looked up to see a rifle, held in black arms, jutting out of an upstairs window. Brumfield, hit in the hip, struggled to the outside stairway of the front building and attempted to climb it. The young man moaned, "Oh, God," then looked up at the window from which the shot came and cried out, "For God's sake, do not shoot!" Charles fired once more, and Brumfield fell dead with a bullet through his lung and heart. Some accounts had it that Brumfield was only a child, and that he had been assisting Father Fitzgerald when Charles shot him ("BLACK FIEND DELIBERATELY MURDERED A PRAYING BOY," headlined the New York *Times*).[22] Neither statement about Brumfield was true, but he was the first unarmed man, and the first civilian, that Charles had put a bullet into. The black man from Mississippi obviously realized that his own death was now inevitable and had decided to take as many whites with him as possible.

About the same moment that Brumfield fell, the telephone in Superintendent Gaster's office transmitted the news that "a policeman had been wounded at the corner of Clio and Saratoga Streets."

21. "Testimony of Rev. Father Fitzgerald," in New Orleans *Daily Picayune*, May 15, 1901; Hazlehurst *Courier*, quoted in Brookhaven *Leader*, August 8, 1900. Brumfield had been a candy and soft-drink salesman on the Illinois Central line, and was caught selling whiskey when the train passed through the dry county of Copiah.

22. Interview with C. A. Kent, in New Orleans *Daily Picayune*, July 29, 1900; Atlanta *Constitution*, July 28, 1900; Boston *Morning Journal*, July 28, 1900; "Record of Inquests," Coroner's Office, July 27, 1900, p. 315; New York *Times*, July 28, 1900.

Gaster sent a patrol wagon from the first precinct, but within fifteen minutes he was informed again by telephone that more than one person had been shot and that firing was still going on. As yet no one was absolutely certain the trouble involved Robert Charles, but every minute the shooting continued the more likely it seemed that he had indeed been cornered. Mayor Capdevielle was enjoying a Turkish bath at the St. Charles Hotel when a telephone message reached him a minute or so after 4 P.M. "that Charles' hideout had been discovered." The Mayor, knowing the mood of the city and fearing that some massive butchery of the black population might take place, called upon the state militia units, which had been mobilized since Thursday, to go to the scene with—and he made a special point of this—their two Gatling guns. Capdevielle declared that if things got completely out of hand, the Gatling guns should be fired into the white mob.[23]

Special police headquarters got the news from Mayor Capdevielle about 4:05 P.M. Since most of the citizen volunteers were not supposed to go on duty for another hour, less than fifty men were in the armory at Camp and Lafayette streets, about twelve blocks from Charles's refuge on Saratoga. W. L. Hughes, in charge of operations at the armory, reported later, "I didn't feel that it was a time when red tape should be insisted upon, and I armed whoever presented himself as a special officer with a Winchester and placed the squad under the leadership of Captain [Charles] O'Connor." One member of O'Connor's command, hurrying to Saratoga Street, was a young medical student at Tulane, Charles A. Noiret.[24]

Before the day was over vicious, degrading things would transpire on and around the 1200 block of Saratoga Street, but there was also one act of genuine heroism. About 4 P.M., not long after Father

23. "Report of Superintendent D. S. Gaster," in New Orleans *Times-Democrat*, August 31, 1900; New Orleans *Daily Picayune*, July 28, 1900.
24. W. L. Hughes to Elmer E. Wood, August 2, 1900, in Mayor's Office Correspondence.

Fitzgerald had administered Extreme Unction to Corporal Lally, a man named Vic Mauberret and a *Times-Democrat* reporter, "Billy" Ball, decided that Lally, Porteous, and Brumfield—it was not certain any of them were actually dead—must be rescued. Father Fitzgerald and the officers who had gone in and out of the lower room had dashed for safety soon after Charles shot Brumfield, leaving Porteous and Lally where they were. Billy Ball had earlier distinguished himself, during the Wednesday night rioting, by saving the life of a black man on Canal Street. Announcing their decision to the crowd of white men now encircling the square, Ball and Mauberret asked those who had weapons and were in a good position to direct a covering fire into the windows of the upper room of the annex, while they attempted to get the fallen men out. For five minutes or so the fusillade into Charles's rooms continued while first Lally's, then Porteous', and finally Brumfield's bodies were carried out to Saratoga Street by Ball and Mauberret. Robert Charles made no effort to fire while this was going on, but several bullets from the crowd came close to the rescuers. Porteous and Brumfield were sent to the morgue; Lally was taken to Charity Hospital, where he died the following afternoon.[25]

The news that police officers had been shot and that Charles's hideout was discovered traveled across town with amazing rapidity. Throngs of white men and boys, many of them armed with rifles, shotguns, or pistols, came running from distances twenty or thirty blocks away. Streetcars of the St. Charles and other lines which passed close to the area became absolutely jammed. By 4 P.M. at least five thousand people were gathered on the streets of the square surrounding Charles's refuge; Saratoga was the most densely packed, but Clio, Erato, and South Rampart were filling up fast. An hour later, with the siege still going on, somewhere between ten and twenty thousand whites had crowded around the block.

25. New Orleans *Times-Democrat*, July 28, 1900.

Thousands more were assembled in front of the *Times-Democrat* building along Camp Street where bulletins on an enormous blackboard were posted at five-minute intervals as to the progress of the seige.[26]

An estimated thousand of the men who surrounded the square block had firearms of some description. The crowd included regular policemen, the special police under Captain O'Connor, and state militiamen; but most of those present had no authority to do any shooting, or even to carry weapons. But shoot they did. And with the forces available it would probably have been impossible to stop them even if anyone had cared to; the police and militia were clearly not planning to act against their fellow whites unless a wholesale massacre of blacks in the neighborhood commenced. Bullets from police, militia, and citizens continued to pepper the upper rooms of the annex. Those standing on the streets were not in a position to do effective shooting and were in little danger of being hit by one of Charles's bullets. The partitioned yard between the two buildings of 1208–1210 had been empty since the rescue work of Ball and Mauberret. But over a hundred men climbed to sheds and house-tops on the square block, and lying on the protected sides of the slopes, were able to shoot into Charles's windows from there. Cartridges of all sorts and sizes were passed up to the rooftops, along with buckets of water to cool the heated rifle and pistol barrels. At intervals of a minute or so, Charles would appear for an instant at one of the windows and fire at his attackers.[27]

Trenchard, the humiliated survivor of the yellow house encounter, made an appearance on South Rampart Street, near the siege, and was immediately recognized by his unforgettably Gallic

26. *Ibid.*; John Smith Kendall, *History of New Orleans* (3 vols.; Chicago: Lewis Publishing Company, 1922), II, 540; letter from the Reverend D. A. Graham, in Indianapolis *Freeman*, August 18, 1900.

27. Richmond *Planet*, August 4, 1900; New Orleans *Daily Item*, July 28, 1900; New Orleans *Times-Democrat*, July 28–29, 1900.

face and Kaiser Wilhelm II moustache. First came individual shouts and then the crowd began chanting: "Trenchard! Trenchard! Trenchard!" Someone in a booming voice, heard above the chanting, roared out: "Now redeem your reputation—let him through!" Corporal Trenchard, carrying a shotgun, seemed to want nothing more than redemption at that moment; rushing through the narrow space between two of the houses back of Charles's hideout, he approached a side of the green annex and fired two barrels of buckshot upward into the room Charles was presently in, but the loads went through the wrong window. After firing again without effect, Trenchard withdrew to seek a better angle. The corporal's progress, however, was impeded by constant advice and recriminations from dozens of amateur strategists.[28]

The one-sided siege continued until a few minutes past 5 P.M. During the almost two hours since he had killed Porteous and fatally wounded Lally, Robert Charles remained in the two upper rooms of the annex, becoming the target of eventually a thousand guns. Observers the next day estimated that the structure was marked by at least five thousand bullet holes, and bullets from the high-powered rifles had torn through the cheap planking. How Robert had survived so long in that place defies logical explanation. He must have been hit several times. But until the end he continued to appear for an instant every minute or so at one of the upstairs windows and get off a shot at his besiegers. Apparently he was never aware of the presence of the hapless George Ford, who all the while lay quietly under the Jackson children's bed.[29]

Under the circumstances, Robert's aim was as remarkable as his hold on life in those little rooms. Not having an unlimited supply of ammunition, and lacking the time to fire repeatedly in any one position, he carefully hoarded his bullets; counting the shots he

28. New Orleans *Times-Democrat*, July 28, 1900.
29. Chicago *Tribune*, July 28, 1900; New Orleans *Daily States*, July 28, 1900; New Orleans *Sunday States*, July 29, 1900.

fired into Porteous and Lally, it was estimated that he pulled the trigger of his Winchester about fifty times between 3:20 and 5 P.M. that Friday afternoon of July 27. Apparently he did not use his Colt revolver. Of the fifty bullets from Charles's Winchester, twenty-four hit human flesh. For in addition to Porteous, Lally, and Brumfield, he fatally wounded two other men and injured nineteen more. The two others who died from his bullets were Andrew Van Kuren, an employee of the city jail, and a civilian from Mississippi named Howell H. Batte. Seven were seriously wounded, but recovered: Patrolman J. W. Bofill, Patrolman F. H. Evans, and five civilians—G. J. Lyons, John Banville, Frank Bertucci, A. S. Leclerc, and Henry David. A dozen other besiegers sustained grazing or superficial wounds from Charles's Winchester and required emergency treatment only. "Not a time was there a flash from his rifle," wrote one eyewitness, "that some besieger was not either hit or had the ball come so close that he knew he was the target."[30]

Counting the deaths of Captain Day and Officer Lamb and the wounding of Officer Mora Monday night, Charles had now left seven dead (four of whom were police officers), eight seriously wounded (three of whom were police officers), and twelve slightly wounded who were not identified by name or occupation.[31] Robert Charles had shot twenty-seven white people since Monday night. But now at 5 P.M. Friday afternoon he was about to die.

Early in the siege the thought of setting fire to Charles's lair had occurred to many in the crowd. A detachment of firemen with chemicals and hoses had arrived, but the firemen expressed strong doubts about such an undertaking, since all residences in the area were closely packed wooden structures. And many of the areas's

30. Bains, "The New Orleans Race Riot of 1900," p. 60; *Annual Report of Board of Police Commissioners, 1900*, pp. 10–11; Rolling Fork *Deer Creek Pilot*, August 3, 1900; New Orleans *Times-Democrat*, July 28, 1900. Lyons and Leclerc were members of the Special Police volunteers.

31. New Orleans *Daily Picayune*, July 28–29, 1900; Boston *Morning Journal*, July 28, 1900; New Orleans *Sunday States*, July 29, 1900.

residents were white. The danger of a general conflagration was obvious. Also there were rumors—unfounded—that more wounded police officers were upstairs in the rooms Charles now occupied. Mayor Capdevielle, who had rushed from his Turkish bath to City Hall, listened to various suggestions during the next hour and a half as to how Charles's resistance might be ended. (Tear gas had not yet been developed.) The fire chief proposed that the structure be blown up, which he insisted would be safer for the neighborhood than starting a fire. One of the state militia officers suggested that the two Gatling guns, already hauled to the area as a means of intimidating the crowd, now be turned upon the two upper rooms of the annex and fired. But Capdevielle cautioned the military against this, pointing out that the spraying effect of these machine guns would "spread destruction far and wide." While the mayor's office debated these and other alternatives, word came to Capdevielle that a fire had already been started, and Charles was smoked out.[32]

Captain William King of the Julia Street Fire Patrol, along with several citizens, had managed to sneak into the bottom floor of the 1208 annex just before 5 P.M. Charles could be heard walking about upstairs. An old horsehair mattress in Burke Jackson's room, where Porteous and Lally had been shot, was carried to the foot of the staircase. Kerosene was poured upon it, and William Porteous, Gabriel's brother, was allowed to strike the match. As soon as the mattress began to blaze, King expertly dribbled water upon it so that the fire would smoulder and produce clouds of black smoke. Carefully, the mattress was positioned so that most of the choking cloud would be drawn upstairs. Then King, William Porteous, and the other men hastily left the room.[33]

32. New Orleans *Daily Picayune*, July 28, 1900.
33. New Orleans *Times-Democrat*, July 28–29, 1900; New Orleans *Daily States*, July 28, 1900.

For the next five minutes the expectant thousands outside watched the black smoke pour out of the little two-story structure. Yet Robert Charles continued, as he had now for almost two hours, to move suddenly or strike a shutter from one window so as to attract gunfire, and then shoot at his besiegers from another window. Somehow, he was able to endure the smoke. But the heat could not much longer be tolerated, for the mattress had caught the staircase on fire, and from there the flames were spreading. Robert came down the stairs on the 1210 side of the annex, since the other stairway was now completely ablaze. Some of the snipers on the rooftops caught glimpses of him through one of the downstairs windows, and then his form was obscured by the smoke and flames.[34]

It began to seem that Robert Charles would be burned alive inside the annex building. Flames were now breaking through the roof. But at last he appeared at the 1210 front door of the annex, holding his Winchester at shoulder level; he was still wearing his brown derby hat, pulled low in front. Before anyone on the rooftops could take aim, he dashed the twenty feet to the rear entrance of the 1210 section of the main building, the downstairs back room of the Joyce residence. Some protection was afforded him by the heavy vines which hung over the pathway between the two buildings.[35]

Just before Robert reached the door, a man in the room he was approaching fired a rifle. Robert stopped momentarily and, reported an eyewitness, "his arms seemed to sink with the weight of his gun." But a second later he had lifted the Winchester again and was at the door. Eight whites were in the little room, three of them city detectives. But the man who killed Robert Charles was Charles A. Noiret, a medical student and a member of the special police.

34. New Orleans *Times-Democrat*, July 28, 1900.
35. New Orleans *Daily Picayune*, July 28, 1900; New Orleans *Times-Democrat*, July 28, 1900.

Noiret may not have fired the shot that struck Robert outside, but it was he who fired when the black man entered the door. Robert fell just inside the room, not two feet from where Noiret was standing; he dropped face first, but continued to clutch his rifle as he fell. Upon hitting the floor, Robert made an attempt to turn over, and Noiret sent three more bullets into him.[36]

Now a wild shooting into the body commenced. First the eight men who had been in the room, and then the dozen or so more who were able to pack themselves into it during the next minute, fired at the corpse, many of them cursing while others gave wordless victory howls. When the ammunition of those in the room ran out, someone suggested that the body be dragged outside. Immediately those nearest lifted Robert up and carried him, dripping, through the Joyce house, to be dumped at the front entrance on Saratoga Street. The crowd outside was quiet for a second or two and then broke into cheers. Men ran up and dragged the body from the doorway into the muddy street. More shots were pumped into the corpse. Then room was made for Corporal Trenchard, who came running up with his double-barreled shotgun. Trenchard placed the muzzle directly against the torso and in a loud, triumphant voice exclaimed: "Now who says I am a coward?" Then he fired both barrels.[37]

Those who possessed no guns cursed at or kicked the corpse, which soon became almost indistinguishable from the trodden mud of Saratoga Street. One woman in a sunbonnet pushed her way forward and tried to do some kicking, but she was led away. A son of one of the dead police officers came up and, with the crowd's permission, stomped upon the face. Shouts of "burn him! burn him!" began to grow louder, and someone brought up a small container of kerosene. (The next day, one of the local papers excused

36. New Orleans *Times-Democrat*, July 28, October 10, 1900. There were three claimants for the "dead or alive" reward money on Charles, but the more reliable witnesses agreed that Noiret was the man who fired the fatal shots.
37. Natchez *Daily Democrat*, July 28, 1900; New Orleans *Daily Item*, July 28, 1900; New Orleans *Daily Picayune*, July 28, 1900.

this conduct by pointing out that "the satisfaction of his capture and death was in a measure embittered by the knowledge that he had suffered less than any of the men he had slain . . . death had come altogether too swiftly and easily to the fiend")[38]

Police did not attempt to discourage the shooting or kicking of the corpse, but were able to prevent its burning. A patrol wagon had been brought up and, related someone who was there, "The police raised the body of the heavy black from the ground and literally chucked it into the space on the floor of the wagon between the seats." When Charles's body landed on the wagon it fell in such a position that the mutilated head hung over the end. Now, as the wagon prepared to move off toward the morgue, people in the crowd began to protest, demanding that the body remain there and be burned, while others ran up with sticks and poked at or stuck the battered head. As soon as the wagon wheels began to turn, hundreds ran after the vehicle; then as it picked up speed on Clio Street, headed toward Baronne Street and the morgue, the crowd chasing it swelled to as many as five thousand for several blocks. But as the wagon moved further away most of the men and boys returned to watch the firemen extinguish the blaze in the duplex on Saratoga, and to look for Negroes within the square block where the shootout had occurred.[39]

The bulletin board of the *Times-Democrat* had informed the other big crowd, on Camp Street, that the body was being carried to the deadhouse, and many who had been watching the bulletins rushed away in that direction. What they saw should have satisfied even the most morbid. The patrol wagon, clattering through the rough streets as rapidly as possible, caused the corpse to sway and bounce, and the head, looking by this time something like a mud-splattered black skillet, swung and jerked over the end of the

38. New Orleans *Times-Democrat*, July 28, 1900.

39. *Ibid.*; Bonnet Carre *Le Meschacebe*, August 4, 1900; Natchez *Daily Democrat*, July 28, 1900; Atlanta *Constitution*, July 28, 1900.

wagon. Outside the morgue another large crowd was gathered, and the police had difficulty preventing the utter destruction of the corpse before it could be taken inside. Afterward the mob outside grew larger and broke the glass on the morgue doors. Some wanted merely to view the cadavers of Charles and the men he had killed, whereas others were still anxious for further vengeance on the body of the black man who had shot almost thirty whites.[40]

The unsated desire for revenge, the feeling on the part of many whites that it was grossly unfair for a black to have died so quickly after having shot so many whites, was to have fatal consequences for two other black men that afternoon. While the siege on Saratoga Street was coming to an end, a roving mob of about a hundred white men saw a black laborer, about thirty years old, passing through the French Market. They began to chase him and the man ran into a residence on Gallatin Street. Climbing the stairs of the house, with some of his pursuers immediately behind him, the Negro leaped from a second-story gallery and upon landing on the sidewalk tried to get up and run, but the mob surrounded him and shot him to death.[41] Not long afterward another innocent person would die, thought at first to be Burke Jackson.

The man police assumed was Burke Jackson was murdered by someone in the crowd along Clio Street only minutes after Charles's body had left the scene. As soon as the patrol wagon with the corpse disappeared down the street, dozens of white men frantically began searching all houses on the block for "accomplices," but at first they found no blacks (most Negroes in the area at the beginning of the shootout had either fled or been taken away by the police). Toward the end of the siege Annie Gant and three other black women still on the block had been placed in a patrol wagon, and reporters present

40. New Orleans *Times-Democrat*, July 28, 1900; Vicksburg *Daily Herald*, July 28, 1900.

41. Boston *Morning Journal*, July 28, 1900; "Record of Inquests," Coroner's Office, July 27, 1900, pp. 320–21.

believed that these women would have been dragged out and killed, except for the determination of a Winchester-carrying city councilman who took charge of their transportation to Parish Prison. By 5:45 P.M. the police and volunteer forces were beginning to show some success in persuading the mob to cease their ransacking of houses and disperse, when little Arthur Baumgarden, a white child who lived at 1205 Saratoga, ran into the street and began shrieking that he had seen two Negroes upstairs in house 1203. Several policemen were able to outrace the mob to the second floor of that residence and they discovered only one black man, about thirty-five years old. The police led him down Clio Street toward a patrol wagon, with the mob tearing at the officers and their prisoner at every step; he was almost safely aboard when one man in the crowd leaned forward and fired a pistol bullet into the back of the Negro's head. The dead man was listed as Burke Jackson, until that individual—who had fled New Orleans—was arrested in Mississippi a few days later.[42] The real name of this victim would never be known to the authorities.

Rumors of racial incidents and reports of arson in black neighborhoods continued throughout the night of July 27. But only one report proved true. The best Negro schoolhouse in Louisiana, named for Thomy Lafon—a philanthropic Creole of color who when he died in 1893 left a fortune for both white and black education and charities in New Orleans—was burned at about midnight. The burning of Lafon school was actually a lesser atrocity than had been planned by the mob which set the fire; earlier, around 10:30 P.M., a crowd of about fifty white men got off the trolley at South Rampart and Fourth, under the leadership of a fierce-looking, one-legged man who carried a shotgun, and this man announced that they were going to set fire to an entire block of

42. New Orleans *Times-Democrat*, July 28, 1900; New Orleans *Daily Picayune*, July 28, August 7, 1900.

Negro homes, then shoot all the inhabitants when they ran out. The proposal was cheered, but much to the man's disgust it was found that his followers were not carrying a sufficient number of guns to accomplish the sort of massacre he had in mind. Then somebody suggested they go to Seventh Street and burn Thomy Lafon school instead. Their leader indignantly demurred, saying that he "was willing to go 'coon hunting,' but would not stand for burning public property." But several mob members went ahead with the idea, especially after someone pointed out that the body of Sergeant Porteous was supposed to be arriving in the neighborhood for a wake about this time; the Negro school, it was declared, would make an appropriate "bonfire in his honor." Soon flames from the three-story wooden structure were visible over much of New Orleans. The firemen arrived too late. A witness insisted that four or five policemen in the vicinity saw the arsonists go to the building, but had made no effort to stop them.[43]

Fortunately, by the next morning, Saturday, July 28, the furious mob spirit among so many New Orleans whites appeared to be ebbing. The 1,500 special police volunteers who had saved the city from total anarchy earlier in the week remained on duty until Sunday morning; but after Friday night there was little for them to do. Property owners among the black and Creole of color population were said to be more gratified at Charles's death than were the whites, since their fear of racial retaliation had grown with each day he remained at large. Poorer blacks, on the other hand, were reportedly regretful only that he had not taken more policemen with him when he died. Among lower class blacks he became an immediate folk hero and "the Robert Charles song," praising his exploits, would occasionally be played at all-black gatherings for

43. Letter from the Reverend D. A. Graham, in Indianapolis *Freeman*, August 18, 1900; Kendall, *History of New Orleans*, II, 540; New Orleans *Daily Picayune*, July 28, August 10, 1900.

years to come. But "that song never did get very far," according to Jelly Roll Morton. "I once knew the Robert Charles song," Morton told Alan Lomax, "but I found out it was best for me to forget it and that I did in order to go along with the world on the peaceful side." [44]

The white daily newspapers of New Orleans, powerful shapers of public opinion, were rather at a loss to explain a black man who had acted with the kind of courageous defiance which it was assumed only white men could display. Charles was not enough of a mulatto to prompt even Major Hearsey to say that his bravery had come from Caucasian blood. The relatively liberal *Item* believed Robert's courage was born of despair and, like some of the other papers, implied that cocaine may have influenced his seeming disregard of death. The *Times-Democrat* had to admit its bewilderment at his marksmanship and his coolness under great stress, but was convinced that his simple Negro mind would never have thought of resistance toward the superior race unless inspired by northern propaganda. "He steeped his little brain in the poison," explained the *Times-Democrat*, "until his lawless lower centres were raw and inflamed." Of course, this paper hastily added, Charles "knew nothing of grievances or oppression until it was drummed into his head by the exaggerated and sentimental writers on the wrongs of the negroes." The *Picayune*, on the other hand, conceded that Charles was an extraordinarily brave and ferociously determined man, but suggested that his deeds were simply the exception which proved the rule that virtually all Negroes were cowards who could never match the fighting abilities of the white race. The *Picayune* insisted that "Robert Charles was the boldest, most desperate and dangerous negro ever known in Louisiana," and

44. *Report of the Operations of the Special Police Force,* in Mayor's Office Correspondence; New Orleans *Times-Democrat*, July 29–31, 1900; Brookhaven *Lincoln County Times*, August 2, 1900; Alan Lomax, *Mister Jelly Roll* (New York: Duell, Sloan and Pearce, 1950), 57.

assured itself and its readers that "there is not another negro in the State who can perform such acts under like circumstances."[45]

Major Hearsey's observations in the *States* on the personality of Robert Charles may have surprised some people. As an extreme Negrophobe of long standing, Hearsey might have been expected to attribute Robert's courage to cocaine, or insanity, or anything except manly qualities. Yet the image of anyone—even a black person—battling so resolutely against such hopeless odds irresistibly appealed to the major's strong romantic and medieval instincts. The day after Robert died, Hearsey confessed to his readers that even though Charles was colored, and despite the fact that he had killed and wounded so many white citizens and police, "[I] cannot help feeling for him a sort of admiration prompted by his wild and ferocious courage." In fact, wrote Major Hearsey, he could think of no instance in history where one person had resisted so many for so long. "Never before," the *States* informed its readers, "was such a display of desperate courage on the part of one man witnessed." Yet, as if suddenly remembering that Charles was not white, Hearsey added that the bravery he was saluting was not that of true manhood but "the courage of the brute the lion or the tiger."[46]

Robert Charles remained at the morgue from late Friday afternoon until shortly before daybreak on Sunday morning. His autopsy report listed thirty-four bullet holes in the torso alone, plus "three large openings undoubtedly due to volleys." Numerous other wounds were found in the arms and legs; the skull had been fractured and shattered "and almost beat to a pulp," wrote the coroner. His penis had been shot. Shortly after Robert's body arrived at the deadhouse (as many New Orleanians still called the morgue) one of the attendants attempted to mold the battered face back into some semblance of humanity, but with no great success. Various black

45. New Orleans *Daily Item*, July 25–28, 1900; New Orleans *Times-Democrat*, July 26, 30, 1900; New Orleans *Daily Picayune*, July 28, 1900.
46. New Orleans *Daily States*, July 28, 1900.

people who had known Charles, including Lenard Pierce, were brought in to identify the body; and because of the clothing and personal effects all made a positive identification except Annie Gant. Miss Gant's assertion that the body was that of Robert's "brother, Si[las] Jackson," was not, however, taken seriously; for she was visibly terror stricken and seemed to have the idea that if she identified the corpse as that of Charles the police would turn her over to the mob outside. All the other identifications were positive; his size and teeth matched descriptions, and the papers and clippings he had about him were concerned with racial wrongs and African emigration. A small-calibre wound about three or four days old was found on his leg, wrapped in green gauze. Some of the black people brought in told authorities that the dead man was also known as "Curtis Robertson."[47]

Friday evening and all day Saturday hundreds of curious white New Orleanians were admitted inside the morgue to view the body of the notorious "black fiend." One of those who filed by was in for quite a shock. Hyman Levy, after the clothing store on Poydras Street closed Friday night, went by the morgue "to take a look," he said, "at the desperate negro." Either Levy had not seen Robert's picture in the paper or — more likely — none of the drawings repro-

47. "Record of Inquests," Coroner's Office, July 27, 1900, p. 322; New York *Times*, July 28, 1900; New Orleans *Times-Democrat*, July 28–29, 1900; New Orleans *Daily Picayune*, July 28, 30, 1900. The *Daily Picayune*, on July 30, claimed to have found a Caroline Robertson living in New Orleans who said she was the mother of a "Curt" Robertson, who was presently in Mississippi and had no connection with Robert Charles. If so, it was simply a case of the alias used by Robert Charles being similar to the real name of another black man, for this Caroline Robertson was not Robert Charles's mother, and evidence from both white and black sources point to the fact that Robert Charles used the Curtis Robertson alias both in Mississippi and in New Orleans, when he first came to the city. Hyman Levy knew him as Curtis Robertson, and several of the black people arrested at the Saratoga Street neighborhood knew he had used that alias. Also, the old Storyville-era black musician Frank Amacker, who in 1974 was still living, recalled in an interview done for Tulane University, that Robert Charles had used the alias of Robertson. Interview with Frank Amacker, July 1, 1965, in William Ransom Hogan Jazz Archive, Tulane University.

duced in the dailies were close likenesses. As soon as he looked at the corpse Levy thought of his friend Curtis Robertson. The salesman then went to one of the morgue attendants and asked to see the clothing the murderer had been wearing. "I immediately recognized a blue serge double-breasted coat that I had sold him last February," Levy related. Talking to a reporter the next day, he said, "You could imagine my surprise when I [realized] it was Robertson, as I never for an instant thought that he was such a desperate scoundrel."[48]

48. Levy interview, New Orleans *Sunday States*, July 29, 1900.

10
AFTERSHOCKS

Robert was taken from the deadhouse in the predawn hours of Sunday, July 29. Knowing that there were many New Orleanians who would still like to capture his body and burn it—or slice it into souvenirs—the authorities took unusual precautions. A cordon of police and a squad of militia stood by as four black prisoners pushed the corpse down into an undersized pine box. The lid was then screwed on and the coffin lifted into a ramshackled wagon. The wagon proceeded slowly until it passed Parish Prison; then the horses were whipped into a trot for the remainder of the journey to Holt's Cemetery, the potter's field of the city. There was no ceremony of any kind. As the cloudbank in the eastern sky began to brighten, the last of the wet earth was shoveled atop the grave.'[1]

For months the exact location of Charles's grave was kept secret, the sexton being under strict instructions to tell no one the number that matched the tiny wooden headboard. A *Picayune* reporter, shown the site in December, wrote that "the body of the negro fiend lies buried about the middle of the cemetery . . . the grave is over-grown with rank weeds, a thistle being the most conspicuous." Today there is no marker at all; untended plots in Holt's Cemetery

1. New Orleans *Times-Democrat*, July 30, 1900; New Orleans *Daily Picayune*, July 30, 1900.

are used over and over again. Probably around 1910, perhaps earlier, Robert would have been disinterred, his coffin destroyed in the ugly brick incinerator to the rear of the cemetery, and his bones allowed to mingle with the soil. But at least New Orleans had spared the remains of Robert Charles—and itself—a far greater indignity. Shortly before Robert was buried, a carnival owner reportedly offered the city "a large price" for the cadaver; he proposed to pickle the disfigured remains in alcohol "and carry it around the country in an air-tight glass case and exhibit it as the body of the archfiend of the century."[2]

The tragedy of Robert Charles by no means ended with the eerie predawn burial in Holt's Cemetery. Aftershocks from his turbulent last five days of life ensued immediately, and continued for many months to come. The air of unreality surrounding what had happened was to some extent matched by reports of peculiar related events elsewhere. In Houston, Texas, the day after Charles's death, a black man was overheard talking about the affair and cursing the white race; he was shot dead by a white passerby. An elderly Chicago black, George Henry, whose mind must have been already unsettled, went to pieces upon hearing of the events in New Orleans and was observed praying for protection in the middle of a street; he said he was "afraid of snakes and white folks." In Battle Creek, Michigan, a Negro boxer named George Baker walked into the office of the chief of police and fired a pistol at the chief's head, but missed; Baker wanted to dramatize his sympathy for Robert Charles, about whom he had read in the papers. Several lynchings in Louisiana during the remaining months of 1900 reportedly had some relationship to the Charles affair. The most bizarre of such deaths was that of one Melby Dotson, black, who seems to have

2. New Orleans *Daily Picayune*, December 22, 1900; New Orleans *Daily Item*, July 29, 1900. Holt's Cemetery, off West Metairie Road, is still being used as a burial ground for the poor of New Orleans. For some reason it is commonly referred to as "Hope" Cemetery. *Soards' New Orleans City Directory for 1900*, XXVII, 1116.

fretted over the New Orleans riot and sometimes had alcoholic nightmares that he was being lynched. While riding on a train through West Baton Rouge Parish, Dotson dreamed a white mob was hanging him and he began shouting, struggling all the while with an imaginary rope around his neck. When the white conductor came down the aisle and demanded quiet, the befuddled Dotson shot him. Placed in jail at Port Allen, Dotson was dragged out the next day by a white mob and hanged from a telegraph pole.[3]

Late on the Sunday afternoon of September 2, Fred Clark, black, sat quietly on his doorstep at 1129 South Rampart Street. He was reading a book. Clark had long been known as an informer for the police, and it was he who had told Superintendent Gaster on July 27 about Robert Charles's possible whereabouts at Silas and Martha Jackson's dwelling. Lewis Forstall, black, lived across the street from Clark at 1118 South Rampart. Forstall, who had known and admired Robert Charles, was a brooding sort of person; he had been unable to put the terrible events of July out of his mind. Seeing Clark sitting there, knowing what he had done, Forstall lost his control. He walked up to the informer and without saying a word, pulled out a revolver, aimed it at Clark's head, and squeezed the trigger. Nothing happened. The weapon had misfired. Forstall squeezed again, and this time the neighborhood heard the loud crack of a bullet. Clark died within minutes.[4]

"TREMBLING WRETCHES ARRAIGNED IN COURT," headlined one of the New Orleans dailies on August 2, over an account of the appearance in criminal district court of nine black people who had been arrested since the previous Friday in the vicinity of the Saratoga Street bloodshed. Lenard Pierce, Charles's companion on the night of the Dryades Street trouble, had already been indicted

3. New Orleans *Times-Democrat*, July 29, October 18, 29, 1900; New Orleans *Daily Picayune*, July 31, 1900; New Orleans *Daily Item*, October 19, 1900.
4. New Orleans *Daily States*, September 3, 1900; New Orleans *Times-Democrat*, September 3, 1900.

on a charge of attempting to murder Sergeant Aucoin. But of the nine from Saratoga Street who were arraigned, one was no longer alive when the indictments were handed down two weeks later. John Willis, who had been mistaken for Robert Charles when he ran down Clio Street just after Porteous and Lally were shot, hanged himself in his cell at Parish Prison on the night of August 4. He had been the most visibly shaken of all those arrested, and when not being interrogated, had spent most of his time in prayer. The fact that Willis appeared to have more white ancestry than the other alleged accomplices of Charles was offered as further proof of the white belief that mulattoes were more suicide-prone than pure Africans.[5]

Even with Willis' death, the list of blacks indicted for supposed participation in Charles's crimes soon increased. For by the time Willis was found hanging in his cell, Burke Jackson had been arrested near Magnolia, Mississippi; and Imogene Nixon had been located by Copiah County authorities and taken back to New Orleans. Since Boss Nixon's white employer swore he was at work several blocks away during the time of the shooting, he was soon released.[6]

The grand jury indictments handed down August 16 charged the ten with first-degree murder. Silas Jackson, Martha Jackson, Charles Jackson, Albert Jackson, Burke Jackson, Annie Gant, George Ford, Imogene Nixon, William Blake, and Sidney Smith all stood accused of murdering Patrolman John Lally. All the Jacksons, as well as Annie Gant and Imogene Nixon, lived at 1208 Saratoga; Ford was the man visiting Mrs. Nixon and discovered later hiding under an upstairs bed in the annex. Blake and Sidney Smith merely

5. New Orleans *Daily Picayune,* August 2, 1900; New Orleans *Daily States,* August 5, 1900; New Orleans *Times-Democrat,* August 5, 1900.
6. New Orleans *Daily States,* August 3, 1900; letter from A. T. Townes, in New Orleans *Daily Picayune,* August 10, 1900.

lived on the same block with the Jacksons, and had the misfortune to be at home on the afternoon of July 27.[7]

There was not the least bit of evidence that any of the accused had participated in the murder of Officer Lally, or anybody else. A strong case could have been made against Silas, Martha, and Burke Jackson for harboring a criminal, and in all likelihood everybody who lived at the 1208 address was aware of Robert Charles's presence. Martha Jackson admitted that she had allowed Robert to come in and gave him a place to hide, but she insisted that her husband did not know of his presence in the house; Silas heartily agreed with this contention. Mrs. Jackson claimed, however, that Charles had only been there since 4 A.M. of Friday morning, the twenty-seventh. And about this she probably lied. Charles, wounded and weak from loss of blood and carrying a rifle, must have gone to the Saratoga Street address no later than the early morning hours of the twenty-fourth, shortly after he left the yellow house on Fourth Street.[8]

White New Orleans—at least the more vocal and influential whites—wanted all these people charged with first-degree murder, despite the lack of evidence for such an accusation; this demand was probably inevitable, considering the fearful, race-centered emotional atmosphere of the time. For one thing, many if not most local whites assumed that Robert Charles was part of some mysterious antiwhite conspiracy; Major Hearsey was by no means alone in supposing that Charles was planning "to stir up a sort of servile war." Holding Charles's friends on a capital offense might eventually break some of them down and squeeze out the truth. In the months that followed all ten, together with Lenard Pierce, would be interrogated repeatedly at Parish Prison. But each continued to tell the

7. "Indictment No. 30,086. For Willful Murder. A True Bill, August 16, 1900," Criminal District Court, Parish of Orleans, Louisiana.

8. New Orleans *Times-Democrat*, July 28, August 2, 1900.

same simple story: that Charles had sought refuge at 1208 Saratoga no earlier than 4 A.M. the morning of the shootout; that Martha Jackson alone had known of his presence that day; and that she had given the killer sanctuary not out of sympathy but out of mortal fear that his violent nature would be turned against her if she tried to refuse him. Sheriff Klock became convinced that Lenard Pierce was now their leader and had drilled them all in this unvarying answer. Their apparent simplicity (most of the prisoners claimed to be illiterate) was interpreted as a mask to deceive the white world. "On the surface," explained the *Item*, "they are innocent, ignorant negroes, but in fact they are wise."[9]

The prisoners also served as surrogate Robert Charleses. True, he had been killed and his body mutilated, but before he died he had shot nearly thirty white people. The racial balance sheet was not yet settled. Consciously or unconsciously, white New Orleans seemed to say that the maintenance of white supremacy demanded that additional Negroes suffer for his deeds. And the blacks who were killed and wounded in the riots had not provided a compensatory total. The desire for racial retribution took little note, at least for the time being, of individual innocence or guilt.

Creoles of color and the more prosperous blacks of New Orleans, for their part, seemed content to let Charles's associates suffer. Indeed, the prisoners from Saratoga Street, along with Pierce, were scathingly denounced by many of their fellow Negroes, and for an obvious reason. There was great fear, in the days following the July violence, that the lives and property of upper- and middle-class people of African descent might be forfeited in New Orleans if white rage were not appeased by lesser victims. Open talk could be heard among more than a few whites about plans to burn Straight and Dillard universities (those "nigger schools"), along with the better black homes and churches. In the immediate aftermath of

9. New Orleans *Daily States*, July 28, 1900; New Orleans *Daily Item*, October 21, 1900.

the Charles affair, Major Hearsey and others spoke of the possibility of a war of extermination; the *States* predicted that New Orleans was close to becoming "a negro Golgotha." Other reports circulated of determined, sober white men making such statements as: "It may not be tonight, it may not be next week or even in a month, but the time will come when a thousand niggers will die for each white man that has been killed." [10]

Although no legitimate case of first-degree murder could be made against any of the indicted blacks, there were certain white men, known by name and identified by witnesses, who had slain unoffending black people during the rioting of July 25 and 26. The police had made no arrests at the time, but during the following week several witnesses—most of them white—testified before the grand jury that they had seen individuals whom they knew by name commit acts of murder. As a result nine white men—Joe Wagner, Robert Brittnacker, Willie Brittnacker, John Emberger, Conrad Schwartz, John Schwartz, Michael Biri, George Flanagan, and Mike Foley—were all indicted for first-degree murder by the August, 1900, session of the Orleans Parish Grand Jury. [11]

Like Lenard Pierce and the ten accused blacks from Saratoga Street, these alleged murderers were denied bail and kept in Parish Prison while awaiting trial. Two other whites were indicted on a riot-connected charge of unlawful assembly: S. M. Cowen, the mayor pro tempore of Kenner; and Ernest F. Carl, who was accused of being the one-legged man who tried to instigate mass murder along South Rampart and Fourth Streets on the night of July 27.

10. See statements of New Orleans black ministers in New Orleans *Southwestern Presbyterian*, August 9, 1900; letter from the Reverend D. A. Graham in Indianapolis *Freeman*, August 18, 1900; New Orleans *Daily States*, August 7, 17, 1900; New Orleans *Daily Item*, July 28–29, 1900.
11. *State of Louisiana* v. *Michael Biri*, Case No. 30,059; *State of Louisiana* v. *Conrad Schwartz and John Schwartz*, Case No. 30,061; *State of Louisiana* v. *George Flanagan and Mike Foley*, Case No. 30,062; *State of Louisiana* v. *Joe Wagner, Robert Brittnacker, Willie Brittnacker, John Emberger*, Case No. 30,074 all in Criminal District Court, Parish of Orleans, Louisiana.

Generally, the more prominent white New Orleanians seemed to approve of these indictments also, although Major Hearsey (who did not deny the men's guilt) complained that Negroes would construe the prosecution of the rioters as an act of white weakness. The major believed that the city's blacks were jubilantly making such statements as: "When some of dem is hung, we won't be pestered anymore." [12] Hearsey frankly disliked the idea of blacks being free of the fear of white hoodlums.

Yet the first people actually found guilty of anything associated with the Robert Charles affair, outside of those jailed or fined for disturbing the peace, were the five policemen who had failed to kill or capture the black man on that night at the yellow house. Sergeant Aucoin, Corporal Trenchard, Corporal Perrier, Patrolman Pincon, and Supernumerary Cantrelle were not, of course, accused of a felony. But it might have been better for them if they had. The charge was cowardice, and on August 8 the Board of Police Commissioners began hearing their cases. Public opinion seemed to demand that Corporal Trenchard be tried first. [13]

In reading the statements made about Corporal Trenchard, the conclusion is unavoidable that he was, to some degree, made a scapegoat not only for the NOPD but for the brutishness that so many whites had demonstrated on Saratoga Street following the death of Robert Charles. Trenchard was not a likable man anyway, and as if by mutual consent he became a favorite target for the daily newspapers. The *Item* ran a savage cartoon showing him hiding in the yellow house, and the fact that he had fired his shotgun into Charles's dead body was acidly commented upon by all the papers.

12. *State of Louisiana* v. *S. M. Cowen*, No. 30, 033; *State of Louisiana* v. *Ernest F. Carl*, Case No. 30,076, both in Criminal District Court, Parish of Orleans, Louisiana; New Orleans *Daily States*, August 26, 1900.

13. Board of Police Commissioners to Mayor Paul Capdevielle, August 7, 1900, in Mayor's Office Correspondence; Superintendent of Police D. S. Gaster to All Stations, undated, *ibid.*; *Annual Report of Board of Police Commissioners, 1900*, pp. 24–25.

In defending himself before the police board, the hapless corporal did, however, make one telling statement. He pointed out that "it took 10,000 men, and a loss of four killed and a number wounded, and then they had to set the house afire in order to get Charles, and that in broad daylight." How, then, could he be expected to take such a creature in the dark with a pistol that did not work?[14]

But Corporal Trenchard was found guilty of cowardice and dismissed from the force. So, later, were Aucoin, Perrier, Pincon, and Cantrelle. All appealed their cases but without success. Of the five, only Trenchard ever made it back on the force; he was appointed a sergeant in 1905, but he was dismissed from the force again, and for the last time, in 1907. The final listing of his name in *Soards' New Orleans City Directory* came in the 1918 edition; his occupation was then "collector" of overdue bills.[15]

Of the five policemen dismissed, old Jules Aucoin fought the hardest to have his name cleared. He took his case up to the Louisiana Supreme Court, in a legal struggle that dragged out until 1903. Eventually Aucoin gave up.[16] Perhaps it never occurred to Aucoin or Trenchard or any of the other officers branded as cowards that they, too, were at least in part the victims of racism. White New Orleans scorned and punished them because they had let a Negro get the best of them.

Robert Charles's deadly aim created difficulties of a less serious nature for Bishop Henry M. Turner of Atlanta and Daniel J. Flummer of Birmingham. Both Turner and Flummer had reason to be concerned, temporarily, that what had transpired in New Orleans

14. New Orleans *Daily Item*, July 29, August 2, 1900; New Orleans *Daily States*, August 9, 1900.

15. *Annual Report of Board of Police Commissioners, 1900*, pp. 24–25; *ibid.*, *1905*, p. 39; *ibid.*, *1907*, pp. 10–11; *Soards' New Orleans City Directory for 1918*, XLV, 1238.

16. New Orleans *Daily Picayune*, February 12, 1903. See also Casper A. Pincon to Board of Police Commissioners, October 15, 1900, in Letterbox File 107, Department of Police and Public Buildings, City Archives Department, New Orleans Public Library.

might enmesh them in legal or personal difficulties, since Robert's association with the *Voice of Missions* and the International Migration Society was indignantly proclaimed by the New Orleans press and was at least briefly mentioned by newspapers across the South. The *States* decided that Bishop Turner was "the one man most responsible for the exaggeration of the murderer's already fiendish disposition toward the whites." *Harlequin* magazine urged Alabama authorities to look into Flummer's activities and also suggested that he be tarred and feathered; in Turner's hometown the Atlanta *Journal* claimed that the bishop had "inspired" Charles to shoot all those whites in New Orleans.[17]

But the outcry against the black bishop and the white promoter had no serious results; after all, neither of them lived in Louisiana and Charles had done nothing in Alabama or Georgia. Nor was there anything illegal or revolutionary about Turner's magazine or Flummer's Liberia literature. For his part, Turner maintained that he had never directly communicated with Robert Charles, nor did he sympathize with Charles's acts of violence. Flummer, interviewed by a *Times-Democrat* reporter who went to Birmingham to see him, was circumspect indeed when the subject of Robert Charles came up.[18] But it may be assumed that both Turner and Flummer made a mental note that it would be best not to visit New Orleans anytime in the near future.

Presently those in New Orleans who preferred to blame the city's racial turmoil on outside agitators discovered a more inviting target than either Turner or Flummer. Twenty-five-year-old Lillian

17. *Harlequin*, II (August 11, 1900), 3; New Orleans *Daily States*, quoted in Natchez *Daily Democrat*, July 28, 1900; Atlanta *Journal*, July 27, 1900. The Atlanta *Constitution*, which thought well of Bishop Turner, gave extensive coverage to the shootings in New Orleans but made no mention of the Bishop's connection with Robert Charles.

18. "Robert Charles," *Voice of Missions*, VIII (September 1, 1900), 2; New Orleans *Times-Democrat*, August 4, 1900. See also, *Voice of Missions*, VIII (October 1, 1900), 2.

C. Jewett of Boston was never near New Orleans and had no connection whatsoever with Robert Charles; but as a sensitive and activist-minded young person she was horrified by reading of the events of late July in the Louisiana city and she resolved to do something about it. She was already active in an organization called the Anti-Lynching League. On the night of the twenty-seventh, a few hours after Charles's death, Miss Jewett presided over a racially mixed gathering which met to protest the treatment of blacks in New Orleans and to raise money for the families of those who had been killed or injured by the mob.[19]

But as initially reported in the southern—especially Louisiana—press, Miss Jewett's gathering took on the character of a latter-day John Brown's frenzy. "INSANE RAVINGS AT A BOSTON NEGRO MEETING," the *Picayune* headlined its account of the affair. Apparently some of the black speakers at the Boston rally did have words of praise for Robert Charles ("If one negro can hold 20,000 at bay what can 10,000 negroes do?") and threatened bloody retribution for the mob murders; but Miss Jewett herself did not talk of violence. Nevertheless, reports reaching New Orleans insisted she was planning to act as a "Joan of Arc of the Negroes" and lead 1,000—or perhaps it was 3,000, or 10,000—armed northern blacks to liberate their oppressed brothers and sisters in Louisiana. This absurd story made headlines across the South; the Natchez *Democrat* solemnly announced that Miss Jewett has "declared war on New Orleans." The sensation that the Boston gathering created led to the rapid expansion of a recently founded organization in New Orleans called the Green Turtle Club.[20]

The Green Turtle Club, made up of young New Orleans white men of good families, had been founded the year before but its

19. New Orleans *Daily Picayune*, August 1, 6, 1900; "Joan of Arc Jewett and Hysteria," *Harlequin*, II (August 4, 1900), 2.
20. Natchez *Daily Democrat*, August 7, 1900; New Orleans *Daily Picayune*, August 1, 5, 6, 16, 1900; New Orleans *Sunday States*, August 26, 1900.

membership remained low until early August of 1900. Its members
took a special oath of allegiance to white supremacy and the Democratic party. Reading of Miss Jewett's Boston rally, the Green
Turtles sent word to her that they were posting a standing offer of
$1,000 for her scalp, and as an afterthought informed her that they
planned to act as a reception committee when she and her "stalwart
coons" approached the city limits of New Orleans. Later, the Green
Turtles were reported as preparing to ship a casket to her in Massachusetts, accompanied by six pallbearers.[21]

Miss Jewett's family became alarmed over these announce-
ments, which some of the Green Turtles later insisted were more
"jocular" than serious. Predictably, the young woman and her
relatives were also upset by an avalanche of hate mail from Louisiana, much of it obscene and some of it urging her not to disappoint
them by failing to come down with her "army." One letter signed
"the mob" pleaded, "We are almost dying for niggers' blood."
Apparently in order to encourage more correspondence for her, one
of the New Orleans dailies gave their readers Miss Jewett's street
address in Boston.[22]

Two lawyers from Boston, hired by the Jewetts, came down by
train in mid-August to investigate the possibility of taking legal
action against the Green Turtles. Everyone in New Orleans seemed
to know of their presence, and business, almost as soon as they
arrived. The lawyers behaved as if ill at ease and they did not remain
long, especially after being subjected to what was termed "unsavory
talk" in a restaurant. They drove by the Green Turtle headquarters
but decided not to stop and enter, which was just as well; several of
the members were waiting inside, hopefully, with fifty feet of rope
and two large iron rings. On returning to Boston, the lawyers

21. New Orleans *Daily Picayune*, August 5, 16, 1900; Port Gibson *Reveille*,
August 23, 1900; Boston *Morning Journal*, August 17, 1900.
22. Boston *Morning Journal*, August 17, 1900; New Orleans *Daily Picayune*,
August 5, 1900; New Orleans *Daily Item*, August 14, 1900.

reported to the Jewett family that prosecution would be fruitless, since no Louisiana jury would convict the club's members for their threats on Lillian's life. But for the Green Turtles, the publicity generated because of Miss Jewett and her Boston lawyers meant unexpected growth and something approaching hero worship of its membership. Applications poured in from white men wishing to join the organization. Offers of military assistance came from various parts of Louisiana, Mississippi, and Alabama. But Miss Jewett proved, finally, to be something of a disappointment; neither she nor her mythical army ever approached New Orleans. The young Bostonian did make one brief trip into the South in September, announcing her intention to "teach [white and black] how to live together." But she got no further than Richmond, Virginia, where she was informed that unless she left immediately, "she might have a very unpleasant experience."[23] In New Orleans, Miss Jewett was soon all but forgotten and the Green Turtle Club settled once more into obscurity.

The Jewett imbroglio simply offered a vivid illustration of how close the South still was, in 1900, to the antebellum condition of mind. Old prewar fears of black insurrection inspired by northern meddlers could be brought to life in an instant by nothing more than the harmless activities of a naive Boston girl. Major Hearsey, who was still angry at William Lloyd Garrison, predictably took the most militant stance against this latest intrusion by a northern busybody. He realized Miss Jewett posed no real "invasion" threat, but he was fearful that southern blacks might derive courage from hearing about her alleged offer of military assistance. "This, " wrote Hearsey, "is the menace of the Charles episode to our peace. The ferocious negro in himself amounted to nothing." It also dawned upon the major that nothing further should be said or written about

23. New Orleans *Daily Item*, August 14, 1900; New Orleans *Daily Picayune*, August 16, 1900; Rayville (La.) *Richland Beacon-News*, August 4, 1900; Boston *Sunday Journal*, September 16, 1900.

Robert Charles, because "if the wild and heroic stories of his bloody triumphs are continued, some Yankee scoundrel will write his life and depict him as the negro Coeur de Lion... to inflame the imitative ambitions of others of his kind."[24]

But in October of 1900 Robert Charles once again became news, and the eyewitness accounts of his last moments of life were quoted yet another time in column after column of the local newspapers. For the time had come to settle the disputed claim for the 250-dollar "dead or alive" reward the city of New Orleans had placed upon Robert's head. There were three serious claimants and their palpable eagerness for this blood money disgusted some observers. Charles A. Noiret, the young medical student, was supported by the more impressive witnesses, but Adolph Anderson, a member of the state militia, had the vocal backing of others who were at the Saratoga Street tragedy. The least-supported claim was that of John Banville, a bailiff in City Court. Mayor Capdevielle finally submitted the matter to a special board of arbitration. Each claimant testified that the honor of killing Charles outweighed monetary considerations.[25] On October 10, a few days before the decision, the *Times-Democrat* thought that the controversy called for a parody of the "Cock Robin" nursery rhyme:

> Who killed Cock Robert?
> "I," said the physician;
> "I took my position
> And shot through his heart as he loped from his lair,
> He promptly expired, and I stamp each edition
> Of different yarns as a fake and a snare!
> I killed Cock Robert!"
>
> Who killed Cock Robert?
> "I," said the bailiff;

24. New Orleans *Daily States*, August 7, 1900.
25. New Orleans *Daily Item*, October 10, 1900; "Report of the Operations of the Special Police Force," Mayor's Office Correspondence; New Orleans *Daily Picayune*, October 16, 1900; New Orleans *Times-Picayune*, December 3, 1922.

"Just put me in jail if
The tale I relate to you now isn't so.
'Twas a detail of riot and done on the quiet;
I only recalled it a few days ago!
I killed Cock Robert!"

Who killed Cock Robert?
"I," said the private;
"Were Robert alive, it
Is certain he'd gladly indorse what I state;
I strolled in and got him,
They'd doubtless forgot him,
For they all were engaged in a silver debate!
I killed Cock Robert!"

Who Killed Cock Robert?
"I think," said the cynic,
"A search at the clinic
Would have shown as clearly as two twos make four,
That these gents are in error;
Cock Robert, the terror,
Was sun-struck, for sure, as he came through the door!
That killed Cock Robert."[26]

The board of arbitration, meeting in the mayor's parlor on the evening of October 15, judged in favor of Charles Noiret. The young man soon afterward left New Orleans and remained away several years, apparently completing his medical education elsewhere. For he reappeared in the city directory in 1906, listed as a physician. Dr. Noiret set up his medical practice at 908 St. Charles Avenue. In addition to the reward money, he was allowed to have the Winchester with which he had slain Robert Charles.[27]

Final decisions concerning the ten blacks and nine whites who were indicted for first-degree murder following the violence in July took somewhat longer. The first of the accused murderers to go on

26. New Orleans *Times-Democrat*, October 10, 1900.
27. *Ibid.*; *Soards's New Orleans City Directory for 1906*, XXXIII, 726; Hughes to Wood, August 2, 1900, in Mayor's Office Correspondence.

trial were Michael Biri, George Flanagan, and Mike Foley, three young men accused of killing unarmed blacks during the rioting. The Biri case resulted in a hung jury; and in the midst of Flanagan and Foley's trial the state abandoned the case because of confused testimony by the key prosecution witness. The indictment against Biri was finally *nol prossed* in December of 1902.[28]

Silas, Martha, and Charles Jackson went on trial for murder in May of 1901, almost a year after the siege at their residence on Saratoga Street. The seven other blacks had been granted a severance from the trial of Silas, his wife, and brother; and it was assumed that the trial of the others would follow quickly if a conviction were obtained in this one. However, at the close of testimony Judge F. D. Chretein directed a verdict of acquittal for Martha and Charles Jackson; the jury then retired and brought in an odd decision that Silas Jackson was guilty of manslaughter. Judge Chretein reversed this verdict and chided the jury for its apparent ignorance of the law and the rules of evidence. "If Jackson was guilty at all," concluded the Judge, "it was as an aider and abettor."[29]

Having failed to convict these three, the state abandoned its murder charge against the other Jacksons, as well as that against Annie Gant, George Ford, William Blake, Imogene Nixon, and Sidney Smith. However, all of them—including Silas, Martha, and Charles Jackson—still had over their heads an indictment for harboring a felon, and this charged remained. But all were released on bond in May of 1901, and the lesser charge against each of them was eventually *nol-prossed* in May of 1902.[30] By this time most if not all of these former residents of Saratoga Street had probably left New Orleans for good.

28. *Louisiana* v. *Michael Biri*, No. 30,059; *Louisiana* v. *George Flanagan and Mike Foley*, No. 30,062.

29. *Louisiana* v. *Silas Jackson et al.*, No. 30,085.

30. "Indictment No. 30,082. For Harboring and Assisting After Murder, etc. A True Bill, August 8, 1900," Criminal District Court, Parish of Orleans, Louisiana; New Orleans *Daily Picayune*, June 7, 1901.

In June of 1901 the last of Charles's indicted associates walked out of Parish Prison. Lenard Pierce, who was accused of attempting to murder Sergeant Aucoin, was released on bond; his case had been set for trial several times, but for one reason or another Aucoin had always been unable to appear. Patrolman Mora always maintained that Pierce was innocent. The charge against Pierce was later dropped and he too probably departed New Orleans soon after his release.[31]

As if it were unfair to prosecute whites accused of murder after the blacks had been released, the district attorney's office, within days after the Jackson trial, dropped murder charges against the remaining white defendants in the riot cases—with the exception of the Biri indictment, which was not abandoned until late 1902. The cases of S. M. Cowen and Ernest F. Carl, accused of unlawful assembly, were never brought to trial; and charges against them were finally *nol-prossed* in November of 1904. With this, the last outstanding charges relating to Robert Charles and the riot had been abandoned. And only one individual was still in confinement, doing time for the sole felony conviction stemming from the Charles affair. Early in 1902 Lewis Forstall, who had killed the informer Fred Clark, was convicted of manslaughter and sentenced to seven years' hard labor in the Louisiana penitentiary by Judge Chretein.[32]

"It all seems like a dream," one New Orleans writer suggested, as he looked back on the Robert Charles troubles and attempted to extract some meaning from what had happened. He found none; the feeling of unreality was too strong. Yet there were many people, white and black, to whom the tragedy had been as real as midsummer heat. The wives and children of the slain policemen; the

31. "Indictment No. 30, 060. For Assault by Willfully Shooting at With Intent to Murder. A True Bill, August 8, 1900," Criminal District Court, Parish of Orleans, Louisiana.

32. *Louisiana* v. *S. M. Cowen*, No. 30,033; *Louisiana* v. *Ernest F. Carl*, No. 30, 076; New Orleans *Daily Picayune*, May 22–23, 1901; New Orleans *Daily States*, February 26, March 4, 1902.

families of the mob victims; the black men and women who spent almost a year in the loathsome Orleans Parish Prison charged with a murder none of them had committed; the policemen branded as cowards—they all remembered, and many nursed their bitterness. Some still hated Robert Charles, and hatred toward a dead man can take strange forms. A few days after the first anniversary of Robert's death, an unknown person went to the abandoned, bullet-marked annex of 1208 Saratoga and poured kerosene into the closet where the black fugitive had hidden. The building was quickly ablaze. But, as had happened the year before, a fire engine arrived and this place that nobody had lived in since that terrible day was once again saved.[33]

33. New Orleans *Times-Democrat*, August 3, 1901.

BIBLIOGRAPHICAL
ESSAY
Exploring the life of an obscure black man who has been dead for seventy-five years is no light task, as I quickly discovered when my research commenced on Robert Charles. All his personal papers and belongings (including composition books filled with his writings) were hauled away by souvenir hunters and apparently lost forever around the time he was killed. Only one letter of his survives—a brief note reprinted in a 1900 pamphlet. He left no wife or children to remember him, and the relatives and friends he did have were understandably not motivated toward leaving recollections about him for future historians. He has no known kin in Mississippi or Louisiana today. I lament the absence of these traditional sources, but I am also aware that if they existed—particularly if his personal writings had been saved—a book probably would have been written about him long before now.

Nevertheless, solid evidence does survive which allowed me to trace the odyssey of Robert Charles from his childhood in a Mississippi share-cropper's cabin to his fiery death in New Orleans. I had to begin at the ending. Most extant sources for the years (1865–1900) and locale (Mississippi and Louisiana) of Charles's life were written by whites, and Charles attracted little notice from white people until the last week of his life. Then, when he began shooting New Orleans policemen and other whites, the press of Louisiana and Mississippi became absorbedly concerned with him.

Only those sources which were of special significance in my search for the life and milieu of Robert Charles are cited in this bibliography. The footnotes accompanying the text show other sources used as evidence for particular statements, but neither the bibliographical essay nor the footnotes list all the primary or secondary materials that were consulted.

NEW ORLEANS

Of all the sources researched, New Orleans newspapers, though often slanted and unreliable, were still the most indispensable. From July 24 through July 28, 1900, the city's four leading dailies — the *Times-Democrat*, the *Picayune*, the *States*, and the *Item* — each published page after page concerning Robert Charles and the police search for him. These papers, especially through their interviews of black and white eyewitnesses to the tragic events of that week, provided most of the basic information about the final days of Robert Charles and the race riot which occurred in the midst of the manhunt for him. Reporters for the New Orleans dailies, though extremely biased against the "black fiend" whose death they avidly anticipated, nevertheless wrote detailed narratives that permit a more objective retelling of what actually happened. The files of the aforementioned newspapers were also carefully searched for the three-year period 1899–1901 (and were examined on particular dates earlier in the 1890s and later in the 1900s) for additional information about those blacks and whites whose paths crossed that of Robert Charles. A superbly edited New Orleans magazine, *Harlequin*, which began publication in 1899, contained many articles that dealt with race relations in the city, particularly during and after the racial crisis triggered by Charles's activities in the summer of 1900.

The only black New Orleans publication of that period whose files have survived, the religiously oriented (Methodist) weekly *Southwestern Christian Advocate*, was not informative about Robert Charles but did provide helpful insights into black life and attitudes in the city. Other black newspapers across the nation became keenly interested in the Charles affair and commented on it extensively. The most valuable of such journals was the Indianapolis *Freeman*, for the reason that it published a lengthly letter from a New Orleans black minister, Reverend D. A. Graham, in which Charles's difficulties and the race riot were perceptively discussed. Another black publication of special usefulness was *Voice of Missions*, a magazine published in Atlanta by Bishop Henry M. Turner of the African Methodist Episcopal Church. It was this journal that Charles peddled in New Orleans in 1899–1900, because Turner's emigrationist philosophy agreed with his own.

Various newspapers outside Louisiana, along with nationally circulated magazines, were searched for stories and commentaries about Charles's last week of life and the attendant race riot. Little additional information was provided by these publications distant from the scene; however, national coverage of the events was rather extensive, and several newspapers in other cities subsequently published letters from New Orleanians that did shed more light on the tragedy in the Crescent City. The most useful non-Louisiana papers were the New York *Times*, the Boston *Morning Journal*, the Atlanta *Constitution*, the Chicago *Tribune*, and the Vicksburg *Daily Herald*. Of the national periodicals, *Outlook* and *Independent* deserve special mention.

Essential though the local dailies were in providing details about Charles and the riot, there were other primary sources that contained information and opinions not available to the press. The City Archives Department of the New Orleans Public Library has many letters and official reports about the riot—and police matters generally—filed in the Mayor's Office Correspondence of Mayor Paul Capdevielle. The Louisiana Division of the New Orleans Public Library also has the following sources which were of great value: the "Record of Inquests" of the Coroner's Office, Parish of Orleans; printed *Annual Reports* (1889–1900) of the Board of Police Commissioners and the Superintendent of Police of the City of New Orleans; and letterbox files of the Department of Police and Public Buildings. The New Orleans Police Department's central records and identification section has on microfilm the "Reports of Arrests" of the city's precincts of 1900, and these records were made available to me. For the legal proceedings against the blacks who were alleged to be Charles's accomplices, and against the whites accused of murder or inciting to riot in the racial violence, it was necessary to disrupt the dusty repose of the 1900–1904 case files located in the attic of the Criminal District Court of the Parish of Orleans. (These files constitute the only source about the final disposition of some indictments, since by 1902 the local press seemingly lost interest in the persons involved in the Charles troubles.)

No graduate thesis or dissertation has ever been written about Charles, although there is one fairly good thesis on the race riot, and in it there is some material concerning Charles that was excerpted from the local press. This study by Parkash Kaur Bains, "The New Orleans Race Riot of 1900" (M.A. thesis, Louisiana State University in New Orleans, 1970) was intriguing because it offered the perspective of a graduate student from Asia upon an American racial conflict.

Few secondary sources mention Robert Charles at all, and none have attempted to examine his life prior to those final days in New Orleans.

However, Edwin S. Redkey's *Black Exodus: Black Nationalist and Back-to-Africa Movements, 1890–1910* (New Haven: Yale University Press, 1969) contains four pages summarizing the events leading to Charles's death. For my purposes, Redkey's book was useful because of his able presentation of black emigrationist thought around the turn of the century, and because of his judicious treatment of the International Migration Society that Charles was associated with. Only two other books have anything more than a passing reference to Charles. Of these, the most valuable to me was a modern reprint of the collected writings of Ida B. Wells-Barnett. In the autumn of 1900 Mrs. Wells-Barnett, a black woman who was an outspoken foe of racial injustice, published in Chicago a pamphlet titled *Mob Rule in New Orleans,* which described the riot and contained accurate speculations that Charles was no "desperado" after all, but a basically decent black workingman who had simply tried to protect his sense of dignity, and his life. This pamphlet is now available as the latter portion of a book titled *On Lynchings,* with a preface by August Meier (New York: Arno Press, 1969). Apparently, Mrs. Wells-Barnett tried to obtain information on Charles's background, but was unsuccessful.

Less revealing, among the three books that give Robert Charles something more than brief mention, is John Smith Kendall's *History of New Orleans* (3 vols.; Chicago: Lewis Publishing Company, 1922). Kendall discusses Charles's troubles on several pages in Volume II; unfortunately, what he provides is little more than a garbled rehash of some of the less-reliable stories that appeared in the *Picayune* issues of late July, 1900.

A large number of books and articles—both contemporaneous accounts and writings by modern scholars—were beneficial in providing background information on black life and race relations in New Orleans. By far the most insightful—although the book ends with 1880—was John W. Blassingame's *Black New Orleans* (Chicago: University of Chicago Press, 1973). I should also note my indebtedness to an article which surveys racial problems in the city during the late nineteenth century: Dale A. Somers, "Black and White in New Orleans: A Study in Urban Race Relations, 1865–1900," *Journal of Southern History,* XL (February, 1974), 19–42. Somers concluded that for New Orleans, the violence touched off by Charles's confrontation with the police "in effect established the pattern for Negro-white relations for the next half century."

MISSISSIPPI

Robert Charles spent all but the last six years of his existence in Mississippi, but the search for him there had to begin with clues provided by incidental information about the end of his life in New Orleans. That he had come to New Orleans from somewhere in Mississippi was agreed upon by the white press, the police, and the blacks who knew him; but precisely where he was from, and for how long he had been in the city, was a matter of much confusion.

After weighing all the reports and speculations about his background that circulated in New Orleans at the time of his death, and adding to these the various accounts that appeared in Mississippi newspapers during this time, I concluded that Robert Charles had been born and had grown up within a three-county area near Jackson, Mississippi: either Hinds, Claiborne, or Copiah County. The best indicators, I thought, pointed to the northwestern portion of Copiah County as the place where Charles had spent his childhood years. With the help of James H. Stone, who was then with the Department of Archives and History of the State of Mississippi, Robert Charles was found—at age fourteen—in the manuscript returns of the United States Tenth Census (1880); he was a sharecropper's son living in northwestern Copiah. Once the fact was established—and the possibility of other black Robert Charleses in that three-county area eliminated by a careful search of the census—it was not too difficult to gather additional information about the family he grew up in. Along with the data provided about the members of the Charles family in the Population Returns of the 1880 census, the agricultural reports in the same manuscript census gave an exact picture of the economic status of this sharecropper family and allowed comparison with the condition of their neighbors. (However, the 1880 census information could not be followed up by reports in the next census, since the 1890 manuscripts for Mississippi were destroyed by fire years ago.) The "Assessment of Personal Property and Polls" for Copiah County during the 1880s, on microfilm in the Mississippi Department of Archives and History (hereinafter referred to as MDAH) was notably useful in providing data on Robert Charles's parents and older brothers.

Reports from New Orleans and from Mississippi at the time of Charles's notoriety in 1900 indicated that as a young man he had spent several years in Vicksburg, possibly as an employee of the LNO & T Railroad. This was confirmed by the Warren County Assessment of Personal Property and Polls in Vicksburg for the period, which are on microfilm in the MDAH.

That Robert Charles had once been in some kind of serious trouble in the vicinity of Rolling Fork, Mississippi (in the Delta region about forty miles to the north of Vicksburg) was a repeated assertion of both the New Orleans press and Vicksburg's chief of police at the time of the manhunt for Charles in 1900. The murder of a railroad brakeman was the "trouble" ascribed to him at Rolling Fork, and 1892 was the year most often mentioned as the time of the deed, although other accounts pointed to 1890, 1894, or 1898. A thorough search of all available Mississippi dailies for each of those years yielded nothing. When I went to Rolling Fork to try to discover the truth of the matter, I was dismayed to learn that the sheriff's records of that period for Sharkey County (Rolling Fork) no longer exist. Luckily, however, the only extant volume of the Rolling Fork newspaper, the *Deer Creek Pilot*, prior to 1900 is that of 1891–1892. The May 28, 1892, issue of that paper carried a story which explained clearly (see Chapter 3) the difficulty that Robert and his brother Henry Charles had with a white flagman (not a brakeman) on a train at Rolling Fork. This account also allowed me to understand why Robert presently went back to Copiah County under the assumed name of Curtis Robertson. Blacks who knew him later in New Orleans—as well as one white man, Hyman Levy—were aware that he called himself Curtis Robertson, but until I read that issue of the *Deer Creek Pilot* I was not sure why he temporarily changed his name.

The encounter with the law that "Curtis Robertson" subsequently had (1894–1896) in Copiah County, which was unrelated to his Rolling Fork difficulty, is inscribed in legal language in the Minutes, Circuit Court, Copiah County, Letterbook W (Copiah County Courthouse, Hazlehurst, Mississippi). No other sources for that two-year period of his life are extant, with the exception of subsequent references in the New Orleans press that indicate he came to the city during that time, using that alias, and became involved in back-to-Africa activities.

No Mississippi newspapers that have survived, and probably none ever, published any information about Robert Charles during the twenty-eight years he lived in that state—with the exception of that one article in the *Deer Creek Pilot* of 1892. But the very lack of evidence about him is, in its own way, evidence that he tended to be a peaceable man who avoided trouble with the whites. When Charles finally achieved untoward publicity in New Orleans there were, of course, stories about him in the Mississippi press—most notably, some statements from black people who had once known him. These reports were helpful in confirming where he had lived prior to 1894, but were otherwise of little worth because the blacks who were interviewed naturally wanted to avoid any suspicion of friendship or sympathy with Robert Charles.

Even so, the extant newspapers published in the places where Charles had lived in Mississippi from 1865 to 1894 were of enormous value to me; their detailed information on race relations, politics, and the social life of whites and blacks helped me to recreate the milieu in which Charles had existed—and thus I was able to reconstruct, at least in part, Charles's life through a description of his environment. All of these papers were white and many were sulfurously racist; yet by a discriminating use of their news stories and commentaries they permit a partial illumination of black life in Mississippi, and they certainly portray the racial climate that blacks had to live under. Fortunately, the files of most of the Copiah County weeklies published at one time or another during the years that Robert Charles lived there (from his birth until he moved away in 1887) are largely intact today, on microfilm in the MDAH. These are: the Hazlehurst *Copiahan* (sometimes titled the *Weekly Copiahan*); Hazlehurst *Mississippi Democrat;* Hazlehurst *Copiah Monitor;* Hazlehurst *Copiah Signal;* Hazlehurst *Signal-Copiahan;* Crystal Springs *Crystal Mirror;* Crystal Springs *Monitor;* Crystal Springs *Meteor;* Wesson *Herald;* Wesson *Mirror.* Of inestimable value for 1887–1892 (the years Charles lived in Vicksburg) were the files of the Vicksburg *Evening Post*, a relatively progressive white daily. Other Mississippi papers of particular usefulness were: the Port Gibson *Reveille;* Vicksburg *Daily Herald;* Jackson *Clarion-Ledger;* Natchez *Daily Democrat;* Woodville *Republican;* Brookhaven *Mississippi Leader;* Raymond *Gazette;* Meadville *Franklin Advocate;* Greenwood *Commonwealth.* The value of Rolling Fork *Deer Creek Pilot*, because of its one story that provided the answer to a major question about Charles's life, has already been cited.

Copiah County's politico-racial crisis of 1883 (described in Chapter II) was the subject of a United States Senate investigation the following year. The hearings, held in New Orleans, were later printed as a federal document under the title "Report of the Special Committee to Inquire into the Mississippi Election of 1883," *Senate Reports,* 48th Cong., 1st Sess., IV, No. 512. Although the investigation was led by partisan Senate Republicans who hoped to make political hay in the 1884 national election by publicizing Democratic outrages in Mississippi, the testimony from black and white witnesses on conditions in Copiah was—for the most part—completely factual, being substantiated by candid admissions in Mississippi Democratic newspapers. Other federal documents pertaining to Mississippi that were examined (in addition to the aforementioned manuscript census returns of 1880) were the manuscript returns of the census of 1860 and of 1870. The latter census is notoriously unreliable, however.

The Alfred Holt Stone Collection at the MDAH, titled "The Negro and Cognate Subjects," includes dozens of pamphlets and clippings that illuminate racial attitudes—both white and black—in the late nineteenth century. In this collection is the booklet *Liberia As It Is* by W. E. De Claybrook (published in Boston in 1884), which helped spread the idea of African emigration among Mississippi blacks during the middle and later 1880s.

Elsewhere in the MDAH shelves are contemporaneous pamphlets and booklets that deal with black life and race relations in Mississippi during the late nineteenth and early twentieth centuries. These include: H. S. Fulkerson, *The Negro: As He Was; As He Is; As He Will Be* (Vicksburg: Commercial Herald Printer, 1887); *The Leading Afro-Americans of Vicksburg, Mississippi* (Vicksburg: Biographica Publishing Company, 1908); S. F. Davis, *Mississippi Negro Lore* (Indianola, Miss.: McCoward-Mercer Publishers, 1914). The MDAH also has two booklets dealing with special topics on Copiah County: S. C. Caldweal, "Copiah County," in *Copiah County, Mississippi: Quarter Century Resource Edition* (Crystal Springs, Miss.: N.p., 1920); and *Report of the Executive Committee of the Associate Society Red Cross, of Copiah County, Miss., On Account of the Great Cyclone of April 22, 1883* (Jackson: Clarion Steam Publishing Company, 1883).

The MDAH, as well as the Department of Archives at Louisiana State University in Baton Rouge, and the Special Collections Division of Tulane University Library, were examined for letters and manuscripts that might assist in reconstructing the black experience at the places where Robert Charles lived. But for the most part these research efforts were futile. Particularly disappointing were the Governor John M. Stone Papers at the MDAH, a collection from which I probably expected too much. However, some very useful information about black and white history in Copiah County was found elsewhere on the shelves of the MDAH: the unpublished Works Progress Administration's Source Material for Mississippi History: Copiah County (*ca.* 1938). The box of material on Copiah County, gathered by WPA writers, contained interviews with elderly blacks who had lived there since the era of slavery.

Every obtainable secondary work and scholarly article dealing with Mississippi between 1865 and the end of the century was consulted. There were three books that were notably useful to me. The standard survey of black history in the state after emancipation is still Vernon Lane Wharton's *The Negro in Mississippi: 1865–1900* (Chapel Hill: University of North Carolina Press, 1947). For political activities during the period, the best overview is provided by Albert D. Kirwan, *Revolt of the Rednecks: Mississippi Politics, 1876–1925* (Lexington: University of Kentucky Press, 1951). An older state history turned out to be valuable because of its references to Copiah County: Dunbar Roland (ed.), *Mississippi: Comprising Sketches of Counties, Towns, Events, Institutions, and Persons, Arranged in Cyclopedic Form* (2 vols.; Atlanta: Southern Historical Publishing Association, 1907).

INDEX

137212